# Windows 7 Portable Command Guide: MCTS 70-680, and MCITP 70-685 and 70-686

Darril Gibson

800 East 96th Street
Indianapolis, Indiana 46240 USA

# Windows 7 Portable Command Guide: MCTS 70-680, and MCITP 70-685 and 70-686

Darril Gibson

Copyright © 2011 by Pearson Education, Inc.

ISBN-13: 978-0-7897-4735-8

ISBN-10: 0-7897-4735-9

Library of Congress Cataloging-in-Publication data is on file.

Printed in the United States of America

First Printing: March 2011

## Trademarks

## Warning and Disclaimer

## Bulk Sales

Pearson IT Certification offers excellent discounts on this book when ordered in quantity for bulk purchases or special sales. For more information, please contact

U.S. Corporate and Government Sales
1-800-382-3419
corpsales@pearsontechgroup.com

For sales outside the United States, please contact

International Sales
international@pearson.com

**Publisher**
Paul Boger

**Associate Publisher**
Dave Dusthimer

**Acquisitions Editor**
Betsy Brown

**Development Editor**
Andrew Cupp

**Series Editor**
Scott Empson

**Managing Editor**
Sandra Schroeder

**Senior Project Editor**
Tonya Simpson

**Copy Editor**
Bill McManus

**Proofreader**
The Wordsmithery LLC

**Technical Editor**
Chris Crayton

**Publishing Coordinator**
Vanessa Evans

**Book Designer**
Gary Adair

**Composition**
Studio Galou, LLC

# Contents at a Glance

Introduction   1

**PART I: Command Prompt Basics**

**CHAPTER 1**   Launching and Using the Command Prompt   3

**CHAPTER 2**   Basic Rules When Using the Command Prompt   15

**CHAPTER 3**   Using Basic Commands   27

**PART II: Working with Files, Folders, and Disks**

**CHAPTER 4**   Manipulating Files and Folders   37

**CHAPTER 5**   Manipulating Disks   55

**PART III: Scripting with Batch Files**

**CHAPTER 6**   Creating Batch Files   63

**CHAPTER 7**   Scheduling Batch Files   81

**PART IV: Managing and Maintaining Windows 7**

**CHAPTER 8**   Using Windows 7 Maintenance Tools   89

**CHAPTER 9**   Retrieving Information About Windows 7   103

**CHAPTER 10**   Managing Security in Windows 7   111

**CHAPTER 11**   Configuring Windows 7 with **netsh**   121

**PART V: Troubleshooting Windows 7**

**CHAPTER 12**   Configuring Windows 7 Using Basic Troubleshooting Tools   135

**CHAPTER 13**   Troubleshooting Network Issues   145

**CHAPTER 14**   Using Recovery Tools   161

**PART VI: Remote Administration**

**CHAPTER 15**   Managing Remote Windows 7 Systems   177

**CHAPTER 16**   Windows Management Instrumentation Command Line   187

**PART VII: Creating and Managing Images**

**CHAPTER 17**  Understanding Images  203

**CHAPTER 18**  Preparing a System to Be Imaged with sysprep  215

**CHAPTER 19**  Installing the Windows Automated Installation Kit  221

**CHAPTER 20**  Using imagex  227

**CHAPTER 21**  Using the Deployment Image Service and Management (DISM) Tool  237

**PART VIII: Working with WinPE and Setup**

**CHAPTER 22**  WinPE Commands  247

**CHAPTER 23**  Installing Windows 7 with **setup**  251

**PART IX: Migrating User Data with USMT**

**CHAPTER 24**  Capturing User Data with **scanstate**  259

**CHAPTER 25**  Restoring User Data with **loadstate**  273

**PART X: Using PowerShell**

**CHAPTER 26**  Understanding PowerShell Commands  279

**CHAPTER 27**  Using the Integrated Scripting Environment (ISE)  299

**CHAPTER 28**  Creating and Running PowerShell Scripts  309

**PART XI: Group Policy and the Command Line**

**CHAPTER 29**  Group Policy Overview  329

**CHAPTER 30**  Group Policy Command-Line Tools  341

**APPENDIX**  Create Your Own Journal Here  347

# Table of Contents

INTRODUCTION   1

**PART I: Command Prompt Basics**

CHAPTER 1   Launching and Using the Command Prompt   3

Launching the Command Prompt   3

Pinning the Command Prompt to the Start Menu and the Taskbar   4

Launching the Command Prompt with Elevated Privileges   4

Responding to the UAC Prompt   5

Using the Built-in Doskey Program   7

Creating Mini Macros in Doskey   9

Copying from and Pasting into the Command Prompt   9

Copy from the Command Prompt Window   10

Paste Text into the Command Prompt Window   10

Changing the Options and Display of the Command Prompt   11

CHAPTER 2   Basic Rules When Using the Command Prompt   15

Using Uppercase or Lowercase   15

Using Quotes to Enclose Spaces   16

Understanding Variables   17

Understanding Switches   18

Understanding Wildcards   18

Getting Help   19

CHAPTER 3   Using Basic Commands   27

Understanding Folders and Directories   27

Understanding Paths   28

Viewing Files and Folders with **dir**   30

Changing the Path with **cd**   31

Using Drag and Drop to the Command Prompt Window   32

Deleting Folders with **rd**   33

Creating Folders with **md**   33

Controlling Output with **more**   34

Redirecting Output   35

Using the Redirect Symbol (>)   35

Using **clip**   **35**

Using **exit**   35

**PART II: Working with Files, Folders, and Disks**

CHAPTER 4    Manipulating Files and Folders    37

Associating File Extensions with **assoc** and **ftype**    37
assoc    39
ftype    39
Viewing Attributes with **attrib**    41
Compressing Files with **compact**    43
Encrypting Files with **cipher**    44
Copying Files with **copy**, **xcopy**, and **robocopy**    46
copy    46
xcopy    47
robocopy    48
Deleting or Removing Files with **del**    50
Expanding Cabinet Files with **expand**    51
Taking Ownership of Files with **takeown**    51
Removing the Windows.old Folder    52
Mapping Drives with **net use**    53

CHAPTER 5    Manipulating Disks    55

Manipulating and Viewing Disks with **diskpart**    55
Creating a VHD File with **diskpart**    56
Modifying the BCD Store for the VHD File    57
Defragmenting Volumes with **defrag**    59
Converting to NTFS with **convert**    61
Managing the File System with **fsutil**    62

**PART III: Scripting with Batch Files**

CHAPTER 6    Creating Batch Files    63

Using Notepad    63
Giving Feedback with **echo**    64
Using Parameters    65
Calling Another Batch File with **call**    68
Clearing the Screen with **cls**    69
Changing the Order of Processing with **goto**    69
Checking Conditions with **if**    70
Logging Events with **eventcreate**    73
Looping Through Tasks with **for**    75

Creating a Menu File   76

   Documenting the Script with **rem**   76

   Pausing for the User   77

   Giving Users a Choice   77

   Creating the Batch File   78


CHAPTER 7   Scheduling Batch Files   81

Scheduling Batch Files with Task Scheduler   81

Scheduling Tasks from the Command Line   82

   Creating a Scheduled Task with **schtasks**   83

   Creating a Scheduled Task from an XML File with **schtasks**   83

   Deleting a Scheduled Task with **schtasks**   85

   Viewing Scheduled Tasks with **schtasks**   85

   Changing Scheduled Tasks with **schtasks**   86

   Running and Ending Scheduled Tasks with **schtasks**   87


**PART IV: Managing and Maintaining Windows 7**


CHAPTER 8   Using Windows 7 Maintenance Tools   89

Controlling Power Settings with **powercfg**   89

   Query the Power Settings with **powercfg**   89

   Modify the Power Settings with **powercfg**   91

   Analyze the Power Settings with **powercfg**   93

Checking Memory with **mdsched**   93

Manipulating Services with **sc**   95

Collecting Events with **wecutil**   97

Restarting Systems with **shutdown**   97

Launching Control Panel Applets from the Command Line   99


CHAPTER 9   Retrieving Information About Windows 7   103

Viewing System Information with **systeminfo**   103

Viewing User Information with **whoami**   106

Launching System Configuration with **msconfig**   107


CHAPTER 10   Managing Security in Windows 7   111

Manipulating Credentials with **cmdkey**   111

Installing Updates with **wusa**   112

Installing Applications with **msiexec**   115

Auditing Systems with **mbsacli**   116

CHAPTER 11   Configuring Windows 7 with netsh   121

    Understanding **netsh**   121

    Understanding Contexts   122

    Configuring a Proxy Server   126

    Configuring the Network Interface with netsh   126


**PART V: Troubleshooting Windows 7**


CHAPTER 12   Configuring Windows 7 Using Basic Troubleshooting Tools   135

    Identifying the System Name with **hostname**   135

    Verifying Core System Files with **sfc**   135

    Checking Digital Signatures with **sigverif**   137

    Viewing Active Tasks with **tasklist**   138

    Terminating Processes with **taskkill**   142

    Viewing Installed Drivers with **driverquery**   144


CHAPTER 13   Troubleshooting Network Issues   145

    Viewing and Manipulating TCP/IP Configuration with **ipconfig**   145

    Viewing the Physical Address with **getmac**   151

    Checking Connectivity with **ping**   152

    Viewing the Router Path with **tracert**   155

    Checking for Data Loss with **pathping**   155

    Checking for Records in DNS with **nslookup**   156


CHAPTER 14   Using Recovery Tools   161

    Manipulating the Boot Process with **bcdedit**   161

        Commands That Operate on a Store   165

        Commands That Control Output   166

        Commands That Control the Boot Manager   167

        Commands That Operate on Entries in the Store   169

        Commands That Operate on Entry Options   170

        Disable Driver Signing   170

    Creating a System Repair Disc with **recdisc**   171

    Checking and Repairing Disks with **chkdsk**   172

    Repairing BitLocker Drives with **repair-bde**   175

**PART VI: Remote Administration**

CHAPTER 15    Managing Remote Windows 7 Systems    177

Configuring Windows 7 for Remote Administration    177

Configuring System for Remote Desktop Connection
(RDC)    177

Configuring System for Remote Access Using an MMC    180

Connecting to Remote Systems with **mstsc**    181

Configuring Windows Remote Management with **winrm**    184

Executing Commands Remotely with **winrs**    185

CHAPTER 16    Windows Management Instrumentation Command Line    187

Understanding **wmic**    187

Configuring the Firewall to Allow **wmic**    188

Running **wmic**    189

Modifying the Format with the /format Switch    191

Retrieving Help from **wmic**    194

Understanding Aliases    194

Operating System Aliases    196

Disk Drive Aliases    197

System Hardware Aliases    198

User, Group, and Domain Aliases    200

Using Verbs    200

**PART VII: Creating and Managing Images**

CHAPTER 17    Understanding Images    203

Understanding WIM Files    203

Using Windows Deployment Services and Images    205

Comparing Boot and Install Images    207

Comparing Thick and Thin Images    213

CHAPTER 18    Preparing a System to Be Imaged with Sysprep    215

Understanding Sysprep    215

Running the Sysprep GUI    216

Running **sysprep** from the Command Line    217

CHAPTER 19   Installing the Windows Automated Installation Kit   221

Downloading the WAIK   221
Installing the WAIK   221
Viewing the WAIK Tools   224


CHAPTER 20   Using **imagex**   227

Creating WinPE on a Bootable USB   227
Capturing Images with **imagex**   231
Appending Images with **imagex**   233
Deleting Images with **imagex**   235
Deploying Images with **imagex**   235


CHAPTER 21   Using the Deployment Image Service and Management
(DISM) Tool   237

Online Servicing Versus Offline Servicing   237
Mounting Images   238
Getting Information About Mounted Images   240
Modifying Images   240
Working with Drivers   241
Working with Packages and Features   242
Miscellaneous Image Modifications   244
Saving Images   245


**PART VIII: Working with WinPE and Setup**


CHAPTER 22   WinPE Commands   247

Add Drivers to WinPE with **drvload**   247
Run Commands Within WinPE with **wpeutil**   248


CHAPTER 23   Installing Windows 7 with **setup**   251

Installing Windows 7 with **setup**   251
Using the Autounattend.xml File   252
Using **slmgr**   253
Basic **slmgr** Commands   254
**slmgr** Activation Commands   255
**slmgr** Commands Used for KMS Clients   256
**slmgr** Commands Used for Token-Based Activation   257

**PART IX: Migrating User Data with USMT**

CHAPTER 24    Capturing User Data with **scanstate**    259

Understanding Migration Stores    259

Reviewing Migration Paths    259

Understanding Hard-Link Migration Stores    263

Capturing Migration Data with **scanstate**    265

Specifying XML Files    266

Modifying XML Files    266

Identifying Users to Migrate with **scanstate**    268

Encrypting the Migration Store with **scanstate**    269

Simple Error Handling with **scanstate**    270

Handling EFS Files    270

Migrating Data from the Windows.old Folder    271

CHAPTER 25    Restoring User Data with **loadstate**    273

Running **loadstate**    273

Specifying XML Files    274

Specifying Hard-Link Options    275

Deleting the Hard-Link Store    275

Identifying Users to Migrate    276

Decrypting an Encrypted Migration Store    277

Handling Errors    278

**PART X: Using PowerShell**

CHAPTER 26    Understanding PowerShell Commands    279

Launching PowerShell    279

Understanding PowerShell Verbs and Nouns    280

Tabbing Through PowerShell Commands    284

Understanding the Different Types of PowerShell Commands    285

Creating Aliases    286

Discovering Windows PowerShell Commands    286

Exploring **get-member**    288

Redirecting Output with Windows PowerShell    291

Understanding PowerShell Errors    291

Understanding PowerShell Variables    293

Using Comparison Operators    295

Understanding Pipelining    296

CHAPTER 27   Using the Integrated Scripting Environment (ISE)   299

Launching the ISE   299

Exploring the ISE   300

Executing Commands in the ISE   302

Creating and Saving a Script in the ISE   303

CHAPTER 28   Creating and Running PowerShell Scripts   309

Setting the Security Context   309

Creating a PowerShell Profile   310

Creating and Modifying the Global PowerShell Profile   312

Running PowerShell Scripts   313

Flushing the DNS Cache   314

Creating a List of Domain Computers   315

Logging Processes with a **get-process** Script   316

Testing for the Existence of a File   318

Creating Output as HTML   318

Running a Script Against Multiple Computers   320

Creating a PowerShell Message Box   322

Scheduling PowerShell Scripts   326

**PART XI: Group Policy and the Command Line**

CHAPTER 29   Group Policy Overview   329

Understanding Group Policy Settings   329

Blocking Inheritance   333

Enforcing GPOs   334

Using Loopback Processing   335

Running Scripts with Group Policy   336

Running PowerShell Scripts via Group Policy   339

CHAPTER 30   Group Policy Command-Line Tools   341

Viewing Group Policy Settings with **gpresult**   341

Refreshing Group Policy Settings with **gpupdate**   343

APPENDIX A   Create Your Own Journal Here   347

# About the Author

**Darril Gibson** is the CEO of Security Consulting and Training, LLC. He regularly teaches, writes, and consults on a wide variety of security and technical topics. He's been a Microsoft Certified Trainer for more than ten years and holds several certifications, including MCSE (NT 4.0, 2000, 2003), MCDBA (SQL Server), MCITP (Windows 7, Server 2008, SQL Server), ITIL v3, Security+, and CISSP. He has authored, coauthored, or contributed to more than a dozen books. You can view a listing of most of his current books on Amazon: http://amzn.to/bL0Obo.

# Dedication

To my wife, who continues to provide me with love and encouragement. I'm thankful we are sharing our lives together.

# Acknowledgments

A book like this is never done in a vacuum. I'm grateful for all the hard work done behind the scenes by the people at Pearson. I'm thankful to Scott Empson, who had the original vision for these books, and grateful that David Dusthimer had faith in me to head up many of the books in the Microsoft series. I especially appreciated the efforts of two key editors, Andrew Cupp and Chris Crayton. This book is much better due to the efforts of these people.

A book like this is never done in a vacuum. I'm grateful for all the hard work done behind the scenes by the people at Pearson. I'm thankful to Scott Empson, who had the original vision for these books, and grateful that David Dusthimer had faith in me to head up many of the books in the Microsoft series. I especially appreciated the efforts of two key editors, Andrew Cupp and Chris Crayton. This book is much better due to the efforts of these people.

## About the Series Editor

**Scott Empson** is the associate chair of the Bachelor of Applied Information Systems Technology degree program at the Northern Alberta Institute of Technology in Edmonton, Alberta, Canada, where he teaches Cisco routing, switching, and network design courses. Scott is also the program coordinator of the Cisco Networking Academy Program at NAIT, a Regional Academy covering Central and Northern Alberta. He has earned three undergraduate degrees: a Bachelor of Arts, with a major in English; a Bachelor of Education, again with a major in English/Language Arts; and a Bachelor of Applied Information Systems Technology, with a major in Network Management. Scott also has a Masters of Education degree from the University of Portland. He holds several industry certifications, including CCNP, CCAI, Network+, and C|EH.

Scott is the series creator and one of the authors of the Portable Command Guide Series. Portable Command Guides are filled with valuable, easy-to-access information to quickly refresh your memory. Each guide is portable enough for use whether you're in the server room or the equipment closet.

## About the Technical Editor

**Christopher A. Crayton** is an author, technical editor, technical consultant, security consultant, trainer, and SkillsUSA state-level technology competition judge. Formerly, he worked as a computer and networking instructor at Keiser College (2001 Teacher of the Year); as network administrator for Protocol, a global electronic customer relationship management (eCRM) company; and at Eastman Kodak headquarters as a computer and network specialist. Chris has authored several print and online books, including *The A+ Exams Guide*, Second Edition (Cengage Learning, 2008), *Microsoft Windows Vista 70-620 Exam Guide Short Cut* (O'Reilly, 2007), *CompTIA A+ Essentials 220-601 Exam Guide Short Cut* (O'Reilly, 2007), *The A+ Exams Guide, The A+ Certification and PC Repair Handbook* (Charles River Media, 2005), *The Security+ Exam Guide* (Charles River Media, 2003), and *A+ Adaptive Exams* (Charles River Media, 2002). He is also co-author of *How to Cheat at Securing Your Network* (Syngress, 2007). As an experienced technical editor, Chris has provided many technical edits/reviews for several major publishing companies, including Pearson Education, McGraw-Hill, Cengage Learning, Wiley, O'Reilly, Syngress, and Apress. He holds MCSE, A+, and Network+ certifications.

# We Want to Hear from You!

As the reader of this book, you are our most important critic and commentator. We value your opinion and want to know what we're doing right, what we could do better, what areas you'd like to see us publish in, and any other words of wisdom you're willing to pass our way.

As an associate publisher for Pearson IT Certification, I welcome your comments. You can email or write me directly to let me know what you did or didn't like about this book—as well as what we can do to make our books better.

Please note that I cannot help you with technical problems related to the topic of this book. We do have a User Services group, however, where I will forward specific technical questions related to the book.

When you write, please be sure to include this book's title and author as well as your name, email address, and phone number. I will carefully review your comments and share them with the author and editors who worked on the book.

Email:  feedback@pearsonitcertification.com

Mail:  David Dusthimer
Associate Publisher
Pearson IT Certification
800 East 96th Street
Indianapolis, IN 46240 USA

# Reader Services

Visit our website and register this book at pearsonitcertification.com for convenient access to any updates, downloads, or errata that might be available for this book.

Thanks for buying *Windows 7 Portable Command Guide*. I'd love to say that this book was my idea, but the real credit goes to Scott Empson, who originally developed the vision of this book with Cisco certifications. I've worked with Scott and Pearson Publishing to help bring the same type of books he created for Cisco products to professionals working on Microsoft products. Scott's vision started with the idea that many IT professionals who have already learned the theory still sometimes need help remembering how to implement it.

The book doesn't go into depth teaching these concepts. The idea is that you already understand them. Instead, the goal is to provide enough information to help you remember what you can do and how to do it in a small, portable, and useful journal, not an encyclopedic-sized volume. However, even if a concept is new to you, there's enough information for you to start typing at the command prompt to gain a better understanding.

As an example, you probably know that you can refresh Group Policy from the command prompt, but you might not always remember the exact command is **gpupdate / force**. You might remember that sysprep is used to prepare a computer for imaging, but you might not always remember that the full command is **sysprep /oobe /generalize**. In other words, you know the theory behind why you'd update Group Policy, and why you'd run sysprep, but you might not always remember the syntax. This book is a ready reference of useful commands and procedures with clear-cut examples. It shows the exact syntax of many of the commands needed for administrative tasks performed regularly by Windows 7 administrators.

I started the outline of this book by ensuring that command-prompt commands covered by the Microsoft Certified Information Technology Professional (MCITP) certifications on Windows 7 were included. This includes the 70-680 and 70-685 exams for the MCITP: Enterprise Desktop Support Technician 7 certification, and the 70-680 and 70-686 exams for the MCITP: Enterprise Desktop Administrator 7 certification. I then added the commands I've found valuable in my day-to-day work on networks and from classroom teaching.

Many IT professionals use an engineering journal to help them remember key information needed on the job. It might include specific commands that they sometimes forget, IP addressing schemes used on their networks, steps for important maintenance tasks that are performed infrequently, or anything else they want to easily recall by looking at the journal. If you already have an engineering journal of your own, you can add this as a Windows 7 addendum. If you don't have one, you can start with this book. It includes the same "Create Your Own Journal Here" appendix that Scott uses in the Cisco series. These are blank pages you can use to add your own notes and make this your journal, not mine.

## Command Syntax Conventions

The conventions used to present command syntax in this book are as follows:

- **Boldface** indicates syntax that is entered literally as shown.
- *Italic* indicates syntax for which you supply actual values.
- Vertical bars (|) separate alternative, mutually exclusive choices.
- Square brackets ([ ]) indicate an optional element.
- Braces ({ }) indicate a required choice.

This chapter provides information and commands concerning the following topics:

- Launching the command prompt
- Pinning the command prompt to the Start menu and the taskbar
- Launching the command prompt with elevated privileges
- Responding to the UAC prompt
- Using the built-in Doskey.exe program
- Creating mini macros in doskey
- Copying from and pasting into the command prompt window
- Changing the options and display of the command prompt

## Launching the Command Prompt

There are several ways you can launch the command prompt within Windows 7:

- Click **Start**, type **cmd** in the Start Search box, and press **Enter**.
- Choose **Start, All Programs, Accessories, Command Prompt**.
- If Command Prompt is on the Start menu, choose **Start, Command Prompt**.

The command prompt opens and looks similar to Figure 1-1.

**Figure 1-1** The Command Prompt Window

## Pinning the Command Prompt to the Start Menu and the Taskbar

If you regularly use the command prompt, you can pin it to the Start menu and the taskbar. If you pin it to the taskbar, it'll appear next to the Internet Explorer, Windows Explorer, and Windows Media Player shortcut links on your taskbar. This makes it easier to access when you need it. To pin it to the taskbar or the Start menu, do the following:

- Click **Start**, type **cmd** in the Start Search box, right-click **CMD**, and choose either **Pin to Taskbar** or **Pin to Start Menu**.

- Choose **Start, All Programs, Accessories**, right-click **Command Prompt**, and choose either **Pin to Taskbar** or **Pin to Start Menu**.

- If Command Prompt is on the Start menu, click **Start**, right-click **Command Prompt**, and choose either **Pin to Taskbar** or **Pin to Start Menu**.

## Launching the Command Prompt with Elevated Privileges

Although there are many commands you can enter using the normal command prompt, some commands require you to have elevated privileges to start them. For example, if you started the command prompt normally and entered **ipconfig /release**, the command would fail. Instead, you'd see the following message:

```
The requested operation requires elevation.
```

This message is letting you know that you must start the command prompt with administrative privileges, or elevated privileges. You need administrative privileges on the system to launch the command prompt with elevated privileges.

To launch the command prompt with elevated privileges, right-click the shortcut and choose **Run as Administrator**.

> **NOTE:**   You can choose Run as Administrator when starting the command prompt from the Start menu or when starting it from the taskbar if you've pinned it to the taskbar.

Figure 1-2 shows how this is done when the command prompt has been pinned to the taskbar.

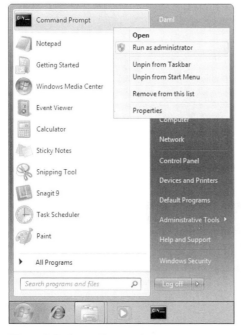

**Figure 1-2**    Launching the Command Prompt with Elevated Privileges from the Taskbar

Figure 1-3 shows how it's done when the command prompt has been pinned to the Start menu.

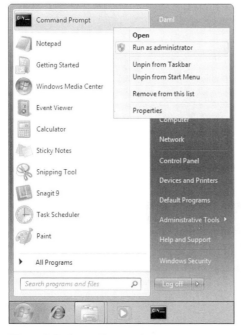

**Figure 1-3**    Launching the Command Prompt with Elevated Privileges from the Start Menu

> **TIP:**    You can also use the Ctrl+Shift+Enter key combination to launch the command prompt with administrative privileges. For example, click **Start**, type **cmd** in the Start Search box, and then press **Ctrl+Shift+Enter**. This works the same as right-clicking and choosing Run as Administrator.

## Responding to the UAC Prompt

By default, User Account Control (UAC) will prompt you to continue. You'll see one of two dialog boxes:

- If you are logged on with an account that has administrative privileges, UAC prompts you to continue with a dialog box similar to that shown in Figure 1-4. Simply click **Yes**.

**Figure 1-4**    Responding to the UAC Prompt

- If you are logged on with an account that does not have administrative privileges, UAC prompts you to enter the username and password of an account that does have administrative privileges.

After you get past UAC, you'll see the command prompt launch and it will look similar to Figure 1-5. Notice that there are subtle differences between the regular command prompt, shown in Figure 1-1, and the elevated command prompt, shown in Figure 1-5.

**Figure 1-5**    Elevated Command Prompt

| Differences Between Regular and Elevated Command Prompts | | |
|---|---|---|
| | **Regular Prompt** | **Elevated Prompt** |
| **Title** | Command Prompt | Administrator: Command Prompt |
| **Path** | Path is user's profile path:<br><br>`C:\Users\Darril>` | Path starts in the Windows\system32 folder:<br><br>`C:\Windows\System32>` |

**NOTE:**   When you launch the command prompt with elevated privileges, all the commands entered in that instance of the command prompt are executed with administrative privileges. When you close the Command Prompt window, the elevated privileges are no longer available.

**NOTE:** If you are logged on as an administrator, the command prompt automatically starts with administrator permissions. It starts in the user's profile path of C:\Users\ Administrator and has a title of Administrator: Command Prompt.

## Using the Built-in Doskey Program

Doskey has been around since the early Microsoft Disk Operating System (MS-DOS) days, and it's just as useful today as it was when it first came out. It keeps a history of the commands you've entered and enables you to easily retrieve them so that you don't have to type them again. This saves a lot of time when you're entering the same commands repeatedly and is especially useful when you're entering long commands, where typos are common.

For example, suppose you're troubleshooting connectivity with another system and you're using either of the following two commands:

```
ping server1
ipconfig /flushdns
```

The next time you want to execute either of these commands, press **Up Arrow** until the command is displayed at the prompt, and then press **Enter**; the same command executes again without requiring you to type it from scratch.

The following table lists and describes the keys you can use to retrieve commands. When reading the descriptions of these commands, imagine that you have already entered the following three lines at the command prompt, in order:

```
ipconfig /displaydns
ipconfig /flushdns
ipconfig /all
```

| Keyboard Key | Description |
| --- | --- |
| Up Arrow | Recalls the previous command. In the example, pressing Up Arrow once recalls **ipconfig /all**. |
| Down Arrow | Recalls the command used after the currently displayed command. For example, if you pressed Up Arrow three times instead of once in the preceding cell, **ipconfig /displaydns** would be displayed. You could then press Down Arrow to display **ipconfig /flushdns**. |
| Page Up | Recalls the oldest command in the current session. In the example, this would display the **ipconfig /displaydns** command. |
| Page Down | Recalls the most recent command in the current session. In the example, this would display the **ipconfig /all** command. |

**TIP:** After you have made an edit to a command, you do not have to reposition the cursor at the end of the line. Simply press **Enter** to continue.

You can use the following keys or key combinations when editing a retrieved doskey. exe command:

| Keyboard Key or Key Combination | Description |
| --- | --- |
| Left Arrow | Moves the cursor back one character at a time. |
| Right Arrow | Moves the cursor forward one character at a time. |
| Ctrl+Left Arrow | Moves the cursor back one word. |
| Ctrl+Right Arrow | Moves the cursor forward one word. |
| Home | Moves the cursor to the beginning of the line. |
| End | Moves the cursor to the end of the line. |
| Esc | Clears the command from the display. |

**NOTE:** The doskey.exe buffer will hold the past 50 commands by default. However, you can change that with the **/listsize** switch. To extend the history buffer to hold 100 commands, use the following command:

```
doskey /listsize = 100
```

**TIP:** You can also change the buffer size by right-clicking the title bar, choosing Properties, and changing the buffer size. The buffer size value is the same as the **listsize** value.

Following are some of the useful commands you can use with doskey:

| Doskey Command | Description |
| --- | --- |
| `C:\>doskey /history` | Lists all commands in the history buffer. |
| F7 | Displays the command history in a selectable pop-up dialog box. |
| `C:\>doskey /reinstall` | Installs a new copy of doskey.exe and clears the command history buffer. |
| `C:\>doskey /listsize = number`<br><br>`C:\>doskey /listsize = 999` | Changes the size of the doskey.exe buffer to the provided number. The example sets the buffer size to 999. |

## Creating Mini Macros in Doskey

You can create mini macros that will be available to you within a command prompt session. For example, imagine that you expect to enter **ipconfig /all** many times. You can create a macro named IP with the following command:

```
doskey ip = ipconfig /all
```

Now, you can simply enter **ip** at the command prompt instead of **ipconfig /all**. After you press Enter, the full **ipconfig /all** command will execute.

| Doskey Command | Description |
|---|---|
| C:\>**doskey** *macroKey* = *command*<br><br>C:\>**doskey ipf = ipconfig**<br>**/flushdns** | Creates a macro that will execute the command when the macro key is entered. The example creates a macro named IPF that can be used to flush the DNS cache. |
| C:\>**ipf** | Executing the macro is the same as executing the command. |
| C:\>**doskey /macros** | Displays all **doskey** macros in the session. |

## Copying from and Pasting into the Command Prompt

You can copy text from and paste text into the Command Prompt window. The process is a little different depending on how the QuickEdit Mode option is configured.

You configure QuickEdit Mode on the Options tab of the Command Prompt Properties window, shown in Figure 1-6. You can access this window by right-clicking the title bar of the Command Prompt window and choosing **Properties**.

The QuickEdit Mode option changes the way that you can cut text from and paste text into the command line. The Insert Mode option below it works just like the Insert key of the keyboard. It allows you to insert characters into the command line when enabled, or overwrite characters in the command line when disabled.

> **TIP:**  If you want your changes to the Options tab to apply any time the Command Prompt window is open instead of applying only to the current session, right-click the title bar of the Command Prompt window, click **Defaults**, and then click the Options tab (if it's not already displayed) and make your changes.

**Figure 1-6**   Options Tab of Command Prompt Properties Window

## Copy from the Command Prompt Window

How you copy text from the command prompt window depends on whether QuickEdit Mode is enabled or disabled.

| If QuickEdit Mode is enabled (checked) | Use the mouse to select text, and then press **Enter** to copy the selected text. |
|---|---|
| If QuickEdit Mode is not enabled (unchecked) | Right-click in the Command Prompt window and click **Mark**. Use the mouse to select text, and then press **Enter** to copy the selected text. |

**NOTE:**  Both of these methods copy the text to the Clipboard. You can then paste the text into any other application, such as Notepad or Microsoft Word.

## Paste Text into the Command Prompt Window

You can paste any text that is on the Clipboard into the command line.

| If QuickEdit Mode is enabled (checked) | Right-click in the Command Prompt window and the data is pasted where you clicked. Caution: If the pasted data includes a new line from the Enter key, you'll execute the command as soon as you paste it. |
|---|---|
| If QuickEdit Mode is not enabled (unchecked) | Right-click in the Command Prompt window and click **Paste**. |

**NOTE:** If you copy the carriage return with the command, the carriage return will be pasted into the Command Prompt window. In other words, when you paste the command, it will execute.

## Changing the Options and Display of the Command Prompt

Figure 1-6 (in the preceding section) shows the Options tab and the edit options of the Command Prompt Properties window. This tab also includes two additional options: Cursor Size and Command History.

| Options Tab Option | Description |
|---|---|
| Cursor Size | You can change this to small, medium, or large. |
| Command History - Buffer Size | The buffer size can be changed to as high as 999 and directly relates to the **/listsize** switch of **doskey**. |
| Command History - Number of Buffers | This identifies how much memory can be used to hold and display the buffer. |
| Command History - Discard Old Duplicates | Duplicate commands are not kept in the history when this is checked. |

Figure 1-7 shows the Font tab of the Properties window. This tab allows you to change the size of the font and pick other fonts, though you don't have many choices available.

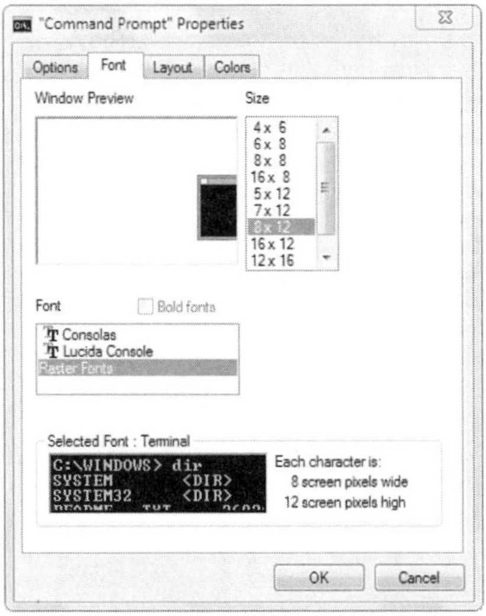

**Figure 1-7**   Font Tab of Command Prompt Properties Window

Figure 1-8 shows the Layout tab of the Properties window. The most valuable setting here is the height of the screen buffer size. If you change this to 9999, the screen buffer will capture as many as 9999 lines. This can be useful when your command has a lot of output data.

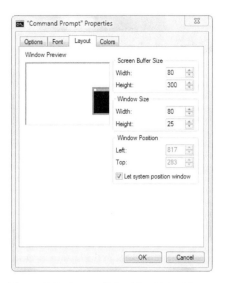

**Figure 1-8**   Layout Tab of Command Prompt Properties Window

**TIP:**   Consider the following command:

```
gpresult /z
```

**gpresult** retrieves detailed results about Group Policy that apply to a system. The **/z** switch specifies super-verbose, resulting in a significant amount of detail. If the output exceeds the buffer, the earlier data sent to the screen is overwritten. However, if you increase the height of the screen buffer size, you'll be able to scroll back to the beginning of the output.

Figure 1-9 shows the Colors tab of the Properties window. You can change the background color and the text color here. This can be especially useful if you're displaying the text for multiple people to see.

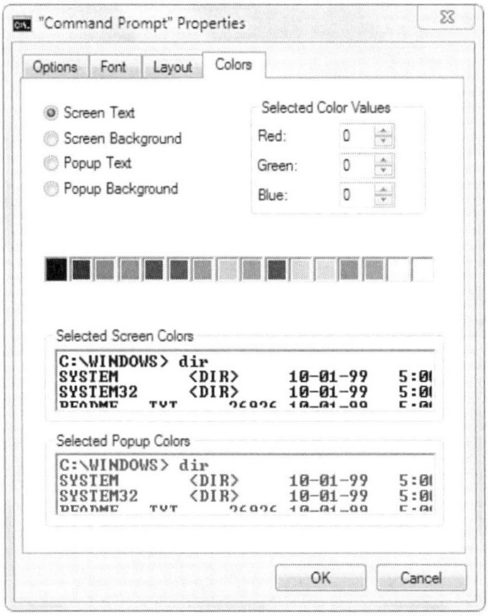

**Figure 1-9**    Colors Tab of Command Prompt Properties Window

**TIP:**   When using an overhead or data projector, text within the command prompt shows up best as black text on a white background.

This chapter provides information and commands concerning the following topics:

- Using uppercase or lowercase
- Using quotes to enclose spaces
- Understanding variables
- Understanding switches
- Understanding wildcards
- Getting help

## Using Uppercase or Lowercase

In almost all instances, you can enter commands as uppercase letters, lowercase letters, or a combination of the two. In other words, the following commands are all interpreted the same:

| Mixed Case | Lowercase | Uppercase |
|------------|-----------|-----------|
| SystemInfo | systeminfo | SYSTEMINFO |
| IPConfig | ipconfig | IPCONFIG |
| RoboCopy | robocopy | ROBOCOPY |

Documentation and help files commonly show the first letter of a command as upper-case, and when a one-word command comprises two words, such documentation might present the first letter of both words as uppercase, such as **SystemInfo**. This is done for readability and doesn't affect how the command is interpreted at the command line.

> **NOTE:** In this book, all commands are shown as all lowercase unless you must enter the command using specific upper- or lowercase letters for the command to work. Such commands are case sensitive.

There are some exceptions where case does matter, but they are rare. For example, if you're using the Deployment Image Servicing and Management (DISM) tool to enable a feature in an offline image, you must enter the name of the feature with its specific case. For example, if you want to enable games on the system, you must enter the feature name as **InboxGames**. The following table shows how to use the **dism** command to enable a feature and presents two examples showing its case sensitivity.

| dism Command | Description |
|---|---|
| `dism /image:c:` <br> `\mountedimage /enable-feature /` <br> `featurename:`*feature* | The **dism** command can be used to manage offline images. Its use is covered in greater depth in Chapter 21, "Using the Deployment Image Service and Management (DISM) Tool." |
| `C:\>dism /image:c:` <br> `\mountedimage /enable-feature /` <br> `featurename:inboxgames` | This command will fail because **inboxgames** isn't entered with the proper case. |
| `C:\>dism /image:c:` <br> `\mountedimage /enable-feature /` <br> `featurename:InboxGames` | This command will succeed because **InboxGames** is entered with the proper case. |

## Using Quotes to Enclose Spaces

The command-line interpreter understands a space as the next part of the command. For example, consider **ping** used in the following command:

| `C:\>ping server1` | The space after **ping** indicates that **ping** is the command and what follows (*server1*) is a parameter for the **ping** command. This will send four echo requests to *server1* and get four echo replies back if the server is operational. |
|---|---|

Some parameters can have spaces. When a parameter does have a space, the parameter must be enclosed in quotes. For example, you can use the **netsh** command to change the configuration of a network interface card (NIC). The default name of the first NIC is Local Area Connection. Because the name has spaces, it must be enclosed in quotes as **"local area connection"** so that the **netsh** command can interpret it correctly.

| netsh Command | Description |
|---|---|
| `netsh interface ipv4 set address` <br> `name = `*name-of-nic*` static` <br> *ip-address subnet-mask* | You can use the **netsh** command to change the configuration of a NIC. It needs the name of the NIC, an IP address, and a subnet mask. Chapter 11, "Configuring Windows 7 with **netsh**," covers **netsh** in more depth. |
| `C:\>netsh interface ipv4 set` <br> `address name = "local area` <br> `connection" static 192.168.1.15` <br> `255.255.255.0` | This command will work because **"local area connection"** is enclosed in quotes. It will set the IP address and subnet mask of the NIC. |
| `C:\>netsh interface ipv4 set` <br> `address name = local area` <br> `connection static 192.168.1.15` <br> `255.255.255.0` <br> `Invalid source parameter (area).` | This command will fail. Because **local area connection** is not enclosed in quotes, **netsh** interprets **local** as the name of the NIC but doesn't understand **area**. |

## Understanding Variables

Multiple variables are available from the command line. Variables always start and end with a percent symbol (%), and you can easily see the value of any variable by using the **echo** command. For example, if you want to see the path to the Program Files folder, you can use this command:

```
echo %programfiles%
```

Some of the commonly referenced variables are listed and described in the following table.

| Variable | Description |
| --- | --- |
| %programfiles% | Shows the path to the Program Files folder (typically C:\Program Files). |
| %systemroot% %windir% | Shows the path to the Windows folder (typically C:\Windows). |
| %systemdrive% | Returns the drive of the root directory (typically C:\). |
| %appdata% | Returns the location where applications store data by default. |
| %userdomain% | Gives the name of the domain that contains the currently logged on user's account. |
| %logonserver% | Lists the name of the domain controller that validated the current logon session (when the system is joined to a domain). |
| %processor_architecture% | Returns the architecture of the processor (such as x86 for 32-bit or AMD64 for 64-bit processors). |
| %userprofile% | Lists the location of the profile for the current user. |
| %allusersprofile% | Lists the location of the All Users profile. |
| %cd% | Lists the current directory string. |
| %date% | Returns the current date. |
| %time% | Returns the current time. |
| %errorlevel% | Gives the error number of the last executed command. Anything other than 0 indicates an error occurred. |

**TIP:** You can view a listing of all variables by typing the **set** command.

It's also possible to create your own variables if desired. This can sometimes be useful within scripts.

| Variable Commands | Comments |
|---|---|
| `set variable-name = value`<br>`C:\>set myvariable = success` | Creates the variable and assigns a value. |
| `C:\>echo %myvariable%`<br>`success` | Shows the value of the variable.<br><br>Because the variable **myvariable** was set to **success**, the **echo** command shows the value of the variable as "success." |

## Understanding Switches

You can modify most commands by using one or more switches. A switch is preceded by a space and a forward slash ( / ) or a space and a dash ( - ). For example, if you wanted to flush the DNS cache, you would use the **ipconfig** command and modify it with the **/flushdns** switch like this:

```
ipconfig /flushdns
```

Some commands can use either a forward slash or a dash, while others work only with one or the other.

| Command | Description |
|---|---|
| `C:\>ipconfig -flushdns`<br>`C:\>ipconfig /flushdns` | Both of these commands will work the same. |
| `C:\>ipconfig/flushdns` | This will work.<br><br>Even though the space is omitted before the slash, the **ipconfig** command recognizes it. |
| `C:\>ipconfig-flushdns`<br>`ipconfig-flushdns is not recognized as an internal or external command, operable program, or batch file.` | This will fail.<br><br>The **ipconfig** command doesn't recognize the dash (-) as the beginning of a switch without a space. |

**TIP:** It's best to always use a space before the switch because this will consistently work. You will have inconsistent results if you use the forward slash (/) or dash (-) without a space preceding it.

## Understanding Wildcards

Wildcards are used to represent one or more characters. Two wildcard characters are available at the command prompt, the asterisk and the question mark.

| Wildcard | Description |
|---|---|
| * | The asterisk takes the place of zero or more characters. |
| C:\>dir *.txt | Shows all files that end with .txt. |
| C:\>dir a* | Shows all files that start with A. |
| C:\>dir a*.txt | Shows all files that start with A and end with .txt. |
| ? | The question mark takes the place of one character. |
| C:\>dir week?.txt | Shows all .txt files that start with "week" and end with one character and .txt (such as week1.txt, week2.txt, and so on).<br><br>**NOTE:** Using the question mark wildcard will not detect a file that has no character where the question mark is used. In other words, if there was a file named week.txt, the **dir week?.txt** command would not detect it. |

# Getting Help

The goal of this book is not to cover every possible switch and every possible command. Instead, the goal is to give you the common commands you'll use on the job and need to know for the Windows 7 exams. If you work with Windows 7 long enough, there will come a time when you'll need a little more information.

Thankfully, the command prompt includes a lot of built-in help if you know how to use it. For example, if you enter just **help**, you'll get a list of commands that you can enter at the command line.

| Command | Description |
|---|---|
| assoc | Displays or modifies file extension associations. |
| attrib | Sets and displays attributes for files. |
| bcdedit | Sets properties in boot configuration data store to control the boot process. |
| call | Calls one batch program from another. |
| cd or chdir | Displays the name of or changes the current directory. |
| chkdsk | Checks a disk and displays a status report, and can also repair disk errors. |
| compact | Displays or alters the compression of files on NTFS partitions. |
| convert | Converts FAT volumes to NTFS. You cannot convert the current drive without rebooting. |
| copy | Copies one or more files to another location. |
| date | Displays or sets the date. |
| del or erase | Deletes one or more files. |
| dir | Displays a list of files and subdirectories in a directory. |
| diskpart | Displays or configures Disk Partition properties. |

| | |
|---|---|
| `doskey` | Edits command lines, recalls Windows commands, and creates macros. |
| `driverquery` | Displays current device driver status and properties. |
| `echo` | Displays messages, or turns command echoing on or off. |
| `exit` | Quits the CMD.EXE program (command interpreter). |
| `for` | Runs a specified command for each file in a set of files. |
| `format` | Formats a disk for use with Windows. |
| `fsutil` | Displays or configures the file system properties. |
| `ftype` | Displays or modifies file types used in file extension associations. |
| `goto` | Directs the Windows command interpreter to a labeled line in a batch program. |
| `gpresult` | Displays Group Policy information that is applied to the local system. |
| `help` | Provides Help information for Windows commands. |
| `icacls` | Displays, modifies, backs up, or restores ACLs for files and directories. |
| `if` | Performs conditional processing in batch programs. |
| `label` | Creates, changes, or deletes the volume label of a disk. |
| `md or mkdir` | Creates a directory. |
| `more` | Displays output one screen at a time. |
| `path` | Displays or sets a search path for executable files. |
| `rd or rmdir` | Removes a directory. |
| `rem` | Records comments (remarks) in batch files or CONFIG.SYS. |
| `ren or rename` | Renames a file or files. |
| `robocopy` | Copies files and directory trees with metadata such as permissions. |
| `set` | Displays, sets, or removes Windows environment variables. |
| `sc` | Displays or configures services (background processes). |
| `schtasks` | Schedules commands and programs to run on a computer. |
| `shutdown` | Allows proper local or remote shutdown of machine. |
| `systeminfo` | Displays machine specific properties and configuration. |
| `tasklist` | Displays all currently running tasks including services. |
| `taskkill` | Kills or stops a running process or application. |
| `time` | Displays or sets the system time. |
| `tree` | Graphically displays the directory structure of a drive or path. |
| `xcopy` | Copies files and directory trees. |
| `wmic` | Displays WMI information inside an interactive command shell. |

There are two ways you can get help on individual commands. You can use the **/?** switch or enter **help** followed by the command. However, only the **/?** switch method works consistently.

| Command | Description |
|---|---|
| `/?`<br>`C:\>assoc /?` | Using the **/?** switch provides help for any command. |
| `help command`<br>`C:\>help assoc` | You can get help for some commands by entering the word **help** followed by the command you want help on. However, not all commands support this syntax. |
| `C:\>help ipconfig`<br>`This command is not supported by the help utility. Try "ipconfig /?".` | This will fail and generate the error shown. In other words, the **ipconfig** command only supports the **/?** switch for help. |

When you ask for help on any command, you'll see that a lot of help is available. However, you need to know how to read it. The following table outlines the conventions used in the **help** output.

| help Notation | Description | Example help Output and Description |
|---|---|---|
| Text without brackets or braces | Items you must type as shown. | `ipconfig [/allcompartments]`<br>`[/all] [/renew[adapter]]`<br>`[/release[adapter]]`<br>`[/renew6[adapter]]`<br>`[/release6[adapter]]`<br>`[/flushdns] [/displaydns]`<br>`[/registerdns]`<br>`[/showclassidadapter]`<br>`[/setclassidadapter`<br>`[classid]]`<br><br>ipconfig is without brackets so it must be entered as **ipconfig**. |
| [Text inside square brackets] | Optional items. | `echo [message]`<br><br>The message is in brackets [ ], indicating it is optional. In other words, you can enter echo to see if echo is turned on or off for the system, or you can enter **echo** with a message to echo to the screen. |

| <Text inside angle brackets> | Placeholder for which you must supply a value. | `echo <message>`<br><br>You provide the message. For example, you could enter echo **%programfiles%** to view the value of the variable. |
|---|---|---|
| {Text inside braces} | Set of required items; choose on. | `gpupdate [/target:{computer | user}] [/force] [/wait:<value>] [/logoff] [/boot] [/sync]`<br><br>If **/target** is used, the user must enter either **computer** or **user**. In this case, **/target** is optional, and if it was omitted, it would execute against both the computer and user. |
| Vertical bar (\|) | Separator for mutually exclusive items; choose one. | `gpresult [/s system [/u username [/p [password]]]] [/scope scope] [/user targetusername] [/r | /v | /z] [(/x | /h) <filename> [/f]]`<br><br>Several items in this command cannot be used with others so they are grouped together in the brackets and separated with the vertical bar. If you want to use **/r**, **/v**, or **/z**, you must choose only one. Similarly, if you want to use **/x** or **/h**, you must choose only one. |
| Ellipsis (...) | Items that can be repeated. | `winrm operation resource_ uri [-switch:value [-switch:value] ...] [@ {key=value[;key=value]...}]`<br><br>The ellipsis indicates that multiple switch values and multiple key values can be entered in the same line. |

Figure 2-1 shows the output of the **ipconfig /?** command. The following table shows this output and breaks down the different elements of the help.

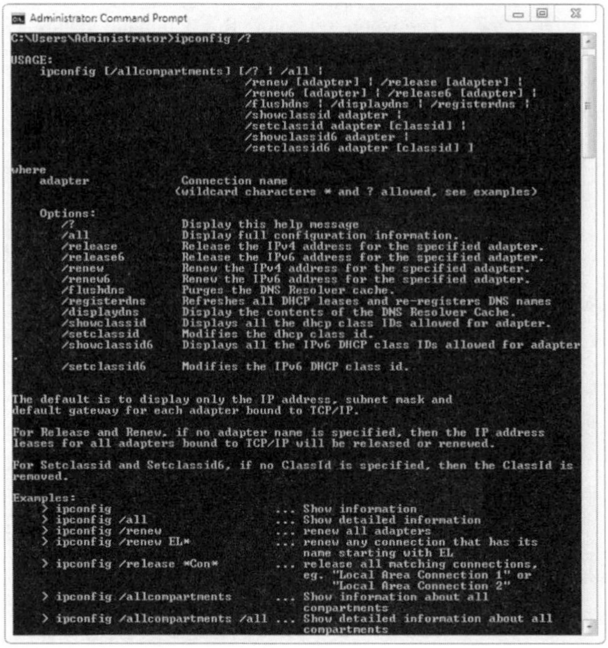

**Figure 2-1** Output of the **ipconfig /?** Command

| help Output | Description |
|---|---|
| USAGE:<br><br>    ipconfig<br><br>        [/allcompartments]  [/?  \|<br><br>        /all  \|<br><br>        /renew [adapter]  \|<br><br>        /release [adapter]  \|<br><br>        /renew6 [adapter]  \|<br><br>        /release6 [adapter]  \|<br><br>        /flushdns  \|<br><br>        /displaydns  \|<br><br>        /registerdns  \|<br><br>        /showclassid adapter  \|<br><br>        /setclassid adapter<br><br>           [classid]  \|<br><br>        /showclassid6 adapter  \|<br><br>        /setclassid6 adapter<br><br>    [classid]  ] | The USAGE section shows the syntax of the command. Notice that all the switches are contained in brackets [ ], indicating that they are all optional. It's possible to enter the command as only **ipconfig**.<br><br>This also shows all the possible switches. Notice that each of the switches is separated from the others by the vertical bar or pipe command. This indicates that you can enter only one of the switches at a time. You can't enter the **ipconfig** command with more than one switch on the same line. This isn't true with all commands.<br><br>Additionally, some of the commands have optional parameters. For example, you can enter the **ipconfig /release** command with or without the name of an adapter.<br><br>**NOTE:** Many systems have more than one network interface card (identified as "adapter" in the help output). Some commands can be entered against all adapters or only specific adapters if you supply the adapter name. |

```
where
    adapter
Connection name
    (wildcard characters *
and ? allowed, see examples)
```

The where section in this command identifies what "adapter" is when referenced by the **ipconfig** command's switches. On a Windows 7 system, the first adapter has a connection name of "Local Area Connection" by default, so you could enter this command to affect only this NIC:

**ipconfig /renew "local area connection".**

You can substitute the name of any adapter on the system, and you can also use wildcard characters. The following example shows how to use a wildcard character to execute the command against all adapters that have a name that starts with "local":

**ipconfig /renew local***

You won't see a where section in all **help** outputs, but it is useful here.

```
    Options:
    /?              Display
this help message
    /all            Display
full configuration
information.
    /release        Release
the IPv4 address for the
specified adapter.
    /release6       Release the
IPv6 address for the specified
adapter.
    /renew          Renew the
IPv4 address for the specified
adapter.
    /renew6         Renew the
IPv6 address for the specified
adapter.
    /flushdns       Purges the
DNS Resolver cache.
    /registerdns    Refreshes all
DHCP leases and re-
registers DNS names
    /displaydns     Display the
contents of the DNS Resolver
Cache.
```

The Options section explains the usage of each of the switches.

This section can often be difficult to interpret if the command developer chose to use just a few words. For example, the **/release** and **/renew** switches refer directly to DHCP and how the TCP/IP configuration information leased from a DHCP server can be released, or a lease can be renewed.

| | |
|---|---|
| `/showclassid     Displays all`<br>`the DHCP class IDs allowed for`<br>`adapter.`<br>`/setclassid          Modifies`<br>`the DHCP class id.`<br>`/showclassid6   Displays all`<br>`the IPv6 DHCP class IDs`<br>`allowed for adapter.`<br>`/setclassid6         Modifies`<br>`the IPv6 DHCP class id.`<br>`The default is to display only`<br>`the IP address, subnet mask`<br>`and default gateway for each`<br>`adapter bound to TCP/IP.`<br>`For release and renew, if no`<br>`adapter name is specified,`<br>`then the IP address leases for`<br>`all adapters bound to TCP/IP`<br>`will be released or renewed.`<br>`For setclassid and`<br>`setclassid6, if no classid is`<br>`specified, then the classid is`<br>`removed.` | |
| `Examples:`<br>`> ipconfig`<br>`... Show information`<br>`> ipconfig /all`<br>`... Show detailed information`<br>`> ipconfig /renew`<br>`... renew all adapters`<br>`> ipconfig /renew EL*`<br>`... renew any connection that`<br>`has its name starting with EL`<br>`> ipconfig /release *Con*   ...`<br>`release all matching con-`<br>`nections,  eg. "Local Area`<br>`Connection 1" or "Local Area`<br>`Connection 2"`<br>`> ipconfig /allcompartments`<br>`... Show information about all`<br>`compartments`<br>`> ipconfig /allcompartments /`<br>`all ... Show detailed informa-`<br>`tion about all compartments` | Most switches include an Examples section that shows you exactly how to enter the command for different purposes. These examples are often useful to get a better understanding of the explanation. |

You can also get additional help on command-line commands through the Windows 7 interface. Choose **Start, Help** and **Support**. Type the name of the command in the **Search Help** text box and press **Enter**.

> **TIP:** You might also like to check out online sources for additional details. For example, you can view a listing of command-line commands from A to Z here: http://technet.microsoft.com/library/cc772390.aspx

This chapter provides information and commands concerning the following topics:

- Understanding folders and directories
- Understanding paths
- Viewing files and folders with **dir**
- Changing the path with **cd**
- Using drag and drop to the Command Prompt window
- Deleting folders with **rd**
- Creating folders with **md**
- Controlling output with **more**
- Redirecting output
- Using **exit**

## Understanding Folders and Directories

The contents of Windows disks are organized into folders. In the early days of MS-DOS, these folders were called *directories*, but as the graphical user interface became prominent, the term *folders* became much more common, in part because the icon looks like a file folder.

Figure 3-1 shows folders within a Windows Explorer window.

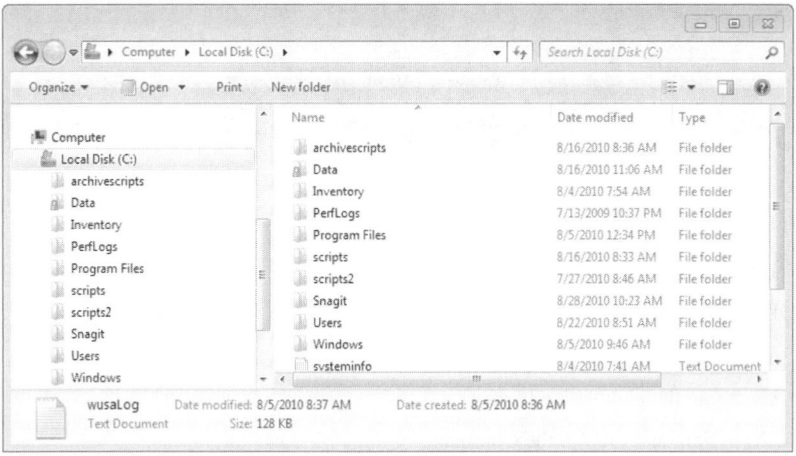

**Figure 3-1**    Folders Viewed in Windows Explorer

Figure 3-2 shows the same folders shown in Figure 3-1. However, the Command Prompt window retains the old-school terminology *directories*.

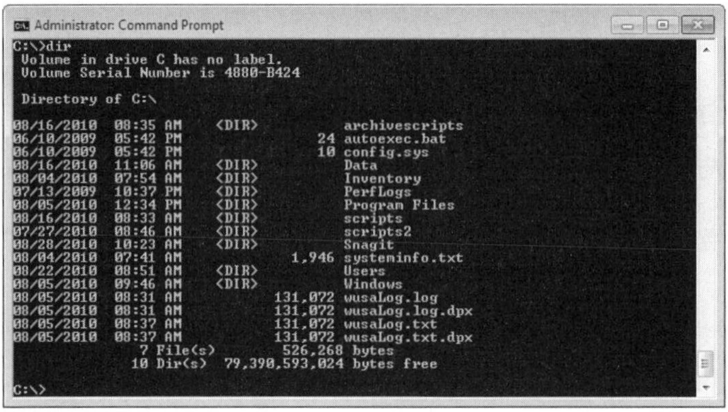

**Figure 3-2**    Directories Viewed in the Command Prompt Window

Even though the term *folder* has replaced *directory* in most current documentation, the command prompt commands still use the term directory. For example, the full names for the **cd**, **rd**, and **md** commands all refer to directories, as in change directory, remove directory, and make directory, respectively.

## Understanding Paths

The command prompt shows the current path at the prompt. For example, if you open a prompt with administrative privileges, you see the following prompt:

```
C:\Windows\System32>
```

When executing a command, the system always looks in the current location for the file or executable command. For example, if you have a file named 70-680.txt in the current path, you could use the following command:

```
notepad 70-680.txt
```

You can also specify a path. For example, if your file is in a folder named studynotes on the C: drive, you could use the following command:

```
notepad c:\studynotes\70-680.txt
```

In this example, it doesn't matter what your current path is because you specified the path for the command to use.

You may notice that the command is **Notepad**, but the path to Notepad is not needed when it is executed. Notepad is located in the C:\Windows folder. Windows 7 is aware of the following paths by default:

- C:\Windows
- C:\Windows\System32
- C:\Windows\System32\Wbem
- C:\Windows\System32\WindowsPowerShell\v1.0\

Windows 7 sets the %**path**% variable to all of these folders when it is first installed. You can view the path with the commands shown in the following table.

| Command | Description |
| --- | --- |
| `C:\>echo %path%` | The output is<br><br>`c:\Windows\system32;c:\Windows;c:\Windows\System32\`<br>`Wbem;c:\Windows\System32\WindowsPowerShell\v1.0\` |
| `C:\>path` | The output is<br><br>`PATH=c:\Windows\system32;c:\Windows;c:\`<br>`Windows\System32\Wbem;c:\Windows\System32\`<br>`WindowsPowerShell\v1.0\` |

You can also modify the path with the commands shown in the following table.

| Command | Description |
| --- | --- |
| `C:\>path = c:\mypath` | Sets the path for the current command prompt session to only `c:\mypath`.<br><br>When you close the session and open another session, the path will revert to the value in the %**path**% variable. |

| | |
|---|---|
| `C:\>path = %path%;c:\mypath` | Appends the current path with the value you include (in the example, **c:\mypath**). |
| | When you close the session and open another session, the path will revert to the value in the **%path%** variable. |

# Viewing Files and Folders with dir

The **dir** command is short for *directory*. It provides a listing of the contents in the current directory or folder.

The simplest usage is

```
dir
```

When executed in a folder named win7study, this is the output:

```
C:\data\win7study>dir
```

```
Volume in drive C has no label.
 Volume Serial Number is 35B2-E2A2
 Directory of c:\data\win7study
07/17/2010  06:43 AM    <DIR>          .
07/17/2010  06:43 AM    <DIR>          ..
07/17/2010  06:42 AM            33,080 70-680 notes.docx
07/17/2010  06:42 AM            42,296 70-685 notes.docx
07/17/2010  06:42 AM            55,662 70-686 notes.docx
07/17/2010  06:43 AM    <DIR>          WhitePapers
07/17/2010  06:42 AM            21,868 Windows 7 Commands.docx
               4 File(s)        152,906 bytes
               3 Dir(s)  21,604,036,608 bytes free
```

This output shows that there are four documents, named 70-680 notes.docx, 70-685 notes.docx, 70-686 notes.docx, and Windows 7 Commands.docx. The date and time shows the last time each file was modified.

Folders or directories are identified by <DIR>. For example, WhitePapers is a folder. There are two additional <DIR> listings. The first one with a single period represents the root of the drive. The second one with two periods represents the parent folder. In this example, the parent folder of C:\data\win7study is c:\data.

The following table lists and describes some switches you might find useful when using the **dir** command.

| dir Switch | Description |
|---|---|
| C:\>dir /p | Shows one page at a time if the listing spans multiple pages. |
| C:\>dir /q | Shows the owner of the file. Normally the owner is the user that created the file. |
| C:\>dir /a:h | Shows only files with the hidden attribute set. You can also use /a:d for directories, /a:s for system files, /a:r for read-only files, and /a:a for files ready for archiving (or that haven't been backed up since they were changed). |
| C:\>dir *.bat | Uses the * wildcard in place of zero or more characters. This will show all the files that have an extension of .bat. Similarly, **dir a\*.bat** shows all the files that start with *a* and have a .bat extension. |

## Changing the Path with cd

Many times when you're working at the command prompt, you need to change the path. The **cd** or change directory command is used to change the path. The syntax is

```
cd path
```

For example, if you want to change the path to the C:\studynotes folder, you can use this command:

```
cd \studynotes
```

The **cd** command changes the path using the current drive by default. In other words, if you're currently using the C: drive, it will change to the path on the current drive. However, you can use the **/d** switch to change to a different drive.

| cd Commands | Description |
|---|---|
| C:\data>cd archive | Changes to the archive folder from within the data folder (C:\data\archive). <br><br> This will fail if the archive folder doesn't exist. |
| C:\data\archive>cd .. | Moves up one folder with **..** <br><br> After executing this command, the path will be C:\data. |
| C:\data\archive>cd \ | Changes to the root of the drive with \. <br><br> After executing this command, the path will be C:\. |
| C:\data\archive>cd /d d:\graphics | Changes to another drive with the **/d** switch. After executing this command, the path will be D:\graphics>. |

## Using Drag and Drop to the Command Prompt Window

You don't always have to type in the path. Instead, you can drag and drop the path from Windows Explorer to the command prompt. This is very useful when you want to change the command prompt path to the location of an open Windows Explorer window.

Consider Figure 3-3. To achieve the same result without dragging and dropping, you would have to enter the following command to change the prompt:

```
cd "c:\data\study\windows 7"
```

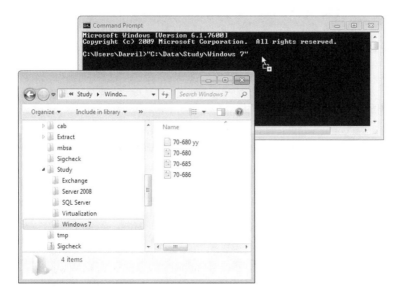

**Figure 3-3**   Dragging and Dropping a Path from Windows Explorer to the Command Prompt

You can use the following steps to drag and drop the path into the command prompt:

**Step 1.**   Open Windows Explorer and a Command Prompt window.

**Step 2.**   Use Windows Explorer to browse to the folder you want to drag and drop.

**Step 3.**   Click and hold the folder in the left pane of Windows Explorer.

**Step 4.**   Drag and drop the folder onto the Command Prompt window.

**Step 5.**   Click in the Command Prompt window.

Press the **Home** key to move the cursor to the beginning of the line.

**Step 6.**   Enter **cd** and a space at the beginning of the line and press **Enter**.

## Deleting Folders with rd

**rd** is the command used to remove or delete directories or folders. You can also enter it as **rmdir**. The basic syntax of the command is

```
rd path
```

**rd** has only two switches, shown in the following table. For these examples, imagine that a folder named oldnotes is in the root of c:\ (as c:\oldnotes).

| Command | Description |
| --- | --- |
| `C:\>rd oldnotes` | Deletes the folder if it is empty. If it is not empty, you'll get this error message:<br><br>`The directory is not empty.` |
| `C:\>rd /s oldnotes` | Deletes the folder and all files and subdirectories in the folder. If there are any folders or files in the folder, you will be prompted to confirm the deletion. |
| `C:\>rd /s /q oldnotes` | This will delete the folder and all files and subdirectories in the folder. It will not prompt you to confirm the deletion.<br><br>The **/q** switch is useful when using the **rd** command within a batch file. It will automatically do the action without requiring a confirmation. |

## Creating Folders with md

**md** is the command used to create (or "make") directories or folders. You can also enter it as **mkdir**. The basic syntax is

```
md path
```

The **md** command works in the context of the current folder by default, but if you include the path, it will create the folder based on the specified path.

| Command | Description |
| --- | --- |
| `C:\Windows\System32>md \data` | Creates a folder named data at the root of the `C:\` drive.<br><br>Notice that the \ character indicates this should be created at the root of the drive, and not in the \System32 folder. |
| `C:\>md data2` | Creates a folder named data2 at the root of the `C:` drive.<br><br>Notice that because the path is currently at `C:`, the folder is created from there. |

| | |
|---|---|
| `C:\>md "\data\studynotes\`<br>`windows 7"` | Creates a folder named windows 7 in the path `C:\data\studynotes`. If none of the folders currently exist, each of the folders (data, studynotes, and windows 7) would be created.<br><br>Notice that because the windows 7 folder includes a space between windows and 7, the entire path must be enclosed in quotes. |
| `Cc:\>md \data\studynotes\`<br>`windows 7` | This is not correct.<br><br>It will create a folder named windows (not windows 7) in the path `c:\data\studynotes`. If none of the folders currently exist, each of the folders (data, studynotes, and windows) would be created.<br><br>Notice that because there is a space in the path, nothing after the space is recognized. Instead of creating a folder named windows 7, it creates a folder named windows and ignores the 7. |

## Controlling Output with more

The **more** command can be used with any other commands issued at the command line to display the output one screen at a time. It's specified at the end of the command with the vertical bar or pipe character ( | ). Press **Shift** and \ on U.S. keyboards to get the | character.

The format of the **more** command is

| | |
|---|---|
| *command* | `more` | Displays the output of the command one page at a time. |
| `gpresult /?` | `more` | Displays the output of **gpresult** help one page at a time. |

The command prompt will show a single page and then display "-- More --" at the bottom of the page, indicating that there is more to display. You can then press one of the keys in the following table to view additional output from the command.

| Key Pressed | Result |
|---|---|
| Spacebar | Displays the next page. |
| Enter | Displays the next line. |
| F | Displays the next file if multiple files are specified in the command, or quits the **more** command if other files aren't specified. |
| Q | Quits the **more** command. |
| = | Shows the current line number. |
| P *n* | Displays the next *n* lines. |
| S *n* | Skips the next *n* lines. |

# Redirecting Output

Many times when you execute a command, you'll want to save the output. There are two primary ways you can do so. You can use the > symbol to redirect the output to a file, or you can use the **clip** command to redirect the output to the Clipboard.

## Using the Redirect Symbol (>)

You can use the > symbol at the end of a command to redirect the output to a file. For example, if you want to view the TCP/IP configuration for a system, you can use **ipconfig /all**. If you want to send the output to a text file named ipconfiguration.txt, you can use the following command:

| | |
|---|---|
| `ipconfig /all > ipconfiguration.txt` | Redirects the output to a file called ipconfiguration.txt. |
| `notepad ipconfiguration.txt`<br>`ipconfiguration.txt` | Both examples open the ipconfiguration.txt file in Notepad. |

> **TIP:** Because Notepad is associated with .txt files by default, you can also simply enter **ipconfiguration.txt** to launch Notepad with the ipconfiguration file opened.

## Using clip

The **clip** command can be used to redirect the output to the Windows Clipboard. The format is

*command* | clip

For example, if you want to send the output of the **gpresult /z** command to the Clipboard, you can use this command:

gpresult /z | clip

After the data is in the Clipboard, you can then paste it into a document. For example, most applications allow you to press Ctrl+V to paste data into an open document.

# Using exit

When you want to close the command prompt or exit a batch file, you can use the **exit** command. When exiting the command prompt, you simply enter

exit

However, if you're using a script, you have two switches you can use:

| exit Switch | Example | Description |
|---|---|---|
| /b | `if exist error.txt exit /b` | The **/b** switch causes the batch file to exit, but the command prompt stays open. If the **/b** switch is omitted, the entire command prompt session closes. The example checks to see if a file named error.txt exists, and if so, exits the batch file.<br><br>Normally, the batch file would run from beginning to end and exit when all the commands have completed. However, you can use this for a conditional exit from a batch file. |
| /b *exitcode* | `set myvar = 5`<br>`if %myvar% equ 5 exit /b 5` | The *exitcode* assigns a value to the **%errorlevel%** variable. This %errorlevel% can be checked after the script is run either directly (such as with an **echo** %errorlevel% command) or within a calling script.<br><br>The example assigns the value of 5 to a variable and then checks to see if the variable is a certain value. It exits the batch file if it meets the condition. It also assigns the **%errorlevel%** variable a value of 5.<br><br>Notice that the **%errorlevel%** variable isn't specified directly in the example. Instead, the **exit /b 5** clause assigns the **%errorlevel%** variable the value of 5.<br><br>After the batch file exits, you can view the value of the **%errorlevel%** variable with this command:<br><br>**echo %errorlevel%** |

This chapter provides information and commands concerning the following topics:

- Associating file extensions with **assoc** and **ftype**
- Viewing attributes with **attrib**
- Compressing files with **compact**
- Encrypting files with **cipher**
- Copying files with **copy**, **xcopy**, and **robocopy**
- Deleting or removing files with **del**
- Expanding cabinet files with **expand**
- Taking ownership of files with **takeown**
- Removing the Windows.old folder
- Mapping drives with **net use**

## Associating File Extensions with assoc and ftype

File extensions are used to tell the operating system what application to open when you double-click a file. For example, if you receive a file named project.docx from a co-worker via e-mail, you can simply double-click the attached file. Microsoft Word 2010 automatically starts and opens the project.docx file, because the .docx extension is associated with Microsoft Word 2010.

Three key points about file extensions and their associated file are

| File Extensions and File Types | Comments |
|---|---|
| Most files have extensions, such as .htm. | Some files do not have an extension, such as the Hosts file used to resolve hostnames to IP addresses. |
| The file extension is mapped to a file type, such as htmlfile. | The extension isn't directly mapped to the application, but instead is mapped to the file type. |
| The file type is mapped to an application. | The application can open the file, such as "c:\program files (x86)\internet explorer\iexplore.exe" -nohome.<br><br>**NOTE:** If you're using a 32-bit system, the path does not need (x86); instead, the path is "c:\program files\internet explorer\iexplore.exe" -nohome. |

**TIP:** The full path and application name can also include any extra parameters or switches supported by the application. For example, If you execute Internet Explorer from the command line as **"c:\program files (x86)\internet explorer\iexplore.exe"** (or **"c:\program files\internet explorer\iexplore.exe"**), Internet Explorer launches with the home page displayed. However, if you enter it as **"c:\program files (x86)\ internet explorer\iexplore.exe" -nohome**, Internet Explorer opens but without any page shown. In other words, the Internet Explorer home page is not displayed.

The two commands you can use to view and manipulate the file extensions and file type associations are as follows:

| Command | Usage |
|---------|-------|
| assoc | View and modify the file extension association |
| ftype | View and modify the association between the file type and application path and name |

You can also set associations to programs for known file extensions from within Windows 7 using the Set Associations tool, as shown in Figure 4-1.

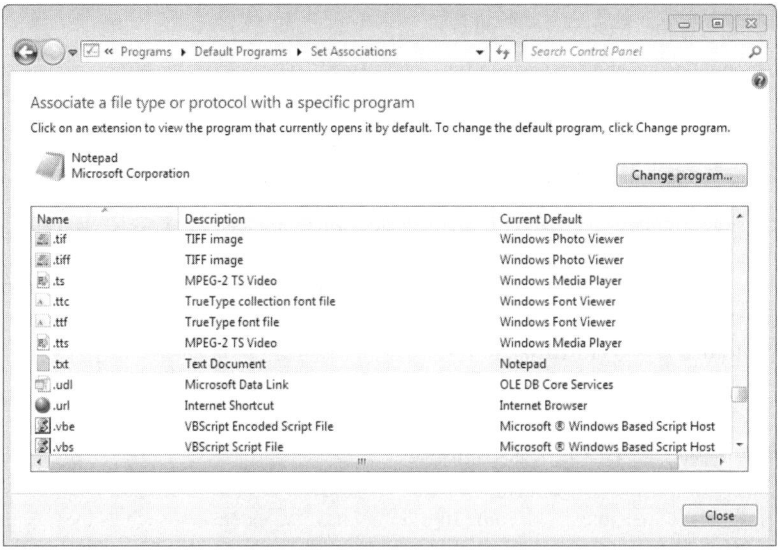

**Figure 4-1** Viewing the Known Extensions

You can access the Set Associations tool by choosing **Start**, **Default Programs** and then clicking **Associate a File Type or Protocol with a Program**.

**NOTE:** The Set Associations tool allows you to associate the program to the file type, but it doesn't allow you to create new associations. You can create new associations with the **assoc** command.

## assoc

You can use the **assoc** command to view and modify file extension associations. When modifying the file extensions, you must run the command from an elevated prompt. The basic syntax is

```
assoc [.ext[=[fileType]]]
```

| assoc Commands | Comments |
| --- | --- |
| `C:\>assoc`<br>`.386=vxdfile`<br>`. . .`<br>`.zip=CompressedFolder` | If you enter **assoc** without any parameters, it shows a listing of all known extensions and the file type that is associated with the extension. This is an extensive list. |
| `C:\>assoc .htm`<br>`.htm=htmlfile`<br>`C:\>assoc .txt`<br>`.txt=txtfile`<br>`C:\>assoc .jpg`<br>`.jpg=jpegfile` | You can add a specific extension and you'll see the file type that is associated with the extension.<br><br>These examples show the file type associated with the .htm, .txt, and .jpg extensions. |
| `C:\>assoc .txt=` | You can delete an association by entering the extension with the = symbol only. This example deletes the association for .txt extensions. |
| `C:\>assoc .txt=txtfile`<br>`.txt=txtfile` | You can create associations by entering the extension and the file type. This example re-creates the association for .txt extensions to the txtfile file type. |

## ftype

The **ftype** command shows the association between a file type and the application that will launch to open that file type. The application is identified with a command string that includes the full path and name of the application. Anyone can view the associations with **ftype**, but you need to run it with elevated privileges to modify the associations. The basic syntax is

```
ftype [fileType[=[openCommandString]]]
```

| ftype Commands | Comments |
| --- | --- |
| `C:\>ftype`<br>`Application.Manifest=rundll32.exe dfshim.`<br>`dll,ShOpenVerbApplication %1`<br>`. . .`<br>`zapfile=%SystemRoot%\system32\notepad.exe %1` | You can view a listing of all known file types and their associated command strings. The command strings include full paths and application names, and can also include parameters. This is an extensive list. |

| | |
|---|---|
| `C:\>ftype htmlfile`<br>`htmlfile="c:\program files\internet explorer\`<br>`iexplorer.exe" -nohome` | If you specify the file type, the command shows the actual command associated with the file type. This example shows that the htmlfile type is associated with Internet Explorer. The **-nohome** switch opens Internet Explorer without opening the home page; instead, it opens the associated file.<br><br>**NOTE:** If you're using a 64-bit system, the path includes (x86), as follows:<br><br>`htmlfile="c:\program files (x86)\internet explorer\ iexplore.exe" -nohome` |
| `C:\>ftype txtfile`<br>`txtfile=%SystemRoot%\system32\notepad.exe %1` | This example shows that the txtfile file type is associated with Notepad. The **%1** parameter indicates to Notepad that a filename is passed as a parameter. In other words, if you double-click a .txt file, the file will be passed as a parameter and opened in Notepad. |
| `C:\>ftype jpegfile`<br><br>`jpegfile=%systemroot%\system32\rundll32.exe`<br>`"%programfiles%\windows photo viewer\`<br>`photoviewer.dll", imageview_fullscreen %1` | The jpegfile file type is associated with Windows Photo Viewer with full screen mode as the default view. This also uses the **%1** parameter similarly to how Notepad uses it. |
| `C:\>ftype txtfile=` | You can delete a file type association by entering the extension with the = symbol only. This example deletes the association for txtfile file types. |
| `C:\>ftype txtfile=%systemroot%\system32\`<br>`notepad.exe %1` | If an association exists for a file type, you can specify the command string. This example creates the command string for the txtfile file type. This command would not work if the txtfile file type wasn't already associated with .txt files. |

## Viewing Attributes with attrib

Every file has several different attributes assigned that you can view and change from the command line with the **attrib** command. You can view all of the existing attributes for files by entering the following command:

```
attrib
```

You can also view and manipulate most of these attributes in Windows Explorer by viewing the properties and advanced attributes, as shown in Figure 4-2.

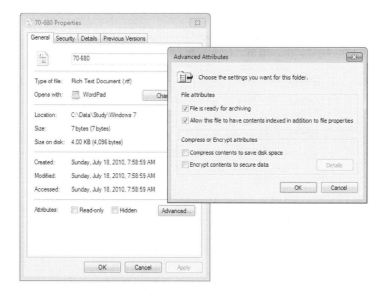

**Figure 4-2** Viewing the Properties and Advanced Attributes of a File

**NOTE:** The extended attributes (compressed and encrypted) are not viewable using the **attrib** command, but you can view them using the **compact** and **cipher** commands, respectively. These commands are covered later in this chapter.

The different attributes that you can see with **attrib** are identified by single capital letters, such as *R* and *H*.

| Attribute Codes | Comments |
|---|---|
| R | Indicates the file is read-only. |
| H | Indicates the file is a hidden file. |
| A | When set, indicates the file has not been backed up or has been modified since it was last backed up. The File Is Ready for Archiving check box, shown in Figure 4-2, will be checked. |
| | When clear, it indicates the file has been backed up. The File Is Ready for Archiving check box will be unchecked. |

| I | When set, indicates the file will not be indexed by the system. The Allow This File to Have Contents Indexed in Addition to File Properties check box, shown in Figure 4-2, will be checked. |
| --- | --- |
| This is the "Not content indexed file attribute." | When not set, indicates the file will be indexed by the system. The Allow This File to Have Contents Indexed in Addition to File Properties check box will be unchecked. |
| | The index attribute can't be set on hidden files. |
| S | Indicates the file is a system file. |

Attributes can be modified with the **attrib** command using the + or - character and the associated letter. Additionally, the **attrib** command has three switches:

| attrib Switches | Comments |
| --- | --- |
| /s | Applies the changes to the files in the current folder and all subfolders |
| /d | Applies the changes to folders in addition to files |
| /l | Applies the changes to the symbolic link instead of to the target of the symbolic link |

**TIP:** A *symbolic link* is a pointer to a different location. For example, in previous editions of Windows, My Documents was located in the C:\Documents and Settings\ folder. However, in Windows 7, the location is in the C:\Users\ folder. If a program is looking for My Documents in the old location, the symbolic link points the application to the new location.

The following table shows some common usage of the **attrib** command.

**NOTE:** Even though the attributes are displayed by the **attrib** command with capital letters, you can change them using either uppercase or lowercase letters.

| Using attrib | Comments |
| --- | --- |
| `C:\>attrib`<br>`A              c:\autoexec.bat`<br>`A              c:\config.sys`<br>`A   SHR    c:\io.sys`<br>`A   SHR    c:\msdos.sys`<br>`A   SH     c:\pagefile.sys`<br>`A              c:\systeminfo.txt`<br>`A      I     c:\wusalog.log` | You can enter the **attrib** command by itself to view the attributes of all the files in the current directory.<br><br>The output shows that all the files have the A attribute set (indicating the file has not been backed up, or has changed since it was backed up).<br><br>Three of the files (io.sys, msdos.sys, and pagefile.sys) are system files. These same files are also hidden. Two of the files (io.sys and msdos.sys) are read-only. Only the wusalog.log file will be indexed. |

| | |
|---|---|
| `C:\data>attrib *.txt` | You can use wildcards with the **attrib** command. This example shows the attributes of all the files ending with the .txt extension in the current directory.<br><br>**NOTE:** The following commands modify files in the C:\Data folder instead of files in the root folder. |
| `C:\data>attrib test.txt +i`<br>`C:\data>attrib *.txt -i` | Attributes can be set with the + character. This example sets the index attribute for the test.txt file. You can remove attributes with the - character. The second example removes indexing for all text files in the folder. |
| `/s`<br>`C:\data>attrib +i /s`<br>`C:\data>attrib -i /s` | Use the **/s** switch if you want to include all files in subfolders. This example sets the index attribute for files in the current folder and subfolders. Similarly, you can remove the attributes for all the files with the **-i** switch. |
| `/d`<br>`C:\data>attrib +i /d /s`<br>`C:\data>attrib -i /d /s`<br>`C:\data>attrib c:\data +i /d /s` | You can use the **/d** attribute to apply the change to folders. It must be applied with the **/s** switch.<br><br>Folder attributes are inherited by new files. For example, if the index attribute is set for a folder, all new files created in the folder will have the index attribute set by default.<br><br>The first two examples set and remove the index attribute for files in the current folder, subfolders, and the folders themselves. However, these first two examples do not set the attribute on the current folder. The third example sets the index attribute on the c:\ data folder by specifying it in the path. |

# Compressing Files with compact

The **compact** command compresses and uncompresses files and folders on NTFS drives. The two primary switches you'll use are **/c** to compress files and **/u** to uncompress them. When files are compressed, Windows Explorer displays them with blue text.

| compact Commands | Comments |
|---|---|
| `C:\data>compact`<br>`Listing c:\Data\`<br>` New files added to this directory`<br>`will not be compressed.`<br>`        3617 :        3617 = 1.0 to`<br>`1   70-680.rtf`<br>`        1641 :        1641 = 1.0 to`<br>`1   70-685.rtf`<br>`        2629 :        2629 = 1.0 to`<br>`1   70-686.rtf`<br>`Of 3 files within 1 directories`<br>`0 are compressed and 4 are not`<br>`compressed.`<br>`7887 total bytes of data are stored`<br>`in 7887 bytes.`<br>`The compression ratio is 1.0 to 1.` | If you enter the command without switches, it shows you the size and current state of compression for files in the current folder.<br><br>The output shows the actual size of the files in bytes and the compression ratio. A compression ratio of 1.0 to 1 indicates the file is not compressed.<br><br>This also shows the uncompressed size and the actual amount of space taken by the files. Compressed files usually take less space on the disk than uncompressed files. |
| `C:\data>compact /c test.txt` | You compress an individual file by using the **/c** switch and then including the name of the file. |
| `C:\data>compact /c` | If you want to compress all files in the current folder, you can use the **/c** switch by itself. This also changes the folder attribute to compressed, causing new files added to the folder to be compressed. |
| `C:\data>compact /c /s` | You can add the **/s** switch to include all files in the folder and subfolders. New files added to any of the folders will be compressed. |
| `C:\data>compact /u /s` | The **/u** switch uncompresses files. This example uncompresses all files in the folder and subfolders. New files added to any of the folders will not be compressed. |
| `C:\data>compact /c /f test.txt` | You can use the **/f** switch to force compression on the file. This is useful if the original attempt to compress the file was interrupted, leaving the file in a partially compressed state. |

# Encrypting Files with cipher

You can encrypt files on NTFS using the **cipher** command. These files are encrypted using the Encrypting File System (EFS) feature of NTFS. The two primary switches you'll use are **/e** to encrypt files and **/d** to decrypt them. When files are encrypted, Windows Explorer displays them with green text.

**NOTE:** Files can be either compressed or encrypted. However, they cannot be compressed and encrypted.

| cipher Commands | Comments |
|---|---|
| C:\data>**cipher**<br>Listing c:\data\study\windows 7\<br>New files added to this directory<br>will not be encrypted.<br>E 70-680.rtf<br>U 70-685.rtf<br>U 70-686.rtf | If you enter **cipher** without any switches, it shows the current state of the encryption attribute.<br><br>Encrypted files are shown with E.<br><br>The U attribute indicates the files are not encrypted.<br><br>The **cipher /c** command provides the same output. |
| **/e**<br>C:\data>**cipher /e** | The **/e** switch used by itself encrypts all the files in the current folder and changes the folder attribute to E. New files added to the folder will be encrypted. |
| **/e** *file*<br>C:\data>**cipher /e 70-685.rtf** | You can add a filename with the **/e** switch to encrypt only the named file. This doesn't affect other files or the folder attribute. |
| **/d**<br>C:\data>**cipher /d** | The **/d** switch decrypts encrypted files and folders. This example decrypts all the files in the current folder, as long as the user has appropriate privileges.<br><br>The user must have encrypted the file, have been added as an authorized user for the file, or be a data recovery agent. |
| **/d** *file*<br>C:\data>**cipher /d 70-685.rtf** | You can decrypt a single file by specifying the file with the **/d** switch. |
| **/u /n**<br>C:\>**cipher /u**<br>C:\data>**cipher /u /n >**<br>**encryptedfileslist.txt** | The **/u** switch can be used to locate all encrypted files on all local drives of a system and update them with the data recovery agent's certificate if it has changed.<br><br>This switch is useful if the keys have changed, such as when a new data recovery agent is designated.<br><br>When used with the **/n** switch, it lists the files but does not update them. This is useful to create a list of encrypted files on a system |
| C:\data>**cipher /k** | Create a new file encryption key for the user. |

| /w | Remove data from available unused disk space on a drive. |
|---|---|
| C:\data>**cipher /w:e:**<br><br>To remove as much data as possible, please close all other applications while running CIPHER /W.<br>Writing 0x00<br>.............................<br>.............................<br>................<br>Writing 0xFF<br>.............................<br>.............................<br>................<br>Writing Random Numbers<br>.............................<br>.............................<br>................ | When files are first encrypted, it's possible that remnants of these files are left on the drive. You can remove all remnants of these files with the **/w** switch. The example sanitizes the unused disk space on drive E. Note that it first writes all 0s (0x00) to the unused disk space, then writes all 1s (0xFF), and then writes random numbers to the drive.<br><br>This can also be done on any NTFS drive even if there aren't any encrypted files on the drive. |

## Copying Files with copy, xcopy, and robocopy

Frequently, you'll need to copy files. There are three primary commands that are useful for copying:

| Copy Methods | Comments |
|---|---|
| copy | Basic file copy. Use when you want to merge multiple files into one. |
| xcopy | Extended copy command. Use when you want to also copy subdirectories. |
| robocopy | Robust file copy command. Use to copy folder structures and include existing permissions. |

### copy

The **copy** command is used for basic file copying. The basic format is

`copy sourceFile [destinationFile]`

> **NOTE:** The destination filename is not needed if you are copying a file from another directory to the current directory. For example, if you want to copy the c:\tmp\70-680.doc file to the current directory of c:\data, you could use this command:
>
> `C:\data>copy c:\tmp\70-680.doc.`

It can also be used to combine multiple files into a single file. The format when copying multiple files is

`copy sourceFile1 + sourceFile2 [+ sourceFileN] destinationFile`

Note that you can include as many source files as desired.

| Merging Files | Comments |
|---|---|
| `C:\>copy test.txt test2.txt` | Creates a new file named test2.txt from an existing source file named test.txt. |
| `C:\>copy test1.txt + test2.txt combined.txt` | Combines test1.text and test2.txt into a single file named combined.txt. The entire contents of test1.txt will be at the beginning of the file, followed by the entire contents of test2.txt at the end. |

## xcopy

**xcopy** extends the basic **copy** command and provides additional capabilities, most notably the capability to copy subdirectories. The basic format of the command is

**xcopy** *sourceFile destinationFile*

| xcopy Commands | Comments |
|---|---|
| `/s`<br>`C:\>xcopy c:\data d:\data /s`<br><br>`C:\>xcopy c:\data d:\data\ /s` | The **/s** switch copies all the files, directories, and subdirectories from the source to the destination. The example copies all the files from c:\data to d:\data.<br><br>Use the trailing backslash (\) on the destination if the destination folder doesn't exist. If the trailing backslash on the destination is omitted (**d:\data** instead of **d:\ data\**) and the destination folder doesn't exist, you will be prompted to send the data to a file or a directory. If you select a file, all of the data will be combined into a single file. If you choose a directory, the entire folder structure will be re-created. |
| `/e`<br>`C:\>xcopy c:\data d:\data\ /s /e` | The **/e** switch includes empty folders. The example copies the entire contents of the c:\data folder, including all empty subfolders, to d:\data. |
| `/t`<br>`C:\>xcopy c:\data d:\data\ /s /e`<br>`/t` | The **/t** switch is used to copy the directory structure only. Files are not copied. |
| `/y`<br>`C:\>xcopy c:\data d:\data\ /s /e`<br>`/y` | The **/y** switch suppresses prompting to overwrite files. This is useful in scripts when you want the process automated without prompting you to take action.<br><br>If the destination folder exists, **xcopy** prompts the user to overwrite it without the **/y** switch. |

**TIP:** When you copy any file, the permissions and compression value are inherited from the target folder. In other words, the permissions and compression attribute never stay the same when copying files with the **copy** command. The only time the permissions and compression attribute stay the same is when you move a file instead of copying it.

**TIP:** When you copy any file, the encryption attribute always wins. In other words, if it was encrypted, it stays encrypted. If the target folder has the encryption attribute set, the file becomes encrypted.

## robocopy

**robocopy** is a robust file copy command. It might seem new to you, because it hasn't been built into the operating system until Windows Vista, but it has been around since the days of Windows NT 4.0 as part of resource kits. The basic syntax is

```
robocopy sourceDirectory destinationDirectory
```

One of the most valuable features of **robocopy** is the ability to copy metadata associated with a file. Metadata is identified by the flags in the following table. Any of the flags can be used with the **/copy** switch to specify what to copy.

| robocopy /copy Switches | Comments |
|---|---|
| d<br>`C:\>robocopy c:\data d:\data\`<br>`/copy:d` | Data flag. The **d** flag identifies the file itself. |
| a<br>`C:\>robocopy c:\data d:\data\`<br>`/copy:da` | Attributes flag. This includes attributes such as hidden or read-only. |
| t<br>`C:\>robocopy c:\data d:\data\`<br>`/copy:dat` | Timestamps flag. Timestamps include when the file was created and when it was modified. |
| s<br>`C:\>robocopy c:\data d:\data\`<br>`/copy:dats` | Security flag. This includes all of the NTFS access control lists (ACLs). In other words, it includes all of the assigned permissions. |
| o<br>`C:\>robocopy c:\data d:\data\`<br>`/copy:datso` | Owner flag. This flag enables you to retain the original owner of the file. If this isn't used, the owner of the copied file is the user that executes the command. |
| u<br>`C:\>robocopy c:\data d:\data\`<br>`/copy:datsou` | Auditing information flag. This includes all of the security ACLs (SACLs), which identify auditing information for files and folders. |

The **d**, **a**, and **t** flags are used by default. In other words, the following two commands are the same:

```
robocopy c:\data d:\data\
robocopy c:\data d:\data\ /copy:dat
```

The following table shows some common usage of the **robocopy** command.

| Common robocopy Commands | Comments |
|---|---|
| `C:\>robocopy c:\data d:\data\`<br>`C:\>robocopy c:\data d:\data\`<br>`/copy:dat` | Copies all the files in the c:\data folder to the d:\data folder. It does not include subfolders. Note that this includes the data, the attributes, and the timestamps and is the same as using the **/copy:dat** switch. |
| `/s`<br>`C:\>robocopy c:\data d:\data\ /s` | The **/s** switch includes non-empty subfolders. It copies the entire contents of the c:\data folder to the d:\data folder. It includes all non-empty subfolders. |
| `/e`<br>`C:\>robocopy c:\data d:\data\ /e` | If you want to include empty folders, use the /e switch. It copies the entire contents of the c:\data folder (including non-empty subfolders) to the d:\data folder. Note that /s is implied and thus does not need to be included. |
| `/purge`<br>`C:\>robocopy c:\data d:\data\ /e`<br>`/purge` | The **/purge** switch deletes files at the destination that no longer exist at the destination. |
| `/mir`<br>`C:\>robocopy c:\data d:\data\ /mir` | Using the **/mir** switch mirrors the source contents at the destination. This is the same as using the **/e** and **/purge** switches. |
| `/mov`<br>`C:\>robocopy c:\data d:\data\ /mov` | The **/mov** switch specifies that the files should be copied to the destination and then deleted from the source. This is similar to a cut and paste operation. It does not include subdirectories. |
| `/move`<br>`C:\>robocopy c:\data d:\data\ /move` | You can add an e to the **/mov** switch (as **/move**) to include all subdirectories, including empty subdirectories. This works like **/mov** but includes all sub-folders. |
| `/copy:`*copyflag(s)*<br>`C:\>robocopy c:\data d:\data\`<br>`/copy:datsou`<br>`C:\>robocopy c:\data d:\data\`<br>`/copy:all` | The **/copy** flag enables you to include additional metadata in the copy operation. The **/copy:datsou** command copies all the metadata and works the same as **/copy:all**. |
| `C:\>robocopy c:\data d:\data\`<br>`/copy:dats`<br>`C:\>robocopy c:\data d:\data\ /sec` | If you want to copy the permissions without the owner and auditing information, you can use the **/copy:dats** switch. This works the same as the **/sec** switch. |

The output of the **robocopy** command provides useful information. It shows how many files and folders were copied, if any files were skipped, if any failures occurred, the speed of the copy, and more, as shown in the following partial output:

```
E:\>robocopy c:\scripts e:\scripts\ /copy:datsou
-------------------------------------------------------------------------

    ROBOCOPY     ::     Robust File Copy for Windows


-------------------------------------------------------------------------

  Started : Mon Aug 16 08:38:45 2010
   Source : c:\scripts\
     Dest : e:\scripts\
    Files : *.*
  Options : *.* /COPYALL /R:1000000 /W:30
-------------------------------------------------------------------------

                      25    c:\scripts\
-------------------------------------------------------------------------

               Total    Copied   Skipped  Mismatch    FAILED    Extras
    Dirs :         1         0         1         0         0         0
   Files :        25         0        25         0         0         0
   Bytes :    53.3 k         0    53.3 k         0         0         0
   Times :   0:00:00   0:00:00                       0:00:00   0:00:00
   Ended : Mon Aug 16 08:38:45 2010
```

As a reminder, you can capture the output of any command using the > symbol to redirect the output, like this:

```
E:\>robocopy c:\scripts e:\scripts\ /copy:datsou > robooutput.txt
```

## Deleting or Removing Files with del

You can delete one or more files with the **del** command (short for delete). The basic syntax is

```
del filename
```

| Using del | Comments |
|---|---|
| C:\data>del **test.txt** | Deletes a single file named test.txt. |
| C:\data>del **\*.txt** | Deletes all files with the .txt extension. |
| C:\data>del **\*.\*** | Deletes all files in the current folder. |
| C:\ >del **\data** | Deletes all files in the specified folder. |
| **/s**<br>C:\data>del **\*.\* /s** | Deletes all files in the specified folder and all subfolders. This does not delete the folders. |

| /q<br>C:\data>**del *.* /q** | Uses quiet mode. This suppresses any prompts for confirmation and is useful in scripts. |

## Expanding Cabinet Files with expand

Microsoft uses cabinet files (.cab) to compress groups of files into a single file. This is similar to the popular zip (.zip) format used to compress files. You can extract files from .cab files with the **expand** command. The basic syntax is

**expand** cabinetFile.cab **/f:*** destinationFolder

The **/f** switch specifies which files to expand and copy and must be included if there is more than one file in the cabinet file. You can copy all of the files if you use the asterisk (*). Also, the destination folder must exist.

| expand Commands | Comments |
| --- | --- |
| C:\data>**expand data1.cab /f:*** **expfolder\**<br>C:\data>**expand data1.cab /f:*** **c:\data\expfolder\** | Extracts the contents of the data1.cab cabinet file to the expfolder. If the expfolder does not exist, the command will fail.<br><br>You can use a relative path or an exact path. In the first example, the relative path is the expfolder\ that is relative to the current path of c:\data. You can also designate the entire path as c:\data\expfolder. |
| C:\data>**expand data1.cab** **expfolder\** | If the data1.cab file includes only one file, this command expands it to the expfolder without the **/f** switch. If there is more than one file in the cabinet file, this command will fail. |
| C:\data>**expand /d data1.cab** | Displays a list of files in the data1.cabinet file. None of the files are extracted. |
| C:\data>**expand data1.cab** **/f:readme.txt expfolder\** | Extracts the readme.txt file from the data1.cab cabinet file to the expfolder. |

**NOTE:** While the online help lists an **extract** command, it is not available at the command line.

## Taking Ownership of Files with takeown

The **takeown** command allows an administrator to take ownership of a file. Owners of files or folders stored on an NTFS drive can change any permissions on these files. If an administrator is denied read or write access to a file, the administrator can take ownership of the file and then modify the permissions to grant the desired permissions. The

**takeown** command must be executed from an elevated prompt. The basic syntax of the command is

```
takeown /f filename
```

| takeown Commands | Comments |
|---|---|
| /f<br>C:\data>takeown /f myfile.txt | The **/f** switch is needed to specify the file or files. This example takes ownership of the myfile.txt file. |
| /f<br>C:\data>takeown /f *.* | You can use wildcards with the **/f** switch. This example takes ownership of all files in the current folder. |
| /r<br>C:\data>takeown /r /f *.* | The **/r** switch includes subfolders. This example takes ownership of all files in the current folder, and all files in all child folders. |
| /a<br>C:\data>takeown /a /f *.* | You can also transfer ownership to the administrators group with the **/a** switch. This example changes ownership for all files in the current folder to the Administrators group. |

# Removing the Windows.old Folder

The Windows.old folder includes files left over from a previous installation. You can delete them with the Disk Cleanup GUI, but it's also possible to do so from the command prompt with administrative privileges. You need to enter two commands:

| Deleting Windows.old | Comments |
|---|---|
| C:\>takeown /f<br>c:\windows.old\* /r /a /d y | Because the files are owned by different security identifiers (SIDs) in a previous installation, you must first take ownership of them. The **/r** switch forces the takeown command to work on the directory and subdirectories, the **/a** switch gives the permission to the Administrators group, and the **/d y** switch forces the takeown command to default to an answer of Yes when prompted for confirmation. This will take some time. |
| C:\>rd /s /q<br>c:\windows.old\ | You can then remove the directory with **rd**. The **/s** switch specifies all subdirectories, and the **/q** switch uses quiet mode, suppressing prompts. |

**TIP:** After completing a migration, you can use these two commands in an automated script to clean up end users' computers, to give them extra space on their hard drive.

## Mapping Drives with net use

There are many times when you'll want to manipulate or access files on a remote share. You can access remote shares with the Universal Naming Convention (UNC) of *\\servername\sharename*. However, some commands don't recognize the UNC path but instead need a drive letter, and sometimes it's just easier to use a drive letter instead of a full UNC path. You can use the **net use** command to map drive letters to UNC paths. The basic syntax is

```
net use x: \\serverName\shareName
```

You can use any drive letter that is not in use on the system, but if the drive letter is in use, the command will fail. Additionally, the UNC path must be reachable or you'll get an error.

| Mapping a Drive with net use | Comments |
| --- | --- |
| `C:\>net use` | You can view all currently mapped drives with this command. |
| `C:\>net use z: \\server1\shareddata` | This maps the drive letter Z: to a share named shareddata on a remote host named server1. |
| `/delete`<br>`C:\>net use z: /delete` | The **/delete** switch deletes the mapped drive and frees up the mapped drive letter. |
| `/persistent`<br>`C:\>net use /persistent: No`<br><br>`C:\>net use /persistent: Yes` | The **/persistent** switch is used by itself and specifies if the mapped drives will be remembered at the next logon. When set to **No**, the **net use** command includes the following line: "New connections will not be remembered." This is the default.<br><br>When set to **Yes**, the **net use** command includes the following line: "New connections will be remembered." |

This chapter provides information and commands concerning the following topics:

- Manipulating and viewing disks with **diskpart**
- Defragmenting volumes with **defrag**
- Converting to NTFS with **convert**
- Managing the file system with **fsutil**

# Manipulating and Viewing Disks with diskpart

The **diskpart** command is a shell command you can access from the command line. After you enter **diskpart**, the DISKPART> prompt appears and you can enter **diskpart** commands from there.

The **diskpart** command requires elevated permissions. If you try to launch it from a normal command prompt, you'll be prompted by User Account Control to continue. If you click **Yes**, another command prompt window will open with elevated permissions.

You can use the commands in the following table to view details on a disk.

| diskpart Commands | Description |
|---|---|
| `C:\>diskpart` | Enters diskpart. |
| `DISKPART>list disk` | Shows a list of disks that are available on the system. Disks are numbered as disk 0, disk 1, and so on. |
| `DISKPART>select disk 0` | Selects disk 0 as the target. |
| `DISKPART>detail disk` | Shows information about the selected disk. This works only if a disk is selected. |
| `DISKPART>rescan` | Rescans the system for disks. This can be useful when the occasional USB drive isn't recognized by the system. |
| `DISKPART>list partition` | Shows a list of partitions on the currently selected disk. Partitions are numbered as partition 1, partition 2, and so on. A disk must be selected before you can get information on partitions. |
| `DISKPART>select partition 1` | Selects partition 1 as the target. |

| `DISKPART>shrink querymax` | Identifies the amount of free space available on the currently selected partition. |
|---|---|
| `DISKPART>shrink desired=500 minimum=250` | Shrinks the drive by 500 MB. If 500 MB of free space isn't available, it shrinks the drive by the highest value between 250 and 500 MB. If 250 MB of free space isn't available, it fails. |

## Creating a VHD File with **diskpart**

You might occasionally want to have another instance of Windows 7 available on your system. You can do this with a virtual hard disk (VHD) file. This has several benefits:

- The VHD file is just like any other file on your system, though much larger than most files. You can copy the VHD file to ensure you can always return it to the original configuration, or copy it to make it available on a different system.

- It configures your system as a dual-boot system. When you reboot, you can choose to boot into the VHD file or boot normally into Windows 7.

- You can use the VHD file for testing. You can test updates, check compatibility of software, or even release and observe malware in an isolated environment. When you're done, you can simply copy your original file back over the modified VHD file.

You can use the following steps to create and attach a VHD file to your system. If you wanted to create a dual-boot or multiboot system with a VHD file, you would perform these steps as part of the installation process. In other words, you would first perform these steps:

**Step 1.**  Boot to the installation DVD as if you are going to install Windows 7.

**Step 2.**  When you get to the screen where you select the language, time and currency format, and keyboard or input method, press Shift+F10. This launches the command prompt.

**Step 3.**  Use the steps in the following table to create the VHD.

**Step 4.**  Install Windows 7 on the VHD.

Use these steps to create a VHD file on your system:

| diskpart Commands | Description |
|---|---|
| `C:\>diskpart` | Launches diskpart. |
| `DISKPART>create vdisk file= c:\win7pcg.vhd maximum=20480 type=expandable` | Creates a virtual hard disk (.vhd) file named win7pcg.vhd in the root of the C: drive. The file will be expandable and can grow to as big as 20 GB if you use a maximum size of 20,480. The initial size is about 40 Kb. |

| | |
|---|---|
| `DISKPART>select vdisk file=`<br>`c:\win7pcg.vhd` | Selects this virtual disk file so that it can be attached and used. |
| `DISKPART>list vdisk` | Shows vdisk 0 with its location. It will have an asterisk (*) on the left indicating it is selected, but it is not attached yet. |
| `DISKPART>attach vdisk` | Attaches the vdisk so that it can be used. |
| `DISKPART>list vdisk` | Shows vdisk 0 as a disk with a state of attached but not open and a type of expandable. |
| `DISKPART>list disk` | Shows all of the disks with the 20-GB vdisk added. |
| `DISKPART>exit` | Exits diskpart. |

You can now continue with the installation of Windows 7. When prompted to select a disk, select the 20-GB disk, which is the vdisk you created. It will not be formatted, so it will show as unallocated space, but the installation will automatically format this disk with the NTFS file system as part of the installation process.

## Modifying the BCD Store for the VHD File

If you install Windows 7 on a VHD file on an existing system, it will modify the boot configuration data (BCD) store to include the new operating system. On the surface this sounds good because it is automatic. However, it changes the configuration so that your system will automatically boot to the VHD file instead of the original Windows 7 installation. You might want to change this.

> **NOTE:** Windows 7 does not use the boot.ini file, but uses the BCD store instead. **bcdedit** is one of the methods used to modify the BCD store.

You can view the contents of the BCD store with the following command:

```
bcdedit /v
```

> **TIP:** You need to run the **bcdedit** command from a command prompt started with administrative privileges.

You'll see the following data:

```
Windows Boot Manager
--------------------
identifier              {9dea862c-5cdd-4e70-acc1-f32b344d4795}
device                  partition=D:
description             Windows Boot Manager
locale                  en-US
inherit                 {7ea2e1ac-2e61-4728-aaa3-896d9d0a9f0e}
```

```
default                 {4dbbe916-9901-11df-948b-8f16cf2e7b02}
resumeobject            {4dbbe915-9901-11df-948b-8f16cf2e7b02}
displayorder            {4dbbe916-9901-11df-948b-8f16cf2e7b02}
                        {18b61673-3f06-11de-b3f5-00242106d5b2}
toolsdisplayorder       {b2721d73-1db4-4c62-bf78-c548a880142d}
timeout                 30


Windows Boot Loader
-------------------
identifier              {4dbbe916-9901-11df-948b-8f16cf2e7b02}
device                  vhd=[D:]\Win7PCG.vhd,locate=custom:12000002
path                    \Windows\system32\winload.exe
description             Windows 7
locale                  en-US
inherit                 {6efb52bf-1766-41db-a6b3-0ee5eff72bd7}
recoverysequence        {4dbbe917-9901-11df-948b-8f16cf2e7b02}
recoveryenabled         Yes
osdevice                vhd=[D:]\Win7PCG.vhd,locate=custom:22000002
systemroot              \Windows
resumeobject            {4dbbe915-9901-11df-948b-8f16cf2e7b02}
nx                      OptIn


Windows Boot Loader
-------------------
identifier              {18b61673-3f06-11de-b3f5-00242106d5b2}
device                  partition=D:
path                    \Windows\system32\winload.exe
description             Microsoft 7
locale                  en-US
inherit                 {6efb52bf-1766-41db-a6b3-0ee5eff72bd7}
osdevice                partition=D:
systemroot              \Windows
resumeobject            {18b61674-3f06-11de-b3f5-00242106d5b2}
nx                      OptIn
```

Notice that the data in the first Windows Boot Loader section includes the data for the Windows 7 VHD file. You can verify this from either the *device* line or *osdevice* line, each of which identifies a device starting with *vhd=[D:]\Win7PCG.vhd*. You'll see something similar to this if you created a VHD boot file using the steps in the previous section.

After you identify which section is for the VHD file and which section is for the native operating system, you can then determine the identifiers. In this example, the installations have the following identifiers:

- VHD file identifier: 4dbbe916-9901-11df-948b-8f16cf2e7b02
- Native OS identifier: 18b61673-3f06-11de-b3f5-00242106d5b2

You can now modify the BCD store with the following steps:

| bcdedit Commands | Description |
|---|---|
| /v<br><br>C:\>bcdedit /v | Lists the different operating systems in the BCD store using verbose mode. You can then use the output to cut the identifier and paste it into the following commands instead of typing it in from scratch. |
| /set<br><br>C:\>bcdedit /set {4dbbe916-9901-11df-948b-8f16cf2e7b02} description "Windows 7 Virtual Hard Disk" | The **/set** command can be used to change the description from the default "Windows 7" to "Windows 7 Virtual Hard Disk" on the boot screen. |
| /default<br><br>C:\>bcdedit /default {18b61673-3f06-11de-b3f5-00242106d5b2} | Changes the default operating system from the VHD to the native operating system. In other words, your system will boot to the native operating system by default instead of to the VHD file. |
| /displayorder<br><br>C:\>bcdedit /displayorder {4dbbe916-9901-11df-948b-8f16cf2e7b02} /addlast | The **displayorder** switch can be used to modify the order in which the installations are displayed on the boot screen. By default, the last installation appears on the top. This example moves the virtual hard disk to last in the displayed boot order on the boot screen. |
| C:\>bcdedit | Displays the changes you've made in the store.<br><br>If you performed the previous steps and restart the system at this point, it will default to the native operating system. You can also use the Down Arrow key to select the VHD file. |

# Defragmenting Volumes with defrag

You can run the **defrag** command to defragment drives. When a system writes a high volume of files to a drive, it's common for the drive to become fragmented. The files become stored in fragments spread around the drive, and when the file is read, the fragments are retrieved and put back together. Excessive fragmentation can cause disk *thrashing*, where the disk is very busy but the overall performance of the system is very slow.

Windows 7 automatically defragments the drives on a regular basis. This is a scheduled task, and you can view and manipulate the properties via Task Scheduler, which you can access by choosing **Start**, **Control Panel**, entering **Schedule** in the **Search Control Panel** text box, and clicking **Schedule Tasks**. Browse to **Task Schedule Library**, **Microsoft**, **Windows**, **Defrag** to view the task, as shown in Figure 5-1. Notice that this runs at 1 a.m. every Wednesday by default.

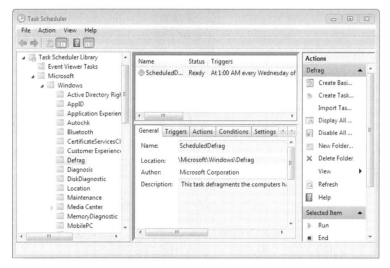

**Figure 5-1**    Viewing the Defrag Scheduled Task

However, there are times when you'll want to check a drive to see whether it's fragmented, or manually start the defragmentation of a drive. The **defrag** command must be run with elevated privileges.

| defrag Commands | Description |
|---|---|
| /a<br>C:\>defrag c: /a | You can use the **/a** switch to analyze the disk without starting the defragmentation. The example command will analyze the C: drive to determine if it needs to be defragmented. It can give you a definitive answer on how fragmented the drive is and whether it needs to be defragmented. |
| /v<br>C:\>defrag c: /a /v | The **/v** switch provides verbose output. The example performs the analysis and provides more detail on fragmentation. |
| /m<br>C:\>defrag c: d: /m | You can defragment multiple drives at the same time using the **/m** switch. The example runs **defrag** on drives C: and D:. The **/m** switch specifies that these operations should run in the background at the same time. |

| /h<br>C:\>defrag c: /h | You can use the **/h** switch to raise the priority of the defrag process. It runs with a low priority by default, but the example shows how to run it to raise the priority to Normal. Normal priority will cause it to run quicker, but will slow down common user tasks. |
|---|---|
| /u<br>C:\>defrag c: /a /u | The **/u** switch causes **defrag** to display progress on the screen.<br><br>Sometimes, it can look like **defrag** has hung and isn't doing anything, but with the **/u** switch, you'll get a display of the progress on the screen. |
| Ctrl+C | Interrupts the defragmentation process. |

**NOTE:**    To fully defragment a drive, you must have at least 15 percent free space. If there is less than 15 percent free space, the drive will be only partially defragmented. The **/f** switch—available in previous operating systems to force a defragmentation even if there is less than 15 percent free—is no longer available. Microsoft recommends keeping at least 20 percent free space for the best performance of defragmentation.

## Converting to NTFS with convert

The NTFS file system provides several different benefits, and using it on Windows 7 drives is highly recommended. The primary benefit is security. You can add permissions to files and folders and even encrypt them.

However, there are several other benefits, such as the capability to work with larger data files. For example, if you try to copy a file larger than 4 GB from an NTFS drive to a FAT32 drive, you'll be informed that the destination drive doesn't have enough space. Even if you have an empty 1-TB drive, you'll still see the same error if you try to copy a file larger than 4 GB. There is a simple solution. Convert the FAT32 drive to NTFS, and you'll be able to copy the larger files.

The basic syntax of the command is

```
convert x: /fs:ntfs
```

You just need to substitute *x* with the drive letter of the target drive.

| convert Commands | Description |
|---|---|
| C:\>convert e: /fs:ntfs | Converts the C: drive to NTFS. If the drive is already NTFS, the output will say so. If the system has the drive locked, you'll be prompted to schedule the conversion. The file system will be converted to NTFS the next time the system is booted. |
| /v<br>C:\>convert e: /fs:ntfs<br>/v | You can run the conversion with verbose mode to provide more details on the conversion process. |

## Managing the File System with fsutil

You can use the file system utility (**fsutil**) to perform advanced tasks on FAT and NTFS file systems. The NTFS file system automatically performs regular checks and maintenance on drives, and when it discovers problems, it fixes them. However, there might be times when you want to use **fsutil** to query the drives.

The **fsutil** command needs to be run with elevated privileges for some of the commands. There are many more commands available with **fsutil**, but this shows some basic commands:

| fsutil Commands | Description |
|---|---|
| `C:\>fsutil` | Returns a list of commands. |
| `C:\>fsutil dirty query c:`<br>`Volume - c: is NOT Dirty` | Determines if the C: drive is dirty or not. If not, it outputs "Volume - c: is NOT Dirty," and if dirty, outputs "Volume - c: is Dirty."<br><br>If the file system is dirty, it indicates it is in an inconsistent state and can cause errors. You should run **chkdsk /f** on the system. If the system is dirty, **chkdsk /f** will automatically run the next time the system is rebooted. |
| `C:\>fsutil dirty set d:`<br>`Volume - c: is now marked dirty` | Marks the D: drive as dirty. This is an indirect way to cause **chkdsk /f** to be run on the system when it's rebooted.<br><br>Note that there isn't a command to mark the drive as not dirty. This can be done only after **chkdsk** has checked the disk. |
| `C:\>fsutil fsinfo drives`<br>`Drives: c:\ d:\ e:\ f:\` | Lists the drives by drive letters in the following format:<br><br>Drives: c:\ d:\ e:\ g:\ h:\ j:\ |
| `C:\>fsutil fsinfo drivetype c:`<br>`c: - Fixed Drive` | Lists the drive type as either a fixed drive, CD-ROM drive, or a removable drive. |
| `C:\>fsutil fsinfo ntfsinfo c:` | Lists details on an NTFS drive such as the number of sectors and clusters. Also lists the bytes per sector, bytes per cluster, and bytes per file record. |

This chapter provides information and commands concerning the following topics:

- Using Notepad
- Giving feedback with **echo**
- Using parameters
- Calling another batch file with **call**
- Clearing the screen with **cls**
- Changing the order of processing with **goto**
- Checking conditions with **if**
- Logging events with **eventcreate**
- Looping through tasks with **for**
- Creating a menu file

## Using Notepad

The difference between a good administrator and a great administrator is that great administrators have learned to script. You don't even have to be a great scripter, and you can start scripting by creating basic batch files in Notepad. One of the great things about the command prompt is that anything you can execute at the command prompt, you can embed as a script in a batch file. Even better, anything you can script, you can automate.

While there are more advanced tools you can use to create batch files, the simplest tool, Notepad, can meet most of your needs. Notepad is a simple text editor that you can use to create batch files easily. As a simple example, you can use the following steps to create a batch file in Notepad:

| Using Notepad | Comments |
| --- | --- |
| `C:\>md c:\scripts` | Creates a folder named scripts at the root of C:. |
| `C:\>cd c:\scripts` | Changes to the c:\scripts folder. |
| `C:\scripts>notepad myfirstscript.bat` | Launches Notepad and creates the batch file named myfirstscript.bat. When prompted to create the file, click **Yes**. |

| Enter the following line in the myfirstcript. bat file: `ipconfig /flushdns` | Creates a one-line script in the batch file. |
| Press **Ctrl+S** to save the batch file. | Saves the batch file. You can now execute it from the command line. |
| `C:\scripts>`**myfirstscript** | Executes the script. The command **ipconfig /flushdns** will run and flush the DNS cache. |

You can also create a batch file by just launching Notepad with the GUI, or typing **Notepad** without specifying the batch filename. The only difference is that when you save it, you need to ensure that you save it with a .bat extension. You do this by entering the file name as *scriptname*.**bat**. Notepad still saves it as a text file, but with a .bat extension. If you don't add the .bat extension, Notepad defaults to a .txt extension, and any file with a .txt extension will not execute as a batch file.

# Giving Feedback with echo

The **echo** command can be used to display messages to users from within a batch file. It's also useful to display the value of variables as shown in Chapter 2, "Basic Rules When Using the Command Prompt." For example, if you just want to know the path to the Program Files folder, you can use this command:

```
echo %programfiles%
```

However, **echo** has a quirk that can be confusing. If you use **echo** with a message from within a batch file, you'll see the **echo** command with the message, and then the message again on the same line. For example, consider a file named echotest.bat with this single line as you look at the following table:

```
echo This will flush the cache
```

| Batch File Contents | Result when Executed at Command Prompt | Description |
|---|---|---|
| `echo This will`<br>`flush the cache` | `C:\>`**echotest**<br>`C:\>echo This will flush`<br>`the cache`<br>`This will flush the cache` | The echo line shows, and then the result of the echo line shows. |
| `echo off`<br>`echo This will`<br>`flush the DNS cache` | `C:\>`**echotest**<br>`echo off`<br>`This will flush the cache` | The **echo off** command shows, but the echo This will flush the DNS cache line isn't shown. |
| `@echo off`<br>`echo This will`<br>`flush the cache` | `C:\>`**echotest**<br>`This will flush the cache` | The **@echo off** command turns off echo but also does not display the line. |

| @echo off<br>echo.<br>echo This will<br>flush the cache | `C:\>echotest`<br>`This will flush the cache` | The **echo.** command will display a blank line. |
|---|---|---|

**TIP:** If you enter **echo off** at the command prompt, the command prompt (C:\>) disappears but you can still enter commands as normal. If you turn echo off from within a batch file, it does not affect the command prompt.

**NOTE:** If you want to include the pipe (|), the less than character (<), the greater than character (>), or the caret (^) symbol in an echo line, you need to precede the character with a caret (^). For example, if you want to include the pipe symbol, you have to list it as ^|. To include the caret, you have to list it as ^^.

## Using Parameters

Windows 7 supports the use of parameters in batch files. You define the parameter within the batch file and then you can pass data to the batch file as a parameter. You can use as many as nine parameters, defined as %1 through %9.

As an example, consider the **whoami** command. You can enter the following command to view the security identifier (SID) of the currently logged-on user:

`whoami /user`

You'll see information similar to the following:

```
USER INFORMATION
----------------

User Name      SID
============== =================================================
win7pcg\darril S-1-5-21-4285671909-4150961583-1987988917-1000
```

You can create a one-line batch file named who.bat with the following line:

`whoami /%1`

| Who.bat<br>Batch File<br>Contents | Result when Executed at Command<br>Prompt | Description |
|---|---|---|
| `whoami /%1` | `C:\>who user`<br>`USER INFORMATION`<br>`----------------`<br><br>`User Name      SID`<br>`===================================`<br>`win7pcg\darril S-1-5-21-4285671909-`<br>`4150961583-987988917-1000` | This command actually runs the following command by substituting **user** for **%1**:<br><br>**whoami /user**. |

Although the previous example is very simplistic, it does show how the parameter is used. The following example shows a more usable batch file that can be used to set the IP address, subnet mask, and default gateway of a Windows 7 system from the command line. Note that even though it runs to two lines in the text, it is entered on a single line.

```
netsh interface ipv4 set address name="local area connection"
   static 10.10.0.10 255.0.0.0 10.10.0.1
```

The previous command sets the IP address to 10.10.0.10, the subnet mask to 255.0.0.0, and the default gateway to 10.10.0.1.

You can create a batch file named setip.bat with the following line using parameters. The batch file will accept three parameters, identified as %1, %2, and %3.

```
netsh interface ipv4 set address name="local area connection"
   static %1 %2 %3
```

| setip.bat Batch File Parameters | Executing setip.bat at Command Prompt | Description |
| --- | --- | --- |
| %1 %2 %3 | C:\>setip 10.10.0.10 255.0.0.0 10.10.0.1 | This command sets the IP address, subnet mask, and default gateway using the setip.bat file. |

You can add a second line to your batch file to also set the address of the DNS server. Notice that the %4 parameter will be the actual IP address of the DNS server.

```
netsh interface ipv4 set address name="Local Area Connection"
   static %1 %2 %3
netsh interface ipv4 set dnsserver "Local Area Connection" static %4
```

| setip.bat Batch File Parameters | Executing setip.bat at Command Prompt | Description |
| --- | --- | --- |
| %1 %2 %3 %4 | C:\>setip 10.10.0.10 255.0.0.0 10.10.0.1 10.10.0.5 | This command sets the IP address, subnet mask, default gateway, and DNS server address using the setip.bat file. |

You can also use several additional codes with parameters. These codes allow you to retrieve specific information about a file passed as a parameter.

The following table shows how to use these codes, with an explanation and sample output. The left column shows sample usage in a batch file named paramtest.bat, and the middle column shows the output you'll see if you execute the batch file to get details on a file named test.txt. The test.txt file exists in the c:\scripts\ folder for this example.

| Parameter Code with Sample Usage in paramtest.bat | Results from Executing paramtest.bat with the Sample Parameter Code | Description |
|---|---|---|
| %1<br><br>Sample usage:<br>echo %1 | C:\scripts>paramtest<br>test.txt<br>test.txt | The normal parameter without any modification. |
| %~f1<br><br>Sample usage:<br>echo %~f1 | C:\scripts>paramtest<br>test.txt<br><br>c:\scripts\test.txt | Shows the full path and filename of the file. |
| %~d1<br><br>Sample usage:<br>echo %~d1 | C:\scripts>paramtest<br>test.txt<br>c: | Shows only the drive letter of the file's path. |
| %~p1<br><br>Sample usage:<br>echo %~p1 | C:\scripts>paramtest<br>test.txt<br>\scripts\ | Shows only the path to the file. |
| %~dp1<br><br>Sample usage:<br>echo %~dp1 | C:\scripts>paramtest<br>test.txt<br>c:\scripts\ | Shows the drive letter of the path and the path to the file. |
| %~n1<br><br>Sample usage:<br>echo %~n1 | C:\scripts>paramtest<br>test.txt<br>test | Shows only the filename, without the extension. |
| %~x1<br><br>Sample usage:<br>echo %~x1 | C:\scripts>paramtest<br>test.txt<br>.txt | Shows only the filename extension, without the name. |
| %~nx1<br><br>Sample usage:<br>echo %~nx1 | C:\scripts>paramtest<br>test.txt<br>test.txt | Shows the filename and extension. |
| %~a1<br><br>Sample usage:<br>echo %~a1 | C:\scripts>paramtest<br>test.txt<br>--a------ | Shows only the attributes of the file, similar to executing attrib test.txt. |
| %~t1<br><br>Sample usage:<br>echo %~t1 | C:\scripts>paramtest<br>test.txt<br>07/29/2010 08:04 AM | Shows the date and time the file was last modified. |
| %~z1<br><br>Sample usage:<br>echo %~z1 | C:\scripts>paramtest<br>test.txt<br>2128 | Shows the file size in bytes. |
| %~ftza1<br><br>Sample usage:<br>echo %~ftza1 | C:\scripts>paramtest<br>test.txt<br><br>--a------ 07/28/2010<br>08:17 AM 2128<br>c:\scripts\test.txt | Shows the attributes, date and time the file was last modified, file size in bytes, and the full path and filename. |

While the **echo** command in the previous table is useful to see what the parameter code is doing, you might want to use the value of the parameter within your script. You can create variables and assign values from within the script as mentioned in Chapter 2. For example, you can use the following line to create a variable named driveletter and then assign the actual drive letter to the variable:

```
set driveletter=%~d1
```

> **TIP:** It's best to not have a space before or after the = sign when setting the variable from these parameter codes. Testing shows inconsistent results when spaces are included when assigning values.

After your variable is populated with a value, you can use it anywhere else in the batch file by referencing it surrounded by percent symbols (%). A simple usage with the **echo** command would be

```
echo drive letter = %driveletter%
```

## Calling Another Batch File with call

You can launch a batch file from within another batch file with the **call** command. The basic syntax is

```
call batchFileName
```

Figure 6-1 shows the order of processing when calling a batch file. calltest.bat will run until it comes to the "call batch2.bat" line. It will stop running and control will then be passed to the called batch file, batch2.bat. After the called batch file runs, control passes back to the calling batch file.

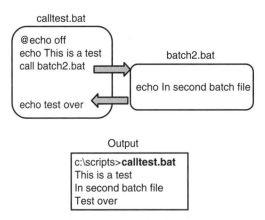

**Figure 6-1** Order of Processing When Calling a Batch File

If the called batch file doesn't exist or somehow fails, control is still returned to the calling batch file. The **call** command only works from within a batch file. If you execute it directly from the command prompt, it is ignored.

The following table shows some example usage of the **call** command within a batch file.

| Using call | Comments |
|---|---|
| `call newbatch.bat` | Calls the newbatch.bat batch file. The file must exist in the current path, or in a path known by the system. |
| `call c:\scripts\newbatch.bat` | Calls the newbatch.bat batch file located in the c:\scripts folder. If the batch file doesn't exist, the call fails and control returns to the calling batch file. |
| `call newbatch.bat batch parameters` | If the called batch program accepts parameters, you can include them in the call. |
| `call newbatch.bat :Label` | Calls the batch program and starts execution at the specified label. |

## Clearing the Screen with cls

The **cls** command is useful within a batch file to clear the screen. It is entered simply as **cls** without any parameters. When entered, it clears the screen and puts the cursor at the top of the screen.

## Changing the Order of Processing with goto

You can use the **goto** statement to change the order of processing of a batch file. Normally, a batch file goes through the lines in the batch file from the first line to the last line. However, there are times you will want some areas of the batch file to be skipped. The basic syntax is

`goto` *label*

The label is listed elsewhere in the document as a string of characters beginning with a colon (:). For example, you could have a label at the end of the batch file named :eof. You could then include the goto eof line in the batch file.

| Script Example | Comments |
|---|---|
| `goto eof` | The next command will be at the :eof label. Notice that the label includes the : (as in :eof), but the **goto** statement does not include the colon. |
| `ipconfig /flushdns` | This command will never execute in this batch file because the **goto eof** statement will always cause it to be skipped. |
| `:eof` | This is the eof label. |
| `echo Exiting batch file` | The **echo** command gives the user feedback. |

## Checking Conditions with if

When creating a batch file, you might occasionally want to check for specific conditions. If a condition exists, you do something. **if** statements are frequently used with **goto** statements.

The basic syntax of the command is

```
if condition command [else command]
```

As a simple example, the following **if** statement could be used in a batch file:

```
if exist log1.txt echo "Log file exists." else echo "No log file."
```

The condition of the **if** command evaluates to either true or false. If the condition is true, it performs the command. If the condition is false, it does not perform the command. If an **else** clause is included, it will be performed if the condition is false. In this example, the condition is a check to see if the file log1.txt exists.

Although you can enter the entire **if** command on the same line, it is sometimes easier to read and understand when entered on separate lines. However, if you're using multiple lines, you must use parentheses around certain areas:

```
if condition (
   command
) else (
   Command
   )
```

For example, the **if** command shown earlier would look like this:

```
if exist log1.txt (
   echo "Log file exists."
) else (
   echo "No log file exist"
   )
```

There are certain conditions you can use, as shown in the following table.

| Condition | Example | Description |
| --- | --- | --- |
| exist | if exist log.txt<br>copy log.txt<br>archive.txt | Checks for the existence of the log.txt file, and if it exists, copies it to the archive.txt file. |
| errorlevel | if errorlevel 4 goto eof<br>This assumes a label of :eof exists in the batch file. | Checks for the value of the %errorlevel% variable. If the value is 4, the batch will go to the eof label and presumably end.<br><br>It's common to use this check to redirect the order of the batch file processing with the **goto** statement. |

| String comparison:<br><br>*string1*==*string2* | `if %1 == abc echo`<br>`"User entered abc"` | Checks the value of one string against another. Notice that two equal signs (==) are required. |
|---|---|---|
| not | `if not exist log.`<br>`txt copy log.txt ar-`<br>`chive.txt`<br>`if not errorlevel 4`<br>`goto end`<br>`if not %1 == abc`<br>`echo "User did not`<br>`enter abc"` | The **not** condition negates the result of the conditional check. If the check resulted in true, the **not** condition changes it to false. If the check resulted in false, the **not** condition changes it to true. |

**NOTE:** You can use any valid command that you want after the condition. In other words, you aren't limited to using only certain commands when you use certain conditions. If it's a valid command from the command line, it's a valid command within the **if** statement.

When using comparison operators, you have several to choose from, as shown in the following table.

| Comparison Operator | Description |
|---|---|
| ==<br>`if string1 == string2`<br>`if abc ==  abc`<br>`if %1 == abc`<br>`if %1 == %myvar%` | Evaluates to true if *string1* and *string2* are the same. These values can be literal strings or batch variables such as %1 or %myvar%. You do not need to enclose literal strings in quotation marks.<br><br>For example, you can check to see what the user entered as a parameter using the %1, and even check to see if it's equal to a variable you created with a statement such as **set myvar= abc**. |
| `if /i string1 ==`<br>`string2` | If you want to ignore the case of the two strings, use the /i switch immediately after the **if** statement. |
| equ<br>`if value1 equ value2` | Equal to<br>Evaluates to true if the two values are equal. |
| neq<br>`if value1 neq value2` | Not equal to<br>Evaluates to true if the two values are not equal. |
| lss<br>`if value1 lss value2` | Less than<br>Evaluates to true if *value1* is less than *value2*. |
| leq<br>`if value1 leq value2` | Less than or equal to<br>Evaluates to true if *value1* is less than or equal to *value2*. |
| gtr<br>`if value1 gtr value2` | Greater than<br>Evaluates to true if *value1* is greater than *value2*. |
| geq<br>`if value1 geq value2` | Greater than or equal to<br>Evaluates to true if *value1* is greater than or equal to *value2*. |

It's common to use **if** statements in combination with **goto** statements and labels. For example, the batch file can accept an input and then check for the value of the input. Based on the input, it could do one of several actions. The following example shows how to do this. You can enter all of these commands in a batch file.

```
@echo off
if %1#==# goto null
if %1==1 goto viewdns
if %1==2 goto flushdns
if %1==3 goto renew
if %1 gtr 3 goto outofrange
:null
echo "No Command entered."
goto eof
:outofrange
echo "Only values 1, 2, and 3 are valid."
goto eof
:viewdns
ipconfig /displaydns
:flushdns
ipconfig /flushdns
:renew
ipconfig /renew
:eof
```

For clarification, the commands used in the previous batch file are explained in the following table. Notice that even though the example shows only one command within each of the labels, you can have as many commands as you like.

| Batch File Command | Description |
|---|---|
| `@echo off` | Turn off **echo** so that the batch file commands don't show. |
| `if %1#==# goto null` | Check for a null value. In other words, if the batch file is entered without a parameter, this will evaluate to true and the batch file will go to the null label. |

| | |
|---|---|
| `if %1==1 goto viewdns`<br>`if %1==2 goto flushdns`<br>`if %1==3 goto renew`<br>`if %1 gtr 3 goto outofrange` | Check for the value of the input. If it is any number, it will use the **goto** statement to process the command. |
| `:null`<br>`echo "No Command entered."`<br>`goto eof` | The **:null** label provides feedback if a parameter isn't provided. It gives feedback to the user and goes to the end of the file. |
| `:outofrange`<br>`echo "Only values 1, 2, and 3`<br>`are valid."`<br>`goto eof` | The **:outofrange** label provides feedback on valid numbers. If a value greater than 3 is entered, it gives feedback to the user and goes to the end of the file. |
| `:viewdns`<br>`ipconfig  /displaydns` | The **:viewdns** label includes the **ipconfig /displaydns** command. |
| `:flushdns`<br>`ipconfig  /flushdns` | The **:flushdns** label includes the **ipconfig /flushdns** command. |
| `:renew`<br>`ipconfig  /renew` | The **:renew** label includes the **ipconfig /renew** command. |
| `:eof` | The **:eof** file label is placed at the end of the file and doesn't have any commands after it. The batch file then exits. |

## Logging Events with eventcreate

There may be times when you want to log information from your batch file in one of the Windows 7 logs. You can do so with the **eventcreate** command. The syntax is

```
eventcreate  [/l {application|system }] /t {error|warning|information }
/id eventid /d description
```

For example, if you wanted to log an error in the application log to indicate that a backup failed, you could use the following command:

```
eventcreate /l application /t error /id 999 /d "Backup failed"
```

When executed, it logs an event similar to the one shown in Figure 6-2.

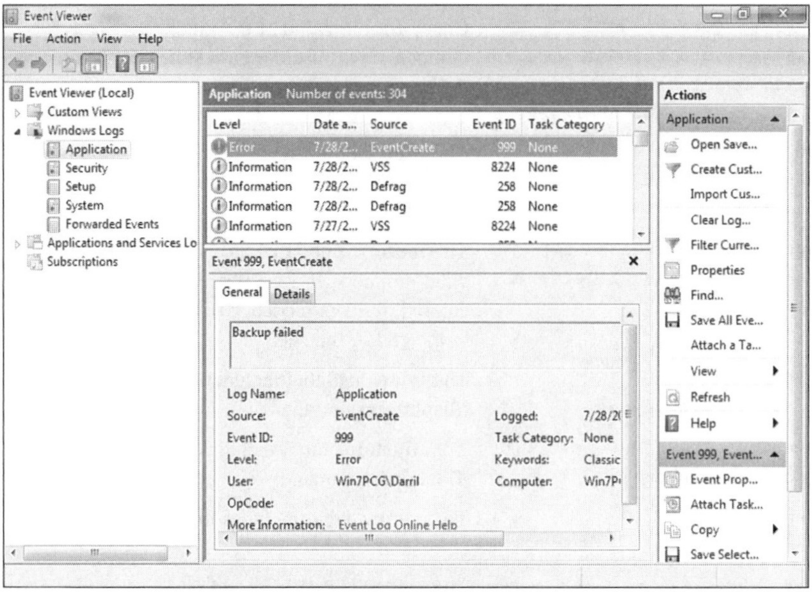

**Figure 6-2** Event Created from the **eventcreate** Command

The following table identifies the different elements within an **eventcreate** command.

**NOTE:** Although you can enter the **eventcreate** command from the command prompt, doing so would be rare. This table shows how you can add the **eventcreate** command to a batch file.

| eventcreate Switches | Comments |
|---|---|
| /l<br>/l application | The **/l** switch specifies the log where you want the event recorded. You can specify either the **application** or **system** log. If you don't specify a log, it defaults to the **application** log. |
| /t<br>/t error | The **/t** switch is used to specify the type of entry. You must specify **error**, **warning**, or **information** as the type. |
| /id<br>/id 999 | **/id** identifies the number for the event. You can use any number between 1 and 1000. |
| /d<br>/d "Backup failed" | A free text description you add. The description is logged with the event and must be enclosed in quotes if it has any spaces. |

| | |
|---|---|
| **/s**<br>**/s** *remote-computer-name or ip-address* | The event is logged on the local computer by default. However, you can use the **/s** switch to have the event logged on a remote computer. You need to include the **/u** and **/p** switches with this switch. |
| **/u**<br>**/u** *domain\username* | Runs the command with the specified user account. The account is specified as just the username, or the domain and username (domain\username). |
| **/p**<br>**/p** *password* | Specifies the password of the user account.<br><br>**CAUTION:** If you put the password in a batch file, it can be read by anyone that has access to the batch file. |

**TIP:** A new feature that you have available with Windows 7 is the ability to attach tasks to events. These tasks can run files or scripts, display a dialog box, or send an email. In other words, if you created an event with an event ID of 999, you can then attach a task to that event to send an email to inform you that the event occurred.

## Looping Through Tasks with for

The **for** command runs a specified command for each file in a set of files. The basic syntax is

```
for %variable in (set) do command [command-parameters]
```

As an example, if you wanted to display the contents of all the text files in a folder, you could use this command:

```
for %x in (*.txt) do type %x
```

**NOTE:** The **type** command will display the text in a file. For example, if you have a file named text.txt, you could enter **type text.txt** to display the contents.

For example, if the previous **for** command is executed within a folder that holds three text files (test1.txt, test2.txt, and test3.txt), it executes the **type** command against each of these files.

| Contents of Folder | for Command | Result of Command |
|---|---|---|
| test1.txt<br>test2.txt<br>test3.txt | `for %x in (*.txt) do`<br>`type %x` | `type test1.txt`<br>`type test2.txt`<br>`type test3.txt` |

**TIP:** If you want the command embedded within a batch file, you need to identify the variable with two percent symbols instead, like this: **for %%x in (*.txt) do type %%x.**

| Identifying Variables | Comments |
|---|---|
| `%variable`<br>`%x`<br>Example:<br><br>`for %x in (*.txt) do type %x` | You can use any single letter (such as a, b, x, or y) as a variable preceded by a percent sign (%) to identify variables.<br><br>For example, %x uses x as the single letter.<br><br>The command then uses this variable to perform the specified command. In the example, the command is **type** %x. |
| `%%variable`<br>`%%x`<br>Example:<br><br>`for %%x in (*.txt) do type %%x` | If you are using the **for** command within a batch file, use two percent symbols for the variable. |
| `(set)`<br>`(file1.txt file2.txt file3.txt)`<br>`(*.txt *.bat)`<br>Example:<br>`for %x in (file1.txt file2.txt`<br>`file3.txt) do type %x` | The *set* clause specifies a set of one or more files. Files can be listed literally, such as file1. txt, file2.txt, and so on, or with wildcards, such as *.txt and *.bat.<br><br>Files in the set are separated by a space, not commas. |
| `command`<br>`type %x`<br>`type %%x`<br>Example:<br><br>`for %x in (*.txt) do type %x` | The *command* clause specifies the command to carry out for each file in the set. For example, you can use the **type** command to display the text. As a reminder, you use one percent symbol at the command prompt and two percent symbols within a batch file. |
| `command-parameters` | If the command can accept parameters such as switches, you can add them in the command. |

# Creating a Menu File

You might want to create a simple batch file that will show the user a menu, allow input, and perform an action based on the input. Based on what you include in the batch file, the user could be you or another administrator. To create the menu file, it's worthwhile knowing a few other simple commands.

## Documenting the Script with rem

It's common to add remarks in a batch file. These are not processed by the batch file, but are instead just notes to yourself. A remark starts with the **rem** command. Any text on the same line after the **rem** command is not executed. The basic syntax is

`rem comments`

> **TIP:** **rem** comments are echoed to the command prompt by default. You can use **@echo off** to prevent comments from being echoed to the command prompt.

In addition to providing documentation to explain what is happening, the **rem** command is useful to remove lines when troubleshooting. Instead of actually deleting the line, you can "rem" it out of execution by simply adding **rem** to the beginning of the line. Later, you can delete **rem** and the line is back in your batch file.

## Pausing for the User

You may occasionally want to give the user a chance to view the output before continuing. For example, if the next command in a script will cause a change or change the display before the reader can see what's happing, you can use **pause** to allow the user to continue when the user is ready. The **pause** command can be used within a batch file to simply wait for the user to press a key. When the **pause** command is executed, the system displays

```
Press any key to continue . . .
```

When the user presses a key, the batch file continues.

## Giving Users a Choice

The **choice** command prompts users to enter one of several single-character choices. You can use this to create a simple menu. The basic syntax of the command is

```
choice /c choice 1 choice 2 choice n /m "text to display"
```

| Using choice | Comments |
|---|---|
| choice /c 1234 /m "Choose menu item to run:" | Prompts the user to press a key from 1 to 4. All other key presses are ignored. |
| choice /c 1234 /m "Choose menu item to run:" /t 30 /d 4 | The /t timeout switch can be used with the /d default switch. As shown, it will wait 30 seconds for the user to press a key. If the user does not press a key within 30 seconds, it will default to a choice of 4. |

The value of the choice is recorded in the errorlevel environment variable. You can then check for the value using an **if** statement and branch to a label with the **goto** statement as follows:

```
if errorlevel 4 goto eof
if errorlevel 3 goto label3
if errorlevel 2 goto label2
if errorlevel 1 goto label1
```

> **TIP:** There is a minor quirk with the **choice** command. You need to list the errorlevel checks in reverse order. In other words, the first check looks for errorlevel 4, then errorlevel 3, then 2, and then 1. If you don't list them in reverse order, the **choice** command doesn't process them correctly.

You may also note that the **if** command is using a shortcut. The same **if** statement can be expressed in several different ways within the **choice** command. All three of these commands will work:

| Different Methods of Comparing | Comments |
| --- | --- |
| `if %errorlevel% == 1 goto label 1` | This method does not use any shortcuts. |
| `if errorlevel == 1 goto label1` | This method omits the % symbols around errorlevel. |
| `if errorlevel 1 goto label1` | This method omits the % symbols around errorlevel and the equal signs (==). |

## Creating the Batch File

The following batch file presents users with a simple menu and gives them a choice. It combines many of the batch file commands presented in this chapter. It gives the user the menu shown in Figure 6-3.

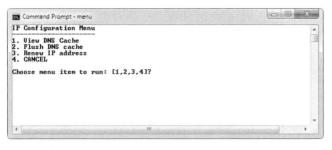

**Figure 6-3** Viewing a Simple Menu

```
@echo off
:menu
rem Show users the menu
cls
echo IP Configuration Menu
echo --------------------
echo 1. View DNS Cache
echo 2. Flush DNS cache
echo 3. Renew IP address
echo 4. CANCEL
echo.
choice /c 1234 /m "Choose menu item to run:" /t 30 /d 4
if errorlevel  4 goto eof
if errorlevel  3 goto renew
if errorlevel  2 goto flushdns
```

```
if errorlevel  1 goto viewdns
:viewdns
ipconfig /displaydns
pause
goto menu
:flushdns
ipconfig /flushdns
pause
goto menu
:renew
ipconfig /renew
pause
goto menu
:eof
```

The contents of the batch file are also shown in the following table.

| Command | Description |
|---|---|
| `@echo off` | Turns off echo and hides the command with the use of the @ symbol. |
| `:menu`<br>`rem Show users the menu` | The **:menu** label is used as a starting point so that the menu can be redisplayed after other commands are issued. The **rem** line is just a comment. |
| `cls`<br>`echo IP Configuration Menu`<br>`echo --------------------`<br>`echo 1. View DNS Cache`<br>`echo 2. Flush DNS cache`<br>`echo 3. Renew IP address`<br>`echo 4. Cancel`<br>`echo.` | **cls** clears the screen each time the menu is displayed. The **echo** commands then display the menu.<br><br>**echo.** is used to display a blank line after the menu choices. |
| `choice /c 1234 /m "Choose menu`<br>`item to run:" /t 30 /d 4` | The **choice** command presents the user with a choice of 1, 2, 3, or 4. It gives the user 30 seconds to make a choice and defaults to a choice of 4 if the user doesn't make a choice.<br><br>If the user presses any key other than 1, 2, 3, or 4, it is ignored. |
| `if errorlevel  4 goto eof`<br>`if errorlevel  3 goto renew`<br>`if errorlevel  2 goto flushdns`<br>`if errorlevel  1 goto viewdns` | The **if** statements check to identify what key was pressed by the user. Based on the key pressed, the **goto** statement redirects the output to a label within the batch file. |

| | |
|---|---|
| ```:viewdns```<br>```ipconfig /displaydns```<br>```pause```<br>```goto menu``` | The **: viewdns** label executes the **ipconfig /displaydns** command. It then pauses to give the user an opportunity to view the data. When the user presses a key, the menu is redisplayed. |
| ```:flushdns```<br>```ipconfig /flushdns```<br>```pause```<br>```goto menu``` | The **: flushdns** label executes the **ipconfig /flushdns** command. It then pauses to give the user an opportunity to view the data. When the user presses a key, the menu is redisplayed. |
| ```:renew```<br>```ipconfig /renew```<br>```pause```<br>```goto menu``` | The **:renew** label executes the **ipconfig /renew** command. It then pauses to give the user an opportunity to view the data. When the user presses a key, the menu is redisplayed. |
| ```:eof``` | The **:eof** label is the last command in the batch file. When the batch file reaches the end, it will exit. |

This chapter provides information and commands concerning the following topics:

- Scheduling batch files with Task Scheduler
- Scheduling tasks from the command line

# Scheduling Batch Files with Task Scheduler

After you've created a batch file, you can automate it. In other words, you don't always have to start the batch file from the command prompt. Instead, you can schedule it to run regularly without any user interaction. As mentioned in Chapter 5, "Manipulating Disks," you use Task Scheduler in Windows 7 to schedule tasks.

You can launch Task Scheduler by clicking Start, entering Task in the Start Search text box, and selecting Task Scheduler. Figure 7-1 shows Task Scheduler with a script in the Task Scheduler Library.

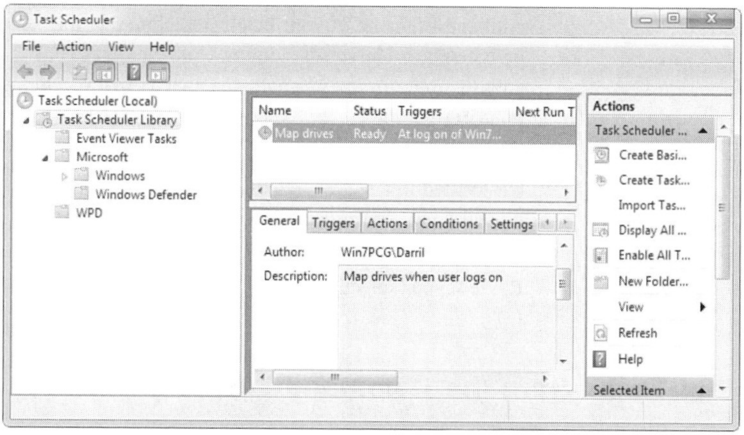

**Figure 7-1**  Task Scheduler with a Script Scheduled to Run When a User Logs On

Task Scheduler doesn't care what the script does. You simply schedule the task and Task Scheduler will run it. You can schedule tasks to run

- Daily
- Weekly
- Monthly

- One time
- When the computer starts
- When a user logs on
- When a specific event is logged

You can use the following steps to schedule a script with Task Scheduler:

| Steps | Remarks |
| --- | --- |
| 1. Launch Task Scheduler. | Click **Start**, enter **Task** in the Start Search text box, and select **Task Scheduler**. |
| 2. Launch the Create a Basic Task Wizard. | Right-click **Task Scheduler Library** and click **Create Basic Task**. |
| 3. Name your task. | Enter a name and description for your task and click **Next**. |
| 4. Identify a trigger to schedule the task. | Choose when you want the script to run. For example, you can choose **When I Log On** to have the script run each time you log on. |
| | If you choose one of the time triggers (**Daily**, **Weekly**, **Monthly**, or **One Time**), you'll be prompted to add additional details for the schedule. |
| 5. Identify the batch file to run. | Select **Start a Program** and click **Next**. Enter the path and filename of your batch file. Note that the path can be a Universal Naming Convention (UNC) path of \\*servername*\*sharename*, such as \\win7computer\scriptsshare\. |
| | For example, if you had a script named mapdrives.bat located in a share named scripts on a computer named win7, you'd use \\win7\scripts\mapdrives.bat. Click **Next**. |
| 6. Complete the wizard. | Review your selections and click **Finish**. |

## Scheduling Tasks from the Command Line

You can also schedule tasks from the command line, but you'll need to launch a command prompt with administrative privileges for most commands. The command is **schtasks** and the basic syntax is

```
schtasks /parameter [arguments]
```

The parameters are essentially commands expressed as switches. Depending on which parameter you use, you will use different arguments. The following table shows most of the parameters you can use with the **schtasks** command.

| Parameter | Description |
|---|---|
| /create | Creates a new scheduled task. |
| /delete | Deletes the scheduled task(s). |
| /query | Displays all scheduled tasks. |
| /change | Changes the properties of the scheduled task. |
| /run | Runs the scheduled task on demand. |
| /end | Stops the currently running scheduled task. |

## Creating a Scheduled Task with schtasks

When you create a scheduled task, you have a lot of optional information that you can add. The required information is

```
schtasks /create /sc schedule /tn taskname /tr task-to-run
```

For example, if you want to create a scheduled task to run a script named logon.bat when a user logs on, you could use this line:

```
schtasks /create /sc onlogon /tn myschtask /tr c:\scripts\logon.bat
```

The following table shows the arguments used to create a schedule.

| /create Argument | Description |
|---|---|
| /sc schedule<br>[/mo modifier] [/d day] [/m months] [/i idletime] | The **/sc** switch specifies the schedule frequency. Valid schedule types are: **minute**, **hourly**, **daily**, **weekly**, **monthly**, **once**, and **onevent**. |
| /tn taskname | The **/tn** switch specifies the name used to uniquely identify the scheduled task. |
| /tr task-to-run | The **/tr** switch specifies the path and filename of the batch file or program to be run at the scheduled time. For example, the task could be C:\scripts\logon.bat. |

## Creating a Scheduled Task from an XML File with schtasks

A very useful feature with **schtasks** is the ability to create a task using an Extensible Markup Language (XML) file. The basic syntax is

```
schtasks /create /tn TaskName /xml xmlfileandpath
```

Creating the XML file from scratch isn't easy, but it is easy to create a task using the Windows 7 GUI and then export the XML file. You can then easily import the XML file into other systems to re-create the task.

You can use the following steps to create a task with the Task Scheduler GUI, export the XML file, and then create the task with an XML file.

| Steps | Remarks |
| --- | --- |
| 1. Create a basic task using Task Scheduler. | Use the detailed steps outlined at the beginning of this chapter. |
| | Name the task **tasktoexport**. |
| 2. Export the XML file of the tasktoexport task. | Right-click the **tasktoexport** task in Task Scheduler and select **Export**. |
| | Browse to a location on your system (such as the C:\scripts folder if it exists) and save the file as tasktoexport.xml. |
| 3. Delete the original tasktoexport task. | Right-click the **tasktoexport** task in Task Scheduler and select **Delete**. |
| | You can then import the same task using the XML file, which simulates importing it into a different system. |
| 4. Launch a command prompt with administrative privileges. | Administrative privileges are required to create a task with the **schtasks** command. |
| 5. Import the task with this command:<br><br>`C:\windows\system32>schtasks / create /tn importedtask /xml c:\ scripts\tasktoexport.xml` | The task name is importedtask, but you can substitute any task name desired. |

This can be especially useful when combining the strengths of Group Policy with scripting. For example, if you wanted to create a scheduled task on all the computers in your domain (or site or organizational unit), you could take the following steps:

| Steps | Remarks |
| --- | --- |
| 1. Create the scheduled task. | Use Task Scheduler to create the task. Test it to ensure it runs as desired. |
| 2. Export the XML file. | Use Task Scheduler to export the task's XML file. |
| 3. Centrally locate the XML file. | You need to place the XML file on a share that is accessible by all computers that will run the script. For example, you could place it on a share named scripts on a server named server1. It is accessible via the UNC path of \\server1\scripts. |

| 4. Create a batch file with these lines:<br><br>`net use z:\\server1\scripts`<br>`schtasks /create /tn importedtask /`<br>`xml z:tasktoexport.xml`<br>`net use z: /delete` | The batch file needs to end with the .bat extension. First, map the UNC path to the letter z with the **net use** command. Then, create the task with the **schtasks** command. Last, delete the mapped drive. |
| 5. Schedule the script with Group Policy. | Chapter 29, "Group Policy Overview," covers how to schedule a script with Group Policy. |

## Deleting a Scheduled Task with schtasks

You can delete a scheduled task with the **/delete** parameter. The only required argument is the **/tn** switch, to identify the task to delete. For example, if you want to delete a task named myschtask, you can use this command:

```
schtasks /delete /tn myschtask
```

The following table shows the arguments used with the **schtasks** command.

| /delete Argument | Description |
|---|---|
| `/tn taskname`<br>`C:\>schtasks /delete /tn myschtask` | The **/tn** switch specifies the name of the scheduled task to delete. You can use an asterisk (*) as a wildcard to delete all tasks. |
| `/f`<br>`C:\>schtasks /delete /tn myschtask`<br>`/f` | The **/f** switch forcefully deletes the task without prompting for confirmation, which is useful if you are deleting a task from within a script. It also suppresses warnings if the specified task is currently running. |
| `/s system`<br>`C:\>schtasks /delete /tn myschtask`<br>`/s dc1` | The **/s** switch enables you to specify a remote system, such as a server named dc1. As long as you have credentials, you can delete a task on the remote system. |
| `/u username`<br>`C:\>schtasks /delete /tn myschtask`<br>`/u administrator` | The **/u** switch specifies the user context under which schtasks.exe should execute. |
| `/p [password]`<br>`C:\>schtasks /delete /tn myschtask`<br>`/u administrator /p P@ssw0rd` | The **/p** switch specifies the password for the given user context. Prompts for input if omitted. |

## Viewing Scheduled Tasks with schtasks

You can view the scheduled tasks that exist on a system with the **/query** parameter. The basic syntax is

```
schtasks /query
```

If you execute this command, you'll see that many more tasks exist on the system than those you've created. You can modify the output with various arguments:

| Using the /query switch | Comments |
| --- | --- |
| schtasks /query /fo value<br>C:\>schtasks /query /fo list<br>C:\>schtasks /query /fo csv | The **/fo** argument is used to format the output. You must specify one of the valid values with the **/fo** argument: **table**, **list**, **csv**. The default value is **table**. In other words, **schtasks /query** and **schtasks /query /fo table** provide the same output. |
| C:\>schtasks /query /fo csv ><br>tasklist.csv | Sends the output to a CSV file that can be opened in Microsoft Excel. |
| C:\>schtasks /query /fo table /nh | Specifies that the column header is not displayed in the output. This is only valid with the table format. |
| C:\>schtasks /query /v | Displays verbose task output. Several additional columns are added that provide significantly more detail on the scheduled tasks. |

## Changing Scheduled Tasks with schtasks

You can modify scheduled tasks with the **schtasks** command. The basic syntax is

```
schtasks /change /tn taskname /option
```

For example, if you wanted to disable a task named importedtask, you could use this command:

```
schtasks /change /tn importedtask /disable
```

Some of the other parameters you can use with **change** are shown in the following table.

| Parameter | Description |
| --- | --- |
| /enable<br>C:\>schtasks /change /tn importedtask<br>/enable | Enables the scheduled task. |
| /disable<br>C:\>schtasks /change /tn importedtask<br>/disable | Disables the scheduled task. |

| `/ru username`<br>`C:\>schtasks /change /tn importedtask`<br>`/ru system` | Changes the username (user context) under which the scheduled task has to run. For the system account, valid values on Windows 7 are as follows:<br><br>blank<br><br>**nt authority\system** or simply **system**<br><br>**nt authority \localservice**<br><br>**nt authority \networkservice**<br><br>You can also use the well-known SID for any of these system accounts. The password is ignored for the system account. |
|---|---|
| `/rp password`<br>`C:\>schtasks /change /tn importedtask`<br>`/rp P@ssw0rd` | Specifies a new password for the existing user context or the password for a new user account. |
| `/tr taskrun`<br>`C:\>schtasks /change /tn importedtask`<br>`/tr c:\scripts\newbatch.bat` | Specifies the new program that the scheduled task will run. You can use this to have the same task run a different program. |

## Running and Ending Scheduled Tasks with schtasks

If you want to run or end a scheduled task from the command line, you can use the **/run** argument or **/end** argument. The only item you must specify is the task name. The basic syntax is

```
schtasks /run /tn taskname
schtasks /end /tn taskname
```

This chapter provides information and commands concerning the following topics:

- Controlling power settings with **powercfg**
- Checking memory with **mdsched**
- Manipulating services with **sc**
- Collecting events with **wecutil**
- Restarting systems with **shutdown**
- Launching Control Panel applets from the command line

## Controlling Power Settings with powercfg

The powercfg.exe utility is a great tool for setting power settings on Windows 7 computers. You can view the power settings without administrative privileges, but the **powercfg** commands that modify settings must be run from an elevated command prompt.

This section shows you the settings to

- Query the power settings with **powercfg**
- Modify the power settings with **powercfg**
- Analyze the power settings with **powercfg**

### Query the Power Settings with powercfg

The following table shows some of the switches you can use with **powercfg** to query the current power settings.

> **NOTE:** As with most command switches, you can use either a dash (-) or a forward slash (/) for the switches. For example, **powercfg /q** works exactly the same as **bercfg -q**.

| Switch | Description |
|---|---|
| `/list`<br>`/l`<br>`C:\>powercfg /list`<br>`Existing Power Schemes (*`<br>`Active)`<br>`------------------------------`<br>`----`<br>`Power Scheme GUID: 381b4222-`<br>`f694-41f0-9685-ff5bb260df2e`<br>`(Balanced) *`<br>`Power Scheme GUID: 8c5e7fda-`<br>`e8bf-4a96-9a85-a6e23a8c635c`<br>`(High performance)`<br>`Power Scheme GUID: a1841308-`<br>`3541-4fab-bc81-f71556f20b4a`<br>`(Power saver)` | Lists all existing power schemes with their globally unique identifier (GUID) and name. The active power scheme is marked with an asterisk (*). By default, there are three schemes: balanced, high performance, and power saver.<br><br>You can also enter this as **powercfg /l**. |
| `/query`<br>`/q`<br>`C:\>powercfg /query`<br>`C:\>powercfg /q` | Displays the contents of the active power scheme. |
| `/q GUID`<br>`C:\>powercfg /q 8c5e7fda-e8bf-`<br>`4a96-9a85-a6e23a8c635c` | Displays the contents of the specified power scheme. The power schemes are identified by their GUID.<br><br>Remember, you can cut and paste the GUID after listing it with the **/l** switch. You don't have to type in the GUID from scratch. |
| `/q GUID sub-GUID`<br>`C:\>powercfg /q  8c5e7fda-e8bf-`<br>`4a96-9a85-a6e23a8c635c 0012ee47-`<br>`9041-4b5d-9b77-535fba8b1442` | Shows the settings for only the hard-disk settings (sub-GUID) of the high-performance settings (primary GUID). |
| `/aliases`<br>`C:\>powercfg /aliases` | Lists aliases with their corresponding GUIDs. You can enter the aliases instead of the GUIDs in some commands. For example, the following are some aliases:<br><br>scheme_max (power saver)<br><br>scheme_min (high performance)<br><br>scheme_balanced (balanced) |

| | |
|---|---|
| `/q alias`<br>`C:\>powercfg /q scheme_max`<br>`C:\>powercfg /q scheme_min`<br>`C:\>powercfg /q scheme_balanced` | Displays contents of specific power settings. Instead of querying the settings using the GUID, you can query using an alias. These show some examples of how the aliases can be used.<br><br>**NOTE:** You can get a listing of all the aliases with the **powercfg /aliases** command. |
| `/getactivescheme`<br>`C:\>powercfg /getactivescheme`<br>`Power Scheme GUID: 8c5e7fda-`<br>`e8bf-4a96-9a85-a6e23a8c635c`<br>`(High performance)` | Identifies the current active scheme by GUID and name. |
| `/waketimers`<br>`C:\>powercfg /waketimers` | Lists any wake timers running on the system. A wake timer wakes the system from sleep and hibernate states when the timer expires. |
| `/requests`<br>`C:\>powercfg /requests` | Lists all active application and driver power requests. A power request prevents the computer from automatically powering off the display or entering a low-power sleep mode. |

## Modify the Power Settings with powercfg

The following table shows some of the methods you can use to modify various power settings.

**TIP:** Remember, you can embed any of these commands in a script and then automate the running of the script with Group Policy. This enables you to easily set the specific power settings for all of the computers in your organization. You can use WMI filters with Group Policy to ensure the settings affect only specific operating systems (such as only Windows 7 systems and not any servers).

| Switch | Description |
|---|---|
| `/setactive scheme_GUID`<br>`/s scheme_GUID`<br>`/s scheme_alias`<br>`C:\>powercfg /s 8c5e7fda-e8bf-`<br>`4a96-9a85-a6e23a8c635c`<br>`C:\>powercfg /setactive scheme_`<br>`max`<br>`C:\>powercfg /s scheme_min`<br>`C:\>powercfg /s balanced` | You can set the active power scheme using either the **/setactive** or **/s** switch. These switches accept either the GUID or the alias. |
| `/h [on \| off ]`<br>`C:\>powercfg /h on` | You can enable or disable the hibernate feature with the **/hibernate** or **/h** switch. |

| | |
|---|---|
| ```/change```<br>```/x```<br>```C:\>powercfg /change```<br>```/monitor-timeout-ac 15``` | The example changes the time to turn off the display when the system is plugged in (AC) to 15 minutes.<br><br>Note that **/monitor-timeout-ac** is the setting and it does not have any spaces.<br><br>You can use either **/change** or **/x** for the change switch. |
| ```C:\>powercfg /change -monitor-```<br>```timeout-dc 5``` | The example changes the time to turn off the display when the system is on battery (DC) power to 5 minutes. |
| ```C:\>powercfg /x```<br>```/disk-timeout-ac 15```<br><br>```C:\>powercfg /x```<br>```/disk-timeout-dc 5``` | The example changes the time to turn off the disk when the system is plugged in (AC) to 15 minutes.<br><br>The second example changes the time to turn off the disk when the system is on battery (DC) power to 5 minutes. |
| ```C:\>powercfg /x```<br>```/standby-timeout-ac 30```<br><br>```C:\>powercfg /x /standby-```<br>```timeout-dc 15``` | The example changes the time to put the system into standby mode when the system is plugged in (AC) to 30 minutes.<br><br>The second example changes the time to put the system into standby mode when the system is on battery (DC) power to 15 minutes. |
| ```C:\>powercfg /x```<br>```/hibernate-timeout-ac 30```<br><br>```C:\>powercfg /x```<br>```/hibernate-timeout-dc 5``` | The example changes the time to hibernate the system when the system is plugged in (AC) to 30 minutes.<br><br>The second example changes the time to hibernate the system when the system is on battery (DC) power to 5 minutes. |

As an example, you could use the following lines in a script to set the power settings for desktop computers. This script will configure the following settings:

- Set the scheme to balanced
- Turn off the monitor after 15 minutes of inactivity
- Turn off disks after 15 minutes of inactivity
- Put the system into standby after 30 minutes of inactivity
- Hibernate the system after 30 minutes

```
powercfg /s balanced
powercfg /change /monitor-timeout-ac 15
```

```
powercfg /x /disk-timeout-ac 15
powercfg /x /standby-timeout-ac 30
powercfg /x /hibernate-timeout-ac 30
```

You could then create a Group Policy object (GPO) and link the script to one or more organizational units (OUs) that include your target desktop computers.

## Analyze the Power Settings with powercfg

You can use the commands in the following table to analyze the power settings and then view the report generated by **powercfg**.

| Command | Description |
|---------|-------------|
| `/energy`<br>`C:\>powercfg /energy`<br>`Enabling tracing for 60 sec-`<br>`onds...`<br>`Observing system behavior...`<br>`Analyzing trace data...`<br>`Analysis complete.`<br>`Energy efficiency problems`<br>`were found.`<br>`4 Errors`<br>`3 Warnings`<br>`9 Informational`<br>`See c:\Windows\system32\`<br>`energy-report.html for more`<br>`details.` | Detects common energy-efficiency and battery-life issues. This includes excessive processor utilization, inefficient power policy settings, ineffective use of suspend by USB devices, and more.<br><br>You can use this to diagnose energy-efficiency problems on user systems. It should be run when the computer is idle, with no open programs or documents. When it completes, it will create an HTML document you can view using any web browser.<br><br>**NOTE:** You can have the file saved in a different location by using the **/output** switch with a path. For example, the following command saves the report in c:\data and names it energy.html:<br><br>`powercfg /energy /output c:\data`<br>`\energy.html` |
| `C:\>c:\windows\system32`<br>`\energy-report.html` | Displays the report created by the **powercfg** **/energy** command. |

# Checking Memory with mdsched

Memory problems often appear as random issues such as random system lockups or random reboots. You can rule out memory problems by launching and scheduling memory diagnostics with the **mdsched** command. The only syntax is

```
mdsched
```

> **NOTE:** Random problems can also indicate other problems, such as the existence of malicious software (malware) on your system, or heat problems due to faulty fans or poor ventilation. This check can verify that memory is, or is not, the source of the problem.

When you execute the command, a dialog box appears, as shown in Figure 8-1.

**Figure 8-1** Scheduling Memory Diagnostics with **mdsched**

You can choose to restart the system immediately and run the diagnostics, or schedule the diagnostics to run the next time the system is rebooted. Figure 8-2 shows the screen that appears after the system has been rebooted and the memory diagnostics begin.

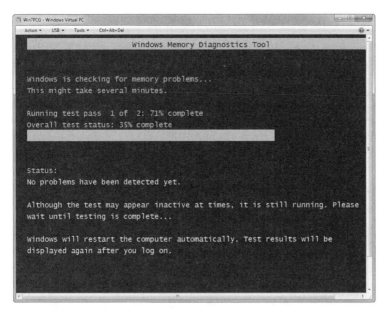

**Figure 8-2** Running Memory Diagnostics

After the diagnostics complete, the system will boot normally. If you're right in front of the screen before it reboots, you'll see the results. However, watching memory diagnostics is about as much as fun as watching paint dry, so you'll probably be somewhere else when it completes. Thankfully, the results are logged.

> **TIP:** You can view the results in the System log using Event Viewer. The Source is MemoryDiagnostics-Results. A good pass will log that the computer's memory was tested and detected no errors.

## Manipulating Services with sc

The service controller (**sc**) command is a rich command you can use to start, stop, and manipulate services from the command line. This allows you to perform many of the same functions from the command line as you can do via the Services console.

Some of the common functions are shown and described in the following table.

| Command | Description |
|---|---|
| `C:\>sc query`<br>`SERVICE_NAME: wsearch`<br>`        TYPE            : 10`<br>`WIN32_OWN_PROCESS`<br>`        STATE           : 4`<br>`RUNNING`<br>`(STOPPABLE, NOT_PAUSABLE,`<br>`ACCEPTS_SHUTDOWN)`<br>`            WIN32_EXIT_CODE    : 0`<br>`(0x0)`<br>`        SERVICE_EXIT_CODE  : 0`<br>`(0x0)`<br>`        CHECKPOINT      : 0x0`<br>`        WAIT_HINT       : 0x0` | Lists all *running* services and drivers. The result on the left shows the results for a single service, but the actual output shows details on all running services and drivers, and the result can be quite extensive.<br><br>Of course, you can capture the entire output with the redirect (>) symbol as follows:<br><br>**sc query > services.txt**<br><br>The service name shows the name of the service that you can use in other commands. |
| `sc query state= all | inactive`<br>`C:\>sc query state= all`<br>`C:\>sc query state= inactive` | Lists all services including services stopped, running, or paused. Notice that there is no space between state and = (**state=**), and there is a space between = and all (**= all**).<br><br>You can also use **state= inactive** to list only services that are stopped or **state= all** to list all services including those that are running and those that are stopped. |

| | |
|---|---|
| `sc query type= service \| driver \| all`<br>`C:\>sc query type= service`<br>`C:\>sc query type= driver`<br>`C:\>sc query type= all` | Lists all running services or drivers. Notice that there is no space between type and = (**type=**), and there is a space between = and service (**= service**).<br><br>You can also use **type= driver** to list drivers instead of services, or **type= all** to list both. |
| `sc query service_name`<br>`C:\>sc query wsearch`<br>`SERVICE_NAME: wsearch`<br>`        TYPE          : 10 WIN32_OWN_PROCESS`<br>`        STATE         : 4 RUNNING`<br><br>`(STOPPABLE, NOT_PAUSABLE, ACCEPTS_SHUTDOWN)`<br>`        WIN32_EXIT_CODE  : 0 (0x0)`<br>`        SERVICE_EXIT_CODE : 0 (0x0)`<br>`        CHECKPOINT       : 0x0`<br>`        WAIT_HINT        : 0x0` | Lists the details on the wsearch service only. You can use the same command for any specific service by specifying the name.<br><br>As a reminder, the *service_name* is the same name you can see in the SERVICE_NAME output from the **sc query** command. |
| `sc start service_name`<br>`C:\>sc start wsearch` | Starts the service.<br><br>This example starts the wsearch service, but you can substitute the service name for any service to start it. |
| `sc stop service_name`<br>`C:\>sc stop wsearch` | Stops a service. The example stops the wsearch service. You can substitute the service name for any service to stop it. |
| `sc pause service_name`<br>`C:\>sc pause winmgmt` | Pauses the service.<br><br>**NOTE:** Not all services can be paused. If the service is listed as PAUSABLE (in the State property), it can be paused. If the service is listed as NOT_PAUSABLE, it cannot be paused. |
| `sc continue service_name`<br>`C:\>sc continue wsearch` | Restarts a paused service. |

## Collecting Events with wecutil

The Windows event collector utility (**wecutil**) is used to create and manage event subscriptions on Windows 7. Windows 7 allows you to use a single system to collect events from several other systems. The system that collects the events is called the *collector computer*. The systems whose events are collected are called the *source computers*.

> **NOTE:** Most of the work for event subscriptions will be through the Event Viewer GUI on the collector computer. The primary thing you'll need to do from the command line is configure the source and collector computers.

When configuring event subscriptions, you need to configure both the source computers and the collector computers.

| Command | Description |
|---|---|
| `C:\>winrm quickconfig` | Use this command to configure source computers for event collection. |
| `C:\>wecutil qc`<br>`C:\>wecutil quickconfig` | Use either of these commands to configure the collector computer. When you enter this command, you'll be prompted to change the startup mode to Delay-Start. Enter **Y** to confirm this change. This command will configure the Windows Event Collector service so that subscriptions can be created and sustained through reboots. The command performs three steps:<br><br>1. Sets the Windows Event Collector service to delay start.<br><br>2. Starts the Windows Event Collector service if it is not running.<br><br>3. Enables the Forwarded Events channel if it is disabled. |

> **TIP:** If the message "The RPC server is unavailable" appears when you try to run **wecutil**, you need to start the Windows Event Collector service (**wecsvc**). You can start **wecsvc** from an elevated prompt with the command **sc start wecsvc**.

## Restarting Systems with shutdown

You can use the **shutdown** command to log off, shut down, and reboot local and remote systems. You can also use the **shutdown** command to start the Shutdown GUI. For example, if you enter the following command, a GUI similar to the one shown in Figure 8-3 will launch:

```
shutdown /i
```

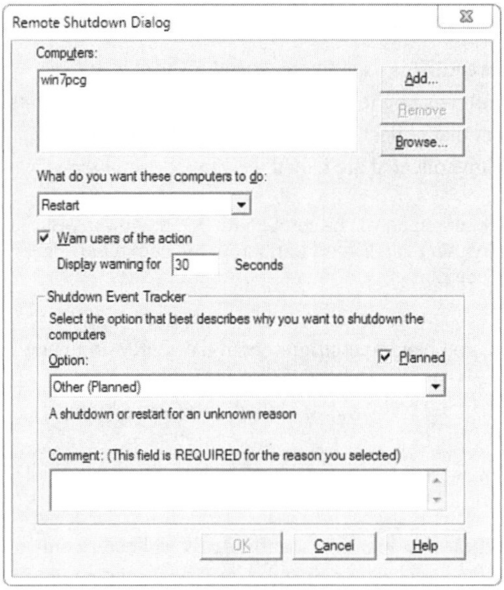

**Figure 8-3**  Using the Shutdown GUI

Other switches used with the **shutdown** command are shown in the following table.

| Switch | Description |
|---|---|
| /1<br>C:\>shutdown /1 | Logs the current user off the local system imme-diately. You can't use this for remote systems. |
| /s<br>C:\>shutdown /s | Shuts down the local computer. |
| /r<br>C:\>shutdown /r | Reboots the local computer. |
| /h<br>C:\>shutdown /h | Hibernates the local computer. |
| /r /t *xxx*<br>C:\>shutdown /r /t 60 | Shuts down the computer (/r) with a time-out period (/t) given in seconds. You can specify any time between 0 and 600 seconds. The default time is 30 seconds. |
| /a<br>C:\>shutdown /a | Cancels a shutdown. You can only use this during a timeout period that hasn't expired. |
| /r /m \\*targetcomputer*<br>C:\>shutdown /r /m \\win7 | Reboots a remote computer. Remote computers are specified with the **/m** switch, followed by two back slashes (\\) and then by the computer name. |

# Launching Control Panel Applets from the Command Line

There might be times when you want to access the Control Panel with administrative permissions while logged on as a regular user. Unfortunately, the Run As Administrator option isn't available for the Control Panel. However, you can start the Command Prompt with administrative permissions and then use the commands in the following table to access the different Control Panel applets.

**TIP:** Many of these commands will work only when executed from a command prompt with administrative permissions. If you execute them from a nonadministrative prompt you often won't see any response at all.

| Command | Control Panel Applet or Tool |
|---|---|
| `C:\>control` | Control Panel |
| `C:\>control sysdm.cpl`<br>`C:\>control sysdm.cpl,,2`<br>`C:\>control sysdm.cpl,,3`<br>`C:\>control sysdm.cpl,,4`<br>`C:\>control sysdm.cpl,,5` | System Properties (advanced system settings)<br><br>**NOTE:** You can directly access specific tabs by using two commas and then the number of the tab. The tabs are<br><br>1 Computer Name<br><br>2 Hardware<br><br>3 Advanced<br><br>4 System Protection<br><br>5 Remote |
| `C:\>control ncpa.cpl`<br>`C:\>control netconnections` | Network Connections (configure NICs and other connections) |
| `C:\>control firewall.cpl` | Windows Firewall |
| `C:\>control appwiz.cpl` | Programs and Features |
| `C:\>control hdwwiz.cpl` | Device Manager |
| `C:\>control desk.cpl` | Display (Screen Resolution) |
| `C:\>control inetcpl.cpl` | Internet Explorer Properties |
| `C:\>control powercfg.cpl` | Power Options |
| `C:\>control sticpl.cpl` | Scanners and Cameras |
| `C:\>control mmsys.cpl` | Sound (including Playback and Recording) |
| `C:\>control modem.cpl` | Modem Properties |
| `C:\>control wscui.cpl` | Action Center |
| `C:\>control desk.cpl,screensaver,@screensaver` | Screensaver |
| `C:\>control tabletpc.cpl` | Pen and Touch Tools for Tablet PC |

| | |
|---|---|
| `C:\>control intl.cpl`<br>`C:\>control international` | Region and Language settings |
| `C:\>control input.dll` | Text Services and Input Languages<br><br>**NOTE:** This uses a .dll extension instead of .cpl. |
| `C:\>control timedate.cpl` | Date and Time properties |
| `C:\>control access.cpl` | Ease of Access Center (Accessibility options) |
| `C:\>control main.cpl`<br>`C:\>control mouse` | Mouse Properties |
| `C:\>control joy.cpl` | Game Controllers |
| `C:\>control nusrmgr.cpl`<br>`C:\>control userpasswords` | User Accounts tool |

**TIP:** Some tools can be run with or without the .cpl extension. Some tools require the extension, and other tools won't launch if it's included. All of the commands in these tables will launch the tool in Windows 7 using the provided command.

The following tools are entered with the **control** command but without the .cpl extension.

| Command | Control Panel Applet or Tool |
|---|---|
| `C:\>control admintools` | Administrative Tools |
| `C:\>control folders` | Windows Explorer Folder Options (configure behavior and views) |
| `C:\>control schedtasks` | Task Scheduler tool |
| `C:\>control telephony` | Phone and Modem settings |
| `C:\>control printers` | Devices and Printers |
| `C:\>control desktop` | Desktop Personalization (themes and background) |
| `C:\>control color` | Windows Color and Appearance |
| `C:\>control keyboard` | Keyboard Properties |
| `C:\>control fonts` | Fonts folder |

Some tools can be accessed using the **/name** switch with the **control** command.

| Command | Control Panel Applet or Tool |
|---|---|
| `C:\>control /name`<br>`microsoft.networkandsharingcenter` | Network and Sharing Center |
| `C:\>control /name`<br>`microsoft.windowsupdate` | Windows Update |

| `C:\>control /name`<br>`microsoft.personalization` | Windows Personalization (themes and background) |
|---|---|
| `C:\>control /name`<br>`microsoft.personalization /page`<br>`pagecolorization` | Windows Color and Appearance (Aero can be turned off through the Advanced Appearance settings) |
| `C:\>control /name`<br>`microsoft.personalization /page`<br>`pagewallpaper` | Desktop background |
| `C:\>control /name`<br>`microsoft.programsandfeatures` | Programs and Features tool |
| `C:\>control /name`<br>`microsoft.defaultprograms` | Default Programs (set default programs, associate file types, and change AutoPlay) |

There are also some direct commands you can use to access different system tools without using the **control** command.

| Command | Control Panel Applet or Tool |
|---|---|
| `C:\>systempropertiesperformance` | Performance Options, Visual Effects<br><br>**NOTE:** The Advanced tab provides access to the paging file. |
| `C:\>systempropertiesremote` | System properties, Remote tab |
| `C:\>systempropertiescomputername` | System properties, Computer Name tab |
| `C:\>systempropertiesprotection` | System properties, System Protection tab |
| `C:\>systempropertiesadvanced` | System properties, Advanced tab |
| `C:\>optionalfeatures` | Windows Features to turn Windows features on or off |

This chapter provides information and commands concerning the following topics:

- Viewing system information with **systeminfo**
- Viewing user information with **whoami**
- Launching System Configuration with **msconfig**

## Viewing System Information with systeminfo

You can use the **systeminfo** command to get detailed information about a system. This includes information on the hardware, the operating system, service packs and hotfixes, and security information. The basic syntax is

```
systeminfo
```

A typical partial output looks like this:

```
Host Name:            Win7LAPTOP
OS Name:              Microsoft Windows 7 Ultimate
OS Version:           6.1.7600 N/A Build 7600
OS Manufacturer:      Microsoft Corporation
OS Configuration:     Standalone Workstation
OS Build Type:        Multiprocessor Free
Registered Owner:     Darril
Registered Organization:
Product ID:           00426-065-0543977-86656
Original Install Date:   8/9/2009, 4:42:31 AM
System Boot Time:     8/4/2010, 4:32:45 AM
System Manufacturer: Hewlett-Packard
System Model:         HP Pavilion dv7 Notebook PC
System Type:          x64-based PC
Processor(s):         1 Processor(s) Installed.
          [01]:       Intel64 Family 6 Model 23 Stepping 6 GenuineIntel
~2401 Mhz
```

```
BIOS Version:          Hewlett-Packard F.26, 2/6/2009
Windows Directory:     c:\Windows
System Directory:      c:\Windows\system32
Boot Device:           \Device\HarddiskVolume1
System Locale:         en-us;English (United States)
Input Locale:          en-us;English (United States)
Time Zone:             (UTC-05:00) Eastern Time (US & Canada)
Total Physical Memory:   6,111 MB
Available Physical Memory:    2,399 MB
Virtual Memory:        Max Size:  21,385 MB
Virtual Memory:        Available: 16,987 MB
Virtual Memory: In Use: 4,398 MB
Page File Location(s): c:\pagefile.sys
                       H:\pagefile.sys
Domain:                WORKGROUP
Logon Server:          \\LAPTOP
Hotfix(s):             2 Hotfix(s) Installed.
          [01]: KB971033
          [02]: KB958559
. . .
                          [68]: KB983590
Network Card(s):          2 NIC(s) Installed.
   [01]: Intel(R) WiFi Link 5100 AGN
          Connection Name:    Wireless Network Connection
          Status:             Media disconnected
   [02]: Realtek RTL8168C(P)/8111C(P) Family PCI-E GBE NIC
          Connection Name:    Local Area Connection
          Status:             Media disconnected
```

**NOTE:** This output doesn't show all the applied hotfixes; hotfixes [3] to [67] were omitted to conserve space. Normal output will include them all.

You can also view the System Information GUI to get detailed information about a system, as shown in Figure 9-1. Click **Start**, type **System** in the Start Search text box, and select **System Information**.

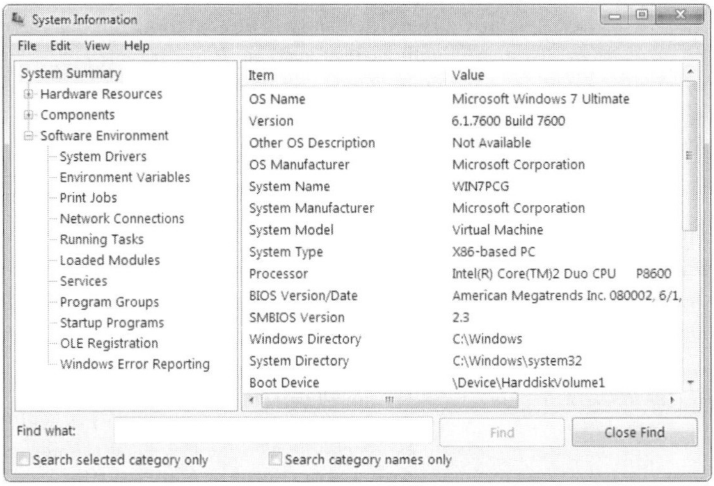

**Figure 9-1**    System Information GUI

Some additional methods you can use with the **systeminfo** command are shown in the following table.

| Switch | Description |
| --- | --- |
| /fo<br>C:\>systeminfo /fo format<br>C:\>systeminfo /fo table<br>C:\>systeminfo /fo csv | The **/fo** switch is used to format the output. You can specify **list**, **table**, or **csv** as the format type. The default format is **list**. |
| /nh<br>C:\>systeminfo /fo csv /nh | The **/nh** switch suppresses the column headers. Only **table** and **csv** formatted outputs have headers, so the **/nh** switch can be used only when formatting the output with **table** or **csv**. |
| /s<br>C:\>systeminfo /s win7pcg | The **/s** switch can be used to specify a remote system or IP address. The default is the local computer. |
| /u<br>systeminfo /s *system* /u *domain\ username*<br>C:\>systeminfo /s win7pcg /u win7pcg\administrator | The **/u** switch specifies the user account to use when running the command. This may be needed when running the command on remote systems.<br><br>You can use either the domain name and specific username with permissions in the domain, or the name of the remote computer and the username of an account that exists on the remote computer. If the **/u** switch is omitted, it will use the current credentials. |

| /u /p<br>`systeminfo /s system /u domain`<br>`\username /p password`<br>`C:\>systeminfo /s win7pcg /u`<br>`win7pcg\administrator`<br>`/p P@ssw0rd` | The **/p** switch specifies the password to use with the user account. If the **/p** switch is omitted, you will be prompted to provide the password. |
| --- | --- |

One way you might want to use the **systeminfo** command is to create inventory files for all the systems in your network. If you have a domain, this can easily be done using Group Policy with the following steps:

| Step | Remarks |
| --- | --- |
| 1. Create a share. | For example, you could create a share named inv on a server named srv1. It will be accessible with the Universal Naming Convention (UNC) path of \\Srv1\Inv. |
| 2. Create a batch file with this one line:<br><br>`systeminfo > \\srv1\`<br>`inv\%computername%.txt` | The **%computername%** variable will retrieve the computer's name and name the file with a .txt extension. For example, if this was run on a system named win7, the file would be named win7.txt. |
| 3. Use Group Policy to schedule the batch file to run as a startup script. You can link the GPO to the domain to run the script on all the computers in your domain. | Chapter 29, "Group Policy Overview," shows how to run scripts with Group Policy. |

# Viewing User Information with whoami

The **whoami** command provides detailed information on the currently logged on user. This includes the user's security identifier (SID), the SIDs for any groups the user belongs to, and a list of privileges granted to the user. The basic syntax is

`whoami`

This will list the username in the format of *domain\username*. If the computer is not a member of a domain, it will list the username as *computername\username*. You can also use several different switches to get additional information.

| whoami switches | Comments |
| --- | --- |
| /all<br>`C:\>whoami /all` | Displays the current username, group member-ship for the user, SIDs for the user and groups, and privileges for the current user access token. |

| /priv<br>`C:\>whoami /priv` | Displays security privileges for the current user access token.<br><br>If you run this from a regular command prompt, you'll see one set of privileges. If you run it from an elevated command prompt, you'll see the additional permissions granted at the prompt with administrator privileges. |
|---|---|
| /upn<br>`C:\>whoami /upn` | Displays the username in user principal name (UPN) format.<br><br>This works only for users in a domain. |
| /fqdn<br>`C:\>whoami /fqdn` | Displays the username in fully qualified domain name (FQDN) format.<br><br>This works only for users in a domain. |
| /user<br>`C:\>whoami /user` | Displays username and the user's SIDs. |
| /groups<br>`C:\>whoami /groups` | Displays group membership for the current user, the type of group account, SIDs for the groups, and group attributes. |
| /fo *format*<br>`C:\>whoami /all /fo list` | Specifies the output format to be displayed. The default format is **table**, but you can also use **list** or **csv**. |
| /nh<br>`C:\>whoami /all /fo csv /nh` | Specifies that the column header should not be displayed in the output. This is valid only for **table** and **csv** formats because the **list** format does not include column headings. |

# Launching System Configuration with msconfig

You can launch the System Configuration tool from the command line with the **msconfig** command. You can't actually manage the System Configuration tool from the command line, so there aren't any switches available to use. However, the System Configuration tool can be valuable when you are troubleshooting system problems.

For example, if you suspect your system is infected with malware, you can use this tool to start the system without starting suspect services or applications. You can then boot into the system and run antivirus software to detect and clean the problem software.

Figure 9-2 shows the General tab of the System Configuration tool. You can use this to modify how the system starts. Normal Startup is selected by default. Diagnostic Startup is similar to starting the system in Safe Mode with only the basic devices and services started. You can use Selective Startup to choose what services and other startup items you want to load on the next boot.

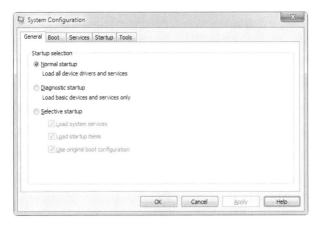

**Figure 9-2**  General Tab of the System Configuration Tool

You can modify the boot configuration data (BCD) store by selecting the Boot tab of
the System Configuration tool. Figure 9-3 shows the choices available. These settings
normally are used only for the next boot. However, you can change this by checking the
Make All Boot Settings Permanent check box. You can also modify the BCD store using
**bcdedit**, which is presented in Chapter 14, "Using Recovery Tools."

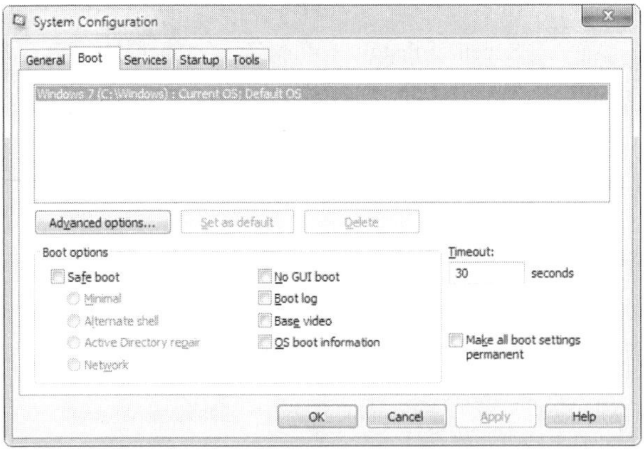

**Figure 9-3**  Boot Tab of the System Configuration Tool

The Services tab, shown in Figure 9-4, lists all the services in the system and indicates
their current status, such as running or stopped. You can uncheck the check box of any
of the services to ensure that it is not started the next time the system is booted. If you
do modify any of these check boxes, the Startup Selection setting on the General tab will
change to Selective Startup.

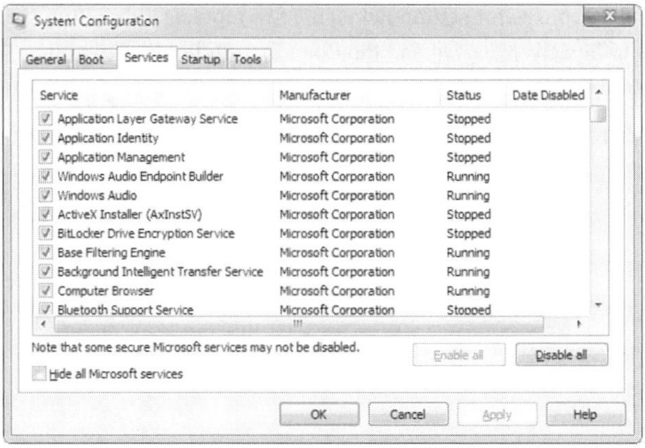

**Figure 9-4**   Services Tab of the System Configuration Tool

If you check the Hide All Microsoft Services check box, you can more easily see all the third-party services that are added to your system. Often, a system is slowed down due to the number of extra services and applications that are scheduled to run when the system boots. If a system is slow, this is a good place to check to see what else is running on the system.

Figure 9-5 shows the Startup tab, which includes all of the applications that are configured to start when the system is booted. Just as additional services configured to start when the system starts can slow down the boot cycle, additional applications configured to start when the system starts can also slow down the boot cycle. Additionally, malware sometimes configures itself as an application to start when the system starts, and can be modified from there.

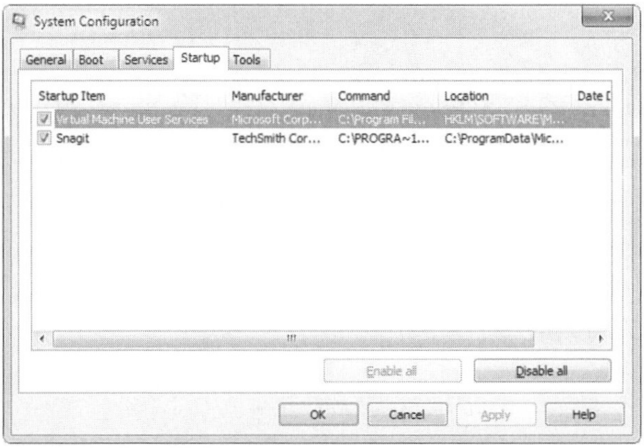

**Figure 9-5**   Startup Tab of the System Configuration Tool

If you do check any of the check boxes for startup items, the Startup Selection setting on the General tab changes to Selective Startup and the Load Startup Items check box changes from a check box to a highlighted check box.

Figure 9-6 shows the Tools tab, which gives you a shortcut to many of the maintenance tools available in Windows 7.

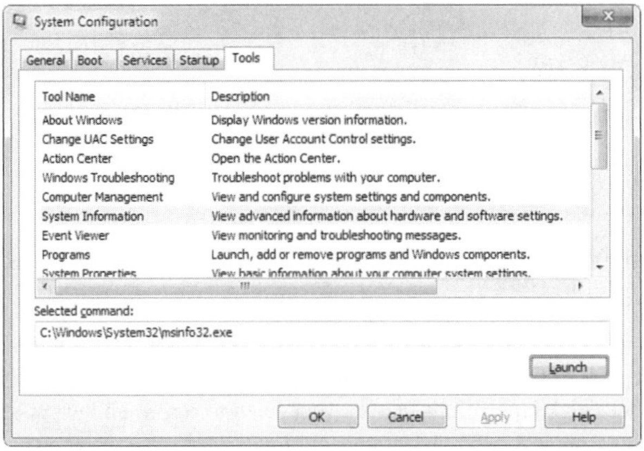

**Figure 9-6**   Tools Tab of the System Configuration Tool

This chapter provides information and commands concerning the following topics:

- Manipulating credentials with **cmdkey**
- Installing updates with **wusa**
- Installing applications with **msiexec**
- Auditing systems with **mbsacli**

## Manipulating Credentials with cmdkey

Windows 7 stores credentials such as usernames and passwords in the Credential Manager vault. For example, if you regularly log onto a website on the Internet, you can save the credentials in Credential Manager. Then, when you access the website, you'll automatically be logged on. Your credentials are stored in special folders called *vaults* and can be managed using either Credential Manager (as shown in Figure 10-1) or the **cmdkey** command.

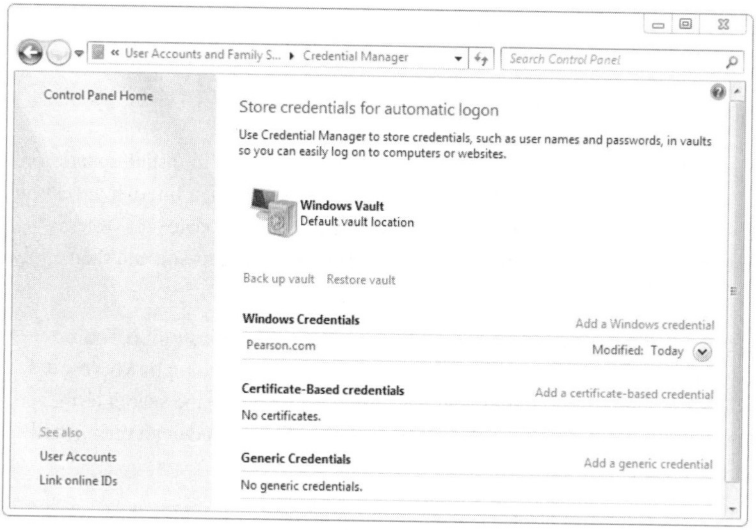

**Figure 10-1** Windows 7 Credential Manager

You can use the **cmdkey** command to create, display, and delete usernames and passwords.

| cmdkey Switches | Comments |
|---|---|
| `/list`<br>`C:\>cmdkey /list`<br>`Currently stored credentials:`<br>`    Target: Domain:target=Pearson.com`<br>`    Type: Domain Password`<br>`    User: DarrilGibson` | Lists all credentials currently stored in the credentials vault. While the target is usually listed as a domain, the actual target can be a website, a domain name, or a computer name. |
| `C:\>cmdkey /list pearson.com` | Displays the credential information for a specific credential stored in the vault. |
| `/delete`<br>`cmdkey /delete` *target*<br>`C:\>cmdkey /delete pearson.com` | Deletes an existing credential listing from the credentials vault. In this example, the target is the domain Pearson.com. |
| `/add`<br>`cmdkey /add:`*target* `/user:`*username*<br>`C:\>cmdkey /add:pearson.com /`<br>`user:darrilgibson` | Adds a username to the credentials vault. Because a password is not included in the example, the user will be prompted to add the password. |
| `cmdkey /add:`*target* `/user:`*username* `/`<br>`pass:`*password*<br>`C:\>cmdkey /add:pearson.com /`<br>`user:darrilgibson /pass:P@ssw0rd` | Adds a username and password to the credentials vault. |

# Installing Updates with wusa

The Windows Update Standalone Installer (**wusa**) tool can be used to install updates on Windows 7 systems. This can be useful for computers that don't have Internet access but need some specific updates, or when you want to install optional updates on systems. You can download the Microsoft update file (.msu) from a Microsoft site and then apply the .msu file to a system.

As an example, you might want to download Remote Server Administration Tools (RSAT) for Windows 7. You can locate and download the file by going to Microsoft's download site (http://microsoft.com/downloads), entering **RSAT** as the search term, and selecting **Remote Server Administration Tools for Windows 7**. You can then install RSAT with the **wusa** command.

Although the **wusa** command has been available in Windows for a while, there are some changes in Windows 7. They include the following:

| wusa Switch Changes | Comments |
|---|---|
| /uninstall | The **/uninstall** switch can be used to uninstall an update. |
| /extract | The **/extract** switch enables you to extract the update to a specific location and then view the files from there. |
| /quiet /option<br>/quiet /norestart<br>/quiet /warnrestart<br>/quiet /promptrestart<br>/quiet /forcerestart | You can use several additional options with the **/quiet** switch:<br><br>**/norestart**: A reboot will not be initiated after the install.<br><br>**/warnrestart**: The installer will warn the user before rebooting.<br><br>**/promptrestart**: The installer will prompt the user to reboot.<br><br>**/forcerestart**: The installer will forcefully close applications and reboot the system. |

The following table shows how **wusa** can be used to manipulate the RSAT .msu installation file.

| wusa Switches | Comments |
|---|---|
| c:\>wusa *full path*<br>C:\>wusa c:\data \x86fre_grmrsat_<br>msu.msu | This example installs the RSAT update named x86fre_grmrsat_ msu.msu located in the C:\data\ folder. |
| /quiet<br>C:\>wusa C:\data\x86fre_grmrsat_<br>msu.msu /quiet<br>C:\>wusa C:\data\x86fre_grmrsat_<br>msu.msu /quiet /norestart<br>C:\>wusa C:\data\x86fre_grmrsat_<br>msu.msu /quiet /warnrestart<br>C:\>wusa C:\data\x86fre_grmrsat_<br>msu.msu /quiet /promptrestart<br>C:\>wusa C:\data\x86fre_grmrsat_<br>msu.msu /quiet /forcerestart | The **/quiet** switch suppresses all user prompts. It can be modified with the different restart options. |
| /uninstall<br>wusa /uninstall *full path*<br>C:\>wusa /uninstall C:\data\x86fre_<br>grmrsat_msu.msu | The **/uninstall** switch checks to see if the update was installed and then uninstalls it by checking the data in the full path of the original .msu file. |
| /extract<br>wusa *path* /extract:*path*<br>C:\>wusa C:\data\x86fre_grmrsat_<br>msu.msu /extract:c:\data\extract | You can use the **/extract** switch to extract the contents of the update. This will not install the update. |

| | |
|---|---|
| `/uninstall /kb ######`<br>`C:\>wusa /uninstall /kb:958830` | You can also uninstall the update using the KB number. Most updates include the KB number, and you can usually view it on the Installed Updates page. |

When you install or uninstall updates using **wusa**, you can view the results in the Windows Setup log via Event Viewer, as shown in Figure 10-2. You can access Event Viewer by clicking **Start**, typing **Event** in the Start Search text box, and selecting **Event Viewer**.

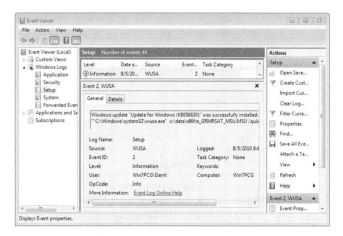

**Figure 10-2** Viewing the Windows Setup Log in Event Viewer Updates Page

Figure 10-3 shows the Installed Updates page. You can access this by choosing **Start**, **All Programs**, **Windows Update**, and selecting **Installed Updates**.

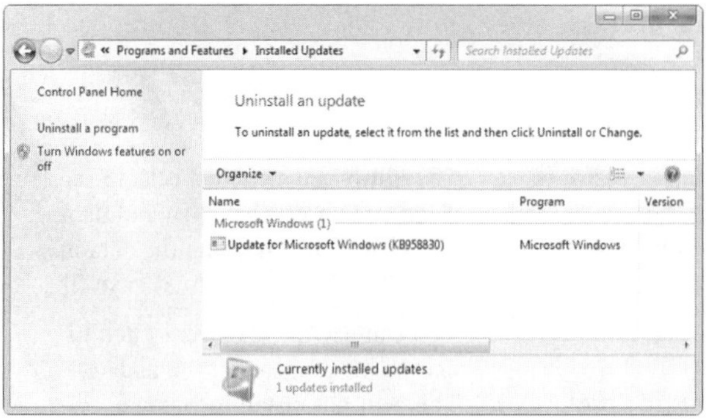

**Figure 10-3** Installed Updates Page

# Installing Applications with msiexec

**msiexec** is the Windows Installer command-line tool. You can use it to install, modify, and perform other operations with Windows Installer from the command prompt. The basic syntax of the command is

```
msiexec /package install package path and name
```

Some of the common switches you'll use with the **msiexec** command are listed in the following table.

| msiexec Switches | Comments |
|---|---|
| `C:\>msiexec /?` | Use this command to launch a help dialog box. The first line identifies the current version. Windows 7 ships with Windows Installer version 5 (V 5.0 7600.16385). |
| `/package`<br>`/i`<br>`msiexec /package package path`<br>`msiexec /i package path`<br>`C:\>msiexec /package C:\data\`<br>`mbsasetup-x86-en`<br>`C:\>msiexec /i c:\data\`<br>`mbsasetup-x86-en` | You can install packages using either the **/package** switch or **/i** switch and specifying the full path and name of the package.<br><br>These examples install the Microsoft Baseline Security Analyzer tool on a 32-bit system. (A 64-bit version is also available.)<br><br>Note that the .msi extension is not needed in the filename. |
| `/quiet`<br>`/passive`<br>`C:\>msiexec /i c:\data\`<br>`mbsasetup-x86-en /quiet`<br>`C:\>msiexec /i c:\data\`<br>`mbsasetup-x86-en /passive` | You can install .msi files using either quiet or passive mode with the **/quiet** or **/passive** switch, respectively. Quiet mode suppresses all user interaction. Passive mode is similar but displays a progress bar so that users know when the installation is completed.<br><br>If the command is not run with elevated privileges, User Account Control (UAC) prompts the user to continue. |
| `/uninstall`<br>`C:\>msiexec /uninstall C:\data\`<br>`mbsasetup-x86-en` | The **/uninstall** switch can be used to uninstall the application. |
| `Restart option`<br>`msiexec /i c:\data\mbsasetup-`<br>`x86-en restart option`<br>`C:\>msiexec /i c:\data\`<br>`mbsasetup-x86-en /norestart`<br>`C:\>msiexec /i c:\data\`<br>`mbsasetup-x86-en /promptrestart`<br>`C:\>msiexec /i c:\data\`<br>`mbsasetup-x86-en /forcerestart` | Some applications need to be restarted after they are installed. If necessary or desired, you can use one of the following restart options:<br><br>**/norestart**: A reboot will not be initiated after the install.<br><br>**/promptrestart**: The installer will prompt the user to reboot.<br><br>**/forcerestart**: The installer will always reboot the system after the installation. |

| | |
|---|---|
| **/l**<br>`msiexec /i c:\data\`<br>`mbsasetup-x86-en` **/l** `flag(s)   log`<br>`file path and name`<br>`C:\>msiexec /i c:\data\`<br>`mbsasetup-x86-en /liwearmo`<br>`installlog.log`<br>`C:\>msiexec /i c:\data\`<br>`mbsasetup-x86-en /l`<br>`installlog.log`<br>`C:\>msiexec /i c:\data\`<br>`mbsasetup-x86-en /l*`<br>`installlog.log`<br>`C:\>msiexec /i c:\data\`<br>`mbsasetup-x86-en /l*vx`<br>`installlog.log` | You can include the **/l** switch to log the results of the install to a specified log file. This is especially useful if the install fails but you're unsure why. The log file path must exist. Note that there are no spaces after the lowercase **l** and the flag(s), but there is a space before the log filename. The flags are<br><br>**i**: Status messages<br><br>**w**: Nonfatal warnings<br><br>**e**: All error messages<br><br>**a**: Startup of actions<br><br>**r**: Action-specific records<br><br>**u**: User requests<br><br>**c**: Initial UI parameters<br><br>**m**: Out-of-memory or fatal exit information<br><br>**o**: Out-of-disk-space messages<br><br>**p**: Terminal properties<br><br>**v**: Verbose output<br><br>**x**: Extra debugging information<br><br>**+**: Append to existing file<br><br>**!**: Flush each line to the log<br><br>**\***: Wildcard, log all information except **v** and **x** options (to include **v** and **x** options, specify **/l\*vx**)<br><br>If no flags are specified, the default is **iwearmo**. |

## Auditing Systems with mbsacli

The Microsoft Baseline Security Analyzer (MBSA) is a valuable tool used to audit security on systems and check for different security vulnerabilities. It's available as a free download from Microsoft's download site (http://microsoft.com/downloads) by entering **MBSA** as the search term and selecting **Microsoft Baseline Security Analyzer 2.2**. **mbsacli** is the command-line equivalent of the MBSA graphical user interface and is installed when you install MBSA.

> **TIP:** Microsoft Baseline Security Analyzer 2.1 has support for Windows Vista and Windows Server 2008. Microsoft Baseline Security Analyzer 2.1.1 and 2.2 has support for Windows 7 and Windows Server 2008 R2.

Figure 10-4 shows the main window of the MBSA tool. The title bar of the window shows the version as 2.2, and the explanation confirms that it supports Windows 7 and Windows Server 2008 R2.

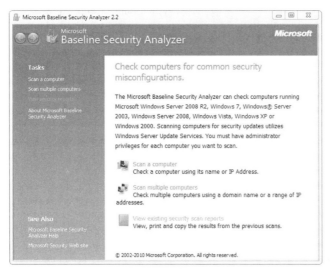

**Figure 10-4**   Microsoft Baseline Security Analyzer

The **mbsacli** tool must be run with administrative privileges on both the computer you're running it from and the computer being scanned.

The mbsacli.exe file is located in the C:\Program Files\Microsoft Baseline Security Analyzer 2 folder. However, this folder is not in the %path% variable. When executing the **mbsacli** tool, you need to do one of the following:

- Include the path in the actual command as follows:

  ```
  C:\>c:\program files\microsoft baseline security analyzer 2\
  mbsacli
  ```

- Change the path as follows:

  ```
  C:\>cd c:\program files\microsoft baseline security analyzer 2\
  ```

- Temporarily modify the **%path%** variable to include the path to mbsacli with this command:

  ```
  C:\>path %path%;"c:\program files\microsoft baseline security
  analyzer 2"
  ```

The following table assumes the path has been temporarily modified using the last method.

| Command | Description |
|---|---|
| `C:\>mbsacli` | Runs **mbsacli** on the local system. |
| `/target`<br>`mbsacli /target name or IP`<br>`C:\>mbsacli /target win7pcg`<br>`C:\>mbsacli /target 192.168.1.10` | Runs **mbsacli** on the target system. The target system can be identified by the name (such as a computer named win-7pcg) or by an IP address.<br><br>The **mbsacli** tool requires administrative privileges on both the computer you're running it from and the computer being scanned. You can use an elevated command prompt for the local system. However, you might need to enter the username and password for the remote system with the **/u** and **/p** switches. |
| `/u /p`<br>`mbsacli /target name or IP`<br>`/u username /p password`<br>`C:\>mbsacli /target win7pcg`<br>`/u pearson\administrator /p P@ssw0rd` | The **/u** switch is used to specify a user. The user can be entered in the *domain\user* format or *computer\user* format. In the example, the domain is named pearson and the account is administrator (pearson\administrator). The **/p** switch is used for the password. |
| `/r`<br>`mbsacli /r IP-IP`<br>`C:\>mbsacli /r 192.168.1.10-`<br>`192.168.1.100` | Scans a range of IP addresses. In the example, all the computers in the range 192.168.1.10 through 192.168.1.100 will be scanned. |
| `/listfile`<br>`mbsacli /listfile file path and name`<br>`C:\>mbsacli /listfile C:\data\`<br>`list.txt` | Scans all the files in the specified text file. Each computer name should be on a separate line such as:<br><br>**Win7PCG1**<br><br>**Win7PCG2** |
| `/l`<br>`/ls`<br>`C:\>mbsacli /l`<br>`C:\>mbsacli /ls` | Any reports you run with **mbsacli** can be viewed from the **mbsacli** tool or from the GUI. The following switches are available:<br><br>The **/l** switch retrieves a list of available reports including the computer name, the IP address, the assessment, and the report name. The report name includes the computer name and the date and time of the scan.<br><br>The **/ls** switch retrieves the header of the most recent report. |

| | |
|---|---|
| `/lr`<br><br>`mbsacli /lr` *report name*<br><br>`C:\>mbsacli /lr "pearson - win7pcg`<br>`(8-5-2010 1-30 pm)"`<br><br>`C:\>mbsacli /lr "workgroup - win7pcg`<br>`(8-5-2010 1-57 pm)"` | The **/lr** switch retrieves an overview of the named report. You can get the report name from the **mbsacli /l** command. Because the report name has spaces in it, it must be enclosed in quotes.<br><br>In the example, the names of the reports shown by the **/l** switch are "pearson - win7 (8-5-2010 1-30 pm)" and "workgroup - win7pcg (8-5-2010 1-57 pm)." |
| `/ld`<br><br>`mbsacli /ld` *report name*<br><br>`C:\>mbsacli /ld "pearson - win7`<br>`(8-5-2010 1-30 pm)"`<br><br>`C:\>mbsacli /ld " pearson - win7`<br>`(8-5-2010 1-30 pm)" > mbsarpt.txt` | The **/ld** switch retrieves a detailed view of the named report.<br><br>Just as with any command-prompt command, you can redirect the output to a text file by using the > symbol. Because the reports are simple text, you can then read them in Notepad. |

**TIP:** You can get much fancier with the **mbsacli** scripting. Microsoft developed a package named MBSA 2.0 Scripting Samples. Even though this was from the version 2.0 release of MBSA, the samples will still work with Windows 7 and Window Server 2008 R2 systems. You can download this package from http://microsoft.com/downloads. Search for **MBSA Scripting Samples**.

This chapter provides information and commands concerning the following topics:

- Understanding **netsh**
- Understanding contexts
- Configuring a proxy server
- Configuring the network interface with **netsh**

## Understanding netsh

The Net Shell (**netsh**) command is a rich command-line scripting tool that enables you to display and modify the network configuration of local and remote computers. You can run **netsh** commands from the netsh prompt, from the command prompt, or from a batch file.

For example, if you wanted to open port 5678 on a firewall, you could do it three different ways using **netsh**, as shown in the following table.

| Opening a Port with netsh | Comments |
|---|---|
| ```
C:\>netsh
netsh>advfirewall
netsh advfirewall>firewall
netsh advfirewall firewall>add rule
name = "open port 5678" dir = in
action = allow protocol = tcp
localport = 5678
Ok.
netsh advfirewall firewall>delete
rule name = "open port 5678"
Deleted 1 rule(s).
Ok.
``` | You can enter the netsh shell and enter the commands. The benefit of doing it this way is that after you enter any context, you can type **help** or **?** to get a list of possible commands and contexts.<br><br>You first type **netsh** to access the shell. Next, you enter **advfirewall** to enter the advfirewall context. You can then create the rule with the **add rule** statement.<br><br>You can delete rules using the **delete rule** statement and the name of the rule. |
| ```
C:\>netsh advfirewall firewall add
rule name = "Open5678" dir = in
action = allow protocol = tcp
localport = 5678
Ok.
C:\>netsh advfirewall firewall delete
rule name = "Open5678"
Deleted 1 rule(s).
Ok.
``` | You can enter the entire line from the command line. You are entering the same data, but instead of entering it one command at a time to reach the netsh advfirewall firewall context, you are entering all the data at the same time.<br><br>Similarly, you can delete the rule with a single-line entry. |

| `C:\>netsh advfirewall firewall add rule name = "Open5678" dir = in action = allow protocol = tcp localport = 5678` | Anything you can enter at the command line can be put into a batch file. You can use Notepad, add the line, and then save the file with a .bat extension. |
|---|---|

Figure 11-1 shows how these commands look when entered at the command prompt. You can see how the context changes as each command is entered in the **netsh** command.

**Figure 11-1**   **netsh** Commands

## Understanding Contexts

**netsh** has multiple command contexts. Each time you enter a context, you have a different set of commands you can use. For example, if you are in the netsh interface context, you have the following commands available to you:

| netsh Interface Context Commands | Description |
|---|---|
| ? or **help** | Displays a list of commands. |
| **6to4** | Changes to the netsh interface 6to4 context. |
| **ipv4** | Changes to the netsh interface ipv4 context. |
| **ipv6** | Changes to the netsh interface ipv6 context. |
| **tcp** | Changes to the netsh interface tcp context. |
| **teredo** | Changes to the netsh interface teredo context. |
| **httpstunnel** | Changes to the netsh interface httpstunnel context. |
| **portproxy** | Changes to the netsh interface portproxy context. |
| **set** | Sets configuration information. |

| show | Displays information. |
|------|----------------------|
| **dump** | Displays a configuration script. |

If you instead entered the **advfirewall** command, you'd have access to a different set of commands associated with the advfirewall context. You can view the available commands by entering **help** or **?** at any context command.

Some of the contexts you may use with Windows 7 are listed in the following table.

| Context | Description |
|---------|-------------|
| Interface (IPv4 and IPv6)<br><br>`netsh>`**`interface ipv4`**<br>`netsh interface ipv4>`<br>`netsh>`**`interface ipv6`**<br>`netsh interface ipv6>` | Display and configure IPv4 and IPv6 information for network interfaces. Previous examples in this book (and examples at the end of this chapter) show how you can configure the TCP/IPv4 configuration for a system. There are also many additional commands that can be used to view information. |
| Windows Firewall with Advanced Security<br><br>`netsh>`**`advfirewall`**<br>`netsh advfirewall>`**`show`**<br>**`allprofiles`** | You can use netsh advfirewall commands to work with Windows Firewall with Advanced Security. These commands help with the creation, administration, and monitoring of Windows Firewall and IPsec. They are useful when configuring Windows Firewall with Advanced Security settings for a large number of computers. These commands can be embedded in batch files to automate the configuration of the systems. |
| Windows Firewall<br><br>`netsh>`**`firewall`** | Display and configure firewall settings.<br><br>**NOTE:** This context has been deprecated in favor of the advfirewall firewall context. It will modify firewall rules only for the domain and private profiles. |
| Wired local area network (LAN)<br><br>`netsh>`**`lan`**<br>`netsh lan>`**`show profiles`** | You can use the netsh local area network (lan) context to configure and manage 802.3 wired Ethernet connectivity. If you have computers that connect IEEE 802.1x servers for authentication, you can configure the security settings. You can also display information about network adapter drivers, network profiles, and more. As an example, the **show profiles** command shows any existing wired profiles on the system.<br><br>**NOTE:** This context needs the Wired AutoConfig Service (dot3svc) to be running. |

| | |
|---|---|
| Wireless local area network (WLAN)<br><br>`netsh>wlan`<br>`netsh wlan>show profiles`<br>`netsh wlan>show all` | You can use commands in the netsh wireless local area network (wlan) context to configure and manage 802.11 wireless connectivity and security settings. Additionally, the **netsh wlan** commands can display information about 802.11 wireless adapter drivers, wireless network profiles, and more.<br><br>As an example, the **show profiles** command shows a list of any existing profiles, and **show all** provides details on all wireless adapters, profiles, and networks.<br><br>**NOTE:** This context needs the Wireless AutoConfig Service (wlansvc) to be running. |
| Windows Hypertext Transfer Protocol (Winhttp)<br><br>`netsh>winhttp`<br>`netsh winhttp>show proxy` | You can use the winhttp context to configure proxy and tracing settings for Windows HTTP. For example, if you want to view current proxy settings, you can use **show proxy**. A result of "Direct access (no proxy server)" indicates a proxy server hasn't been configured. |

No matter which context you enter, you have several core commands available to you. Some of these commands are shown in the following table.

| Command | Description |
|---|---|
| `..`<br>`netsh winhttp>..`<br>`netsh>` | Moves the context up one level. |
| `alias`<br>`netsh>alias nic "local area`<br>`connection"`<br><br>`netsh>alias`<br>`nic     local area connection` | Creates an alias that can be used within the netsh session. An alias is one string of characters that can take the place of another string of characters. The example shows how to create an alias named nic to represent "local area connection".<br><br>When entered by itself, **alias** lists all known aliases, just like **show alias**. |
| `unalias` *alias name*<br>`netsh>unalias nic` | You can delete an existing alias with the **unalias** command. The alias will also be deleted if you exit netsh.<br><br>The existing alias name must be entered with the exact case (uppercase and lowercase). |
| `bye, exit,` or `quit`<br>`netsh>bye`<br>`C:\>` | Exits netsh. |

| | |
|---|---|
| **dump**<br>netsh>**dump**<br>netsh>**dump** > c:\data\config.txt | Displays all the current netsh context configuration data. You can execute this from the command prompt to redirect the output to a text file. The text file can then be used to reconfigure the system with the **exec** command. |
| **exec** *scriptfile*<br>netsh>**exec** c:\data\config.txt | Executes a script file. This can be used to reconfigure a computer using the settings in the script file. You can create the script file from the **dump** command. |
| **help** or **?**<br>netsh>**help** | Displays help. Help information includes commands that can be listed in any context, and the current context. |
| **set file** [**open** \| **append** \|<br>**close**] *file*<br>netsh>**set file open** c:\data\<br>netsh.txt<br>netsh>**set file append** c:\data\<br>netsh.txt<br>netsh>**set file close** | Copies all data from the netsh session to a file. You can use the **set file** command to capture all the activity in your session. The **open** command creates a new file. **append** appends the data to an existing file.<br><br>**close** stops sending the data to the file. Note that you don't enter the name of the file in the **close** command. |
| **set machine**<br>**set machine** [**name** =] *computer*<br>[**user** = *DomainName\UserName*]<br>[**pwd** = ] [*Password* \| *\**]<br><br>netsh>**set machine name** = dc1<br>**user** = pearson\administrator<br>**pwd** = P@ssw0rd<br>[dc1] netsh> | You can use the **set machine** command to connect to a remote system and perform the tasks on it. The default is the local system.<br><br>For example, if you want to use **netsh** to administer a server named DC1 in the Pearson domain, you can use the Pearson\ Administrator account with the administrator's password (P@ssw0rd in the example). The prompt changes to include the remote computer's name. |
| **set mode** [ **online** \| **offline** ]<br>netsh>**set mode online**<br>netsh>**set mode offline** | You can set the mode to online or offline. In online mode, **netsh** commands are run immediately after you type them and press Enter. In offline mode, **netsh** commands are saved and can be run with the **commit** command, or aborted with the **abort** command. |
| **abort**<br>netsh>**abort** | The **abort** command discards any changes made in offline mode. It does not have any effect if executed in online mode. |
| **commit**<br>netsh>**commit** | The **commit** command commits any changes made in offline mode. It does not have any effect in online mode. |

| show<br><br>netsh>**show alias**<br>netsh>**show helper**<br>netsh>**show mode** | You can view alias, helper, and mode information with the **show** command. Aliases aren't created by default, but many default helper.dll files are available by default to provide help in different contexts. The default mode is online. |
|---|---|

# Configuring a Proxy Server

You can view and configure proxy server settings using the **netsh** command as shown in the following table.

| Command | Description |
|---|---|
| C:\>**netsh winhttp show proxy**<br>Current WinHTTP proxy settings:<br>    Proxy Server(s)  :<br>ProxySrv1:8080<br>      Bypass List    :  Pearson.Int | This command shows details on the currently configured proxy server.<br><br>If a proxy server is not currently configured, it gives this message: "Direct access (no proxy server)." |
| C:\>**netsh winhttp set proxy proxy-server="proxysrv1:8080" bypass-list="pearson.Int"**<br>Current WinHTTP proxy settings:<br>    Proxy Server(s)  :<br>ProxySrv1:8080<br>      Bypass List    :  Pearson.Int | This command sets the proxy server to a server named ProxySrv1, which is listening for HTTP requests on port 8080.<br><br>If you have any URLs that you don't want to use the proxy server, such as an internal web server, you can create a bypass list. In this example, any HTTP addresses using an internal name of Pearson.Int will not use the proxy server. |
| C:\>**netsh winhttp reset proxy**<br>Current WinHTTP proxy settings:<br>    Direct access (no proxy server). | This command resets the proxy server settings to the default. In other words, it removes the proxy server settings. |

**NOTE:** The Microsoft Windows HTTP Services (WinHTTP) proxy configuration tool (proxycfg.exe) was used in previous operating systems to configure proxy settings for HTTP applications. However, if you try to run proxycfg.exe in Windows 7, you'll find that the command is no longer available.

# Configuring the Network Interface with netsh

**netsh** is presented briefly in Chapters 2 and 6. Chapter 2, "Basic Rules When Using the Command Line," shows how you could use the following command to set the IP address and subnet mask of a network interface card (NIC) that has the default name of "local area connection":

```
netsh interface ipv4 set address name = "local area connection" static
192.168.1.15 255.255.255.0
```

> **NOTE:** As a reminder, because the NIC's name (local area connection) has spaces
> within it, it must be enclosed in quotes.

Some other commands you can use to configure the NIC are shown in the following
table.

| Command | Description |
|---------|-------------|
| `C:\>netsh interface ipv4 set address name = "local area connection" static 10.10.0.10 255.0.0.0 10.10.0.1` | This command sets the IP address to 10.10.0.10, the subnet mask to 255.0.0.0, and the default gateway to 10.10.0.1 for the NIC. |
| `C:\>netsh interface ipv4 set dns-server "local area connection" static 10.10.0.200` | This command sets the IP address of the preferred DNS server. |
| `C:\>netsh interface ipv4 set address name = "local area connection" source = dhcp` | This command changes the NIC to get the TCP/IP configuration automatically from DHCP. |
| `C:\>netsh interface ipv4 set dnsserver = "local area connection" source = dhcp` | This command changes the NIC to get the DNS address automatically from DHCP. |

If you want to identify the names of the interfaces on the system, you can use the following command:

```
netsh interface ipv4 show interfaces
```

You'll see an output similar to this:

```
Idx    Met         MTU          State         Name
---    ----------  ----------   -----------   --------------------
10     20          1500         Connected     Local Area Connection
```

Chapter 6, "Creating Batch Files," also showed how you could use parameters in a batch
file named setip.bat to set the NIC. You could then just pass the parameters to the batch
file to set the TCP/IP configuration for any system. The following batch file expands
this by adding some parameters and some basic error checking. You can then use the
batch file to manually set the IP address, subnet mask, default gateway, and DNS server
address for any system with a single command-line command.

The script will accept four parameters:

- **%1**: IP address
- **%2**: Subnet mask

- **%3**: Default gateway
- **%4**: Address of DNS server

```
@echo off
if "%4"=="" goto nodns
netsh interface ipv4 set address name="local area connection" static %1
%2 %3
if %errorlevel% gtr 0 goto error
echo.
echo IP address set to %1
echo Subnet mask set to %2
echo Default Gateway set to %3
netsh interface ipv4 set dnsserver "local area connection" static %4
if %errorlevel% gtr 0 goto errordns
echo DNS set to %4
goto end
:nodns
if "%3"=="" goto nodefaultgateway
netsh interface ipv4 set address name="local area connection" static %1
%2 %3
if %errorlevel% gtr 0 goto error
echo.
echo IP address set to %1
echo Subnet mask set to %2
echo Default Gateway set to %3
echo.
echo You can also configure a DNS address
echo Example: Setip 192.168.1.0 255.255.255.0 192.168.1.1 192.168.1.100
goto end
:nodefaultgateway
if "%2"=="" goto error
netsh interface ipv4 set address name = "local area connection" static
%1 %2
if %errorlevel% gtr 0 goto error
echo.
echo IP address set to %1
echo Subnet mask set to %2
echo.
echo You can also configure a default gateway, or a default gateway and
DNS address
echo Example with default gateway:
echo Setip 192.168.1.0 255.255.255.0 192.168.1.1
echo Example with default gateway and DNS:
echo Setip 192.168.1.0 255.255.255.0 192.168.1.1 192.168.1.100
```

```
goto end
:error
echo.
echo You must enter at least a valid IP address and subnet mask
echo Example:
echo Setip 192.168.1.0 255.255.255.0
echo.
echo You can configure a default gateway by adding a valid IP address
echo Example:
echo Setip 192.168.1.0 255.255.255.0 192.168.1.1
echo.
echo You can also configure a default gateway and DNS address
echo Example:
echo Setip 192.168.1.0 255.255.255.0 192.168.1.1 192.168.1.100
echo.
:errordns
echo.
echo The DNS server was not configured.
echo Please rerun the command with a valid IP address for the DNS
Server.
:end
```

The following table provides some comments on the lines within the script.

| Batch File Contents | Remarks |
| --- | --- |
| `@echo off` | This command turns echo off so that the user doesn't see all the commands. |
| `if "%4"=="" goto nodns` | The "%4"=="" check determines if a fourth parameter was entered. Because the fourth parameter is the address of the DNS server, it will branch to the nodns section if an address for DNS is not entered. |
| `netsh interface ipv4 set address name="local area connection" static %1 %2 %3` | If there is a fourth parameter, the configuration is set using the **netsh** command.<br><br>The **netsh** command sets the configuration of the IP address (using the parameter passed in as %1), the subnet mask (using the parameter passed in as %2), and the default gateway (using the parameter passed in as %3). |

| | |
|---|---|
| `if %errorlevel% gtr 0 goto error` | After the first **netsh** command is executed, the **if %errorlevel%** statement checks to see if an error occurred. A 0 indicates success, so anything other than a 0 indicates an error. If an error occurred, the batch file branches to the error label. |
| `echo.`<br>`echo IP address set to %1`<br>`echo Subnet mask set to %2`<br>`echo Default Gateway set to %3` | After **netsh** sets the configuration, **echo** commands are used to let the user know what occurred. |
| `netsh interface ipv4 set dnsserver`<br>`"local area connection" static %4` | The second **netsh** command sets the address of the DNS server to the parameter passed in as **%4**. |
| `if %errorlevel% gtr 0 goto errordns` | After the second **netsh** command is executed, the **if %errorlevel%** statement checks to see if an error occurred. A 0 indicates success, so anything other than a 0 indicates an error. If an error occurred, the batch file branches to the errordns label. |
| `echo DNS set to %4`<br>`goto end` | After **netsh** sets the configuration, the **echo** command is used to let the user know the DNS address was set. |
| `:nodns`<br>`if "%3"=="" goto nodefaultgateway` | If a fourth parameter wasn't passed in, processing continues here. This checks to see if a third parameter (**%3** for the default gateway) was passed in. If not, the batch file branches to the nodefaultgateway label. |
| `netsh interface ipv4 set address`<br>`name="local area connection" static`<br>`%1 %2 %3` | The **netsh** command sets the configuration of the IP address (using the parameter passed in as **%1**), the subnet mask (using the parameter passed in as **%2**), and the default gateway (using the parameter passed in as **%3**). |
| `if %errorlevel% gtr 0 goto error` | After the **netsh** command is executed, the **if %errorlevel%** statement checks to see if an error occurred. A 0 indicates success, so anything other than a 0 indicates an error. If an error occurred, the batch file branches to the error label. |

| | |
|---|---|
| `echo.`<br>`echo IP address set to %1`<br>`echo Subnet mask set to %2`<br>`echo Default Gateway set to %3`<br>`echo.`<br>`echo You can also configure a DNS`<br>`address`<br>`echo Example: Setip 192.168.1.0`<br>`255.255.255.0 192.168.1.1`<br>`192.168.1.100`<br>`goto end` | After **netsh** sets the configuration, **echo** commands are used to let the user know what occurred.<br><br>Additional **echo** commands are used to let the user know how the DNS server could also be configured.<br><br>The **goto end** statement branches the batch file to the end of the file. |
| `:nodefaultgateway`<br>`if "%2"=="" goto error` | If a third parameter (**%3** for the default gateway) wasn't passed in, processing continues here. This checks to see if a second parameter (**%2** for the subnet mask) was passed in. If not, the batch file branches to the error label. |
| `netsh interface ipv4 set address`<br>`name = "local area connection"`<br>`static %1 %2` | The **netsh** command sets the configuration of the IP address (using the parameter passed in as **%1**) and the subnet mask (using the parameter passed in as **%2**). |
| `if %errorlevel% gtr 0 goto error` | After the **netsh** command is executed, the **if %errorlevel%** statement checks to see if an error occurred. A 0 indicates success, so anything other than a 0 indicates an error. If an error occurred, the batch file branches to the error label. |
| `echo.`<br>`echo IP address set to %1`<br>`echo Subnet mask set to %2`<br>`echo.`<br>`echo You can also configure a`<br>`default gateway, or a default`<br>`gateway and DNS address`<br>`echo Example with default gateway:`<br>`echo Setip 192.168.1.0`<br>`255.255.255.0 192.168.1.1`<br>`echo Example with default gateway`<br>`and DNS:`<br>`echo Setip 192.168.1.0`<br>`255.255.255.0 192.168.1.1`<br>`192.168.1.100`<br>`goto end` | After **netsh** sets the configuration, **echo** commands are used to let the user know what occurred.<br><br>Additional **echo** commands are used to let the user know how the default gateway and DNS server could also be configured.<br><br>The **goto end** statement branches the batch file to the end of the file. |

| | |
|---|---|
| `:error`<br>`echo.`<br>`echo You must enter at least a`<br>`valid IP address and subnet mask`<br>`echo Example:`<br>`echo Setip 192.168.1.0`<br>`255.255.255.0`<br>`echo.`<br>`echo You can configure a default`<br>`gateway by adding a valid IP`<br>`address`<br>`echo Example:`<br>`echo Setip 192.168.1.0`<br>`255.255.255.0 192.168.1.1`<br>`echo.`<br>`echo You can also configure a`<br>`default gateway and DNS address`<br>`echo Example:`<br>`echo Setip 192.168.1.0`<br>`255.255.255.0 192.168.1.1`<br>`192.168.1.100`<br>`echo.` | If incorrect data is used for the **netsh** commands, **goto** statements branch the processing of the batch file to the error label.<br><br>**echo** statements are used to let the user know how to enter valid data for the batch file. |
| `:errordns`<br>`echo.`<br>`echo The DNS server was not`<br>`configured.`<br>`echo Please rerun the command with`<br>`a valid IP address for the DNS`<br>`Server.` | If a valid IP address, subnet mask, and DNS server are entered, but incorrect data is passed in for the DNS server, the batch file branches to there. It lets the user know that the address of the DNS server was not configured. |
| `:end` | The batch file finishes. |

After you create the setip.bat file, you can then call it to set different parameters. You may like to first position the batch file on a share and then map a drive to the share. For example, if you place the setip.bat file on a share named scripts on a server named server1, you could map the Z: drive to the share with the following command:

```
net use z: \\server1\scripts
```

You could then use the following commands to execute the batch file and configure TCP/IP configuration for systems in your network:

| Command to Use Batch File | Description |
|---|---|
| `C:\>z:\setip 192.168.1.10`<br>`255.255.255.0` | Sets the IP address to 192.168.1.10 and the subnet mask to 255.255.255.0. |
| `C:\>z:\setip 192.168.1.10`<br>`255.255.255.0 192.168.1.1` | Sets the IP address to 192.168.1.10, the subnet mask to 255.255.255.0, and the default gateway to 192.168.1.1. |

| `C:\>z:\setip 192.168.1.10`<br>`255.255.255.0 192.168.1.1`<br>`192.168.1.100` | Sets the IP address to 192.168.1.10, the subnet mask to 255.255.255.0, the default gateway to 192.168.1.1, and the address for the DNS server to 192.168.1.100. |

When you're done, you can delete the mapped drive with this command:

```
net use z: /delete
```

This chapter provides information and commands concerning the following topics:

- Identifying the system name with **hostname**
- Verifying core system files with **sfc**
- Checking digital signatures with **sigverif**
- Viewing active tasks with **tasklist**
- Terminating processes with **taskkill**
- Viewing installed drivers with **driverquery**

## Identifying the System Name with hostname

There are times when you simply want to know the name of the system you're working on. One of the easiest ways to determine this from the command prompt is with the **hostname** command as follows:

```
c:\>hostname
```

The **hostname** command doesn't have any switches.

## Verifying Core System Files with sfc

The sfc tool can be used to check the integrity of all protected system files and registry keys. If any of the files have been modified or corrupted, **it** can replace them with the correct version of the file. The basic syntax of the command is

```
sfc /scannow
```

> **TIP:** Knowledge base article 929833 provides some additional information on the System File Checker, including some other uses. You can check it out here: http://support.microsoft.com/kb/929833.

Malicious software often attempts to modify system files. If it succeeds, the malware may have extensive control over the system. The **sfc** utility can be very useful in repairing system files that have been corrupted by malware. While some files can be repaired using the internal protected source files, you may be prompted to provide the installation DVD to restore system files.

> **NOTE:** You can view the results of a scan in the cbs.log file, which is located in the %windir%\Logs\CBS folder.

The **sfc** command must be run from an elevated command prompt.

There are several switches that can be used with the **sfc** command, as shown in the following table.

| Command | Description |
|---|---|
| /scannow<br><br>C:\>sfc /scannow | The **/scannow** switch initiates a full check of all the system resources. It checks the integrity of the resources and repairs problems when possible. This check does take some time. |
| /verifyonly<br><br>C:\>sfc /verifyonly | This is similar to the **/scannow** switch but doesn't attempt repairs. It only scans the files and reports any issues. If it finds problems, it reports the following:<br><br>Windows Resource Protection found integrity violations. Details are included in the CBS.Log windir\ Logs\CBS\CBS.log. For example C:\Windows\Logs\CBS\CBS.log. |
| /scanfile<br><br>sfc /scanfile=path and filename<br><br>C:\>sfc /scanfile=c:\windows\system32<br>\kernel32.dll | You can scan specific files and check for integrity problems on these specific files. Just as the **/scannow** switch repairs any detected problems, the **/scanfile** switch repairs the file if problems are identified. You must specify the full path to the file.<br><br>**NOTE:** You cannot include spaces before or after the = sign in this command. In other words, this command will not work: **sfc /scanfile** = path. |
| /verifyfile<br><br>sfc /verifyfile=path and filename<br><br>C:\>sfc /verifyfile=c:\windows\system32<br>\kernel32.dll | The **/verifyfile** switch checks specific files for integrity problems and reports the results. It does not attempt a repair. You must specify the full path to the file.<br><br>**NOTE:** You cannot include spaces before or after the = sign in this command. In other words, this command will not work: **sfc /verifyfile** = path. |

| | |
|---|---|
| `/offbootdir`<br>`/offwindir`<br>`sfc /scannow /offbootdir=`*driveletter* `:\`<br>`/offwindir=`*drive letter and folder*<br>`C:\>sfc /scannow /offbootdir=d:\`<br>`/offwindir=d:\windows` | You can also scan an offline instance of Windows. In other words, if you have a dual-boot system, you can boot into one system and scan the other system. The **/offbootdir** switch specifies the offline drive and the **/offwindir** switch specifies the offline Windows folder.<br><br>These switches are used in conjunction with other switches, such as the **/scannow** switch shown in the example.<br><br>**NOTE:** You cannot include spaces before or after the = sign in this command. |

## Checking Digital Signatures with sigverif

The **sigverif** command launches the File Signature Verification tool, which can detect which files have been digitally signed and which files are not digitally signed. The syntax is

```
sigverif
```

There aren't any switches used with **sigverif**. Instead, it launches the graphical user interface shown in Figure 12-1. You can then run the tool by clicking **Start**.

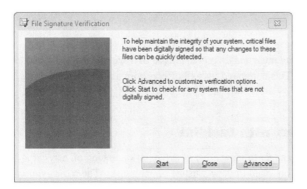

**Figure 12-1** The File Signature Verification Tool

If all the files are digitally signed, a dialog box appears indicating "Your files have been scanned and verified as digitally signed." If any of the files are not digitally signed, you'll see a dialog box indicating which files are not digitally signed. The most common files you're likely to see that are not digitally signed are those related to display drivers because they are often newer. The display shows the name of the files, the path, the file type, and the version.

Figure 12-2 shows the logging options for **sigverif**. You can view this screen by clicking **Advanced**. It enables you to view the results of **sigverif** scans by clicking the View Log button. The sigverif.txt log file is located in the %systemdrive%\Users\Public\ Documents folder.

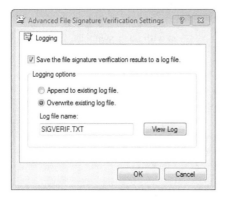

**Figure 12-2** File Signature Verification Logging Options

> **TIP: sigverif** can't be run exclusively from the command line. However, Microsoft has a free download available called **sigcheck** that was written by Mark Russinovich at Sysinternals. You can get it from http://technet.microsoft.com/bb897441.aspx. After you download and extract it, you can execute it from the command line. For example, you could use the following command to check for unsigned files in the system32 folder and log the results into a file named sigcheck.txt: **sigcheck -u c:\windows\ system32 > sigcheck.txt**.

You can also identify signed and unsigned drivers using the **driverquery /si** command, as shown later in this chapter. This command lists all drivers with an IsSigned column indicating True or False.

## Viewing Active Tasks with tasklist

You've probably used Task Manager to view a list of active tasks running on a system. You can also use the **tasklist** command to view a list of running tasks. The basic syntax is

```
tasklist
```

The output includes the tasks identified with their image name, process ID (PID), session name, session number, and memory usage. The following text shows partial output. Note that the system refers to the running tasks as images (under the column Image Name).

```
Image Name         PID    Session Name      Session#     Mem Usage
===============    ====   =============     =========    ============
System Idle Proc   0      Services          0            24 K
System             4      Services          0            3,592 K
smss.exe           288    Services          0            724 K
csrss.exe          440    Services          0            3,104 K
. . .
wininit.exe        500    Services          0            1,760 K
csrss.exe          536    RDP-Tcp#0         1            11,720 K
services.exe       560    Services          0            6,552 K
lsass.exe          576    Services          0            10,160 K
```

You have several different options that you can use with the **tasklist** command, as shown in the following table.

| Command | Description |
| --- | --- |
| /m [*module name*]<br>C:/>**tasklist /m**<br>C:/>**tasklist /m ntdll.dll** | You can use the **/m** switch to determine what DLL modules are being used by the different tasks. When you omit the module name, all of the tasks are listed, and if any of the tasks are using modules, the modules are also included.<br><br>You can also specify the module to determine which tasks are using the specific DLL module. |
| /svc<br>C:/>**tasklist /svc** | You can list all of the associated services (if any) that are running to support each task in the task list. |
| /fi<br>**tasklist /svc /fi "imagename eq** *taskname*"<br>C:\>**tasklist /svc /fi "imagename eq svchost.exe"** | You can use the **/fi** switch to filter the output. The filter options are explored in greater depth later in this section, but this example might be useful. It's common to have multiple instances of the **svchost** process running, and you might want to know what services are related to the process.<br><br>You can combine the **/svc** switch with **/fi** switch to show specifically what services are running for each instance of the **svchost** task. |
| /v<br>C:\>**tasklist /v** | The **/v** switch (verbose) will give you more detailed task information. It cannot be combined with the **/m** or **/svc** options. |

| `/fo`<br>`tasklist /fo table \| list \| csv`<br>`C:\>tasklist /fo list`<br>`C:\>tasklist /fo csv > c:\data\`<br>`tasks.csv` | You can use the **/fo** switch to change the format of the output. The default format is **table**. The comma-separated value (**csv**) format can be combined with the redirect symbol (>) to create a file that can easily be viewed using Microsoft Excel. |
|---|---|
| `/nh`<br>`C:\>tasklist /fo csv /nh` | The **/nh** switch suppresses headers in the output. It is only valid when used with the **table** or **csv** outputs because the **list** output does not use headers. |
| `/s`<br>`/u`<br>`/p`<br>`tasklist /s system  /u user /p`<br>`password`<br>`C:/>tasklist /s dc1 /u pearson\`<br>`administrator /p P@ssw0rd` | You can use the **/s** switch to run the command on a different computer. You'll also need to specify the username and password of an account that has permissions on the remote system.<br><br>In the example, the command is run on the computer named dc1 in the pearson domain with the administrator account. |

The **tasklist /svc /fi "imagename eq svchost.exe"** command shown in the preceding table can be used to only show services with an image name of svchost.exe. However, you have several additional options you can use to filter the output. These filters use the following operators:

- **eq**: Equal
- **ne**: Not equal
- **gt**: Greater than
- **lt**: Less than
- **ge**: Greater than or equal to
- **le**: Less than or equal to

**TIP:** When using filters, you need to enclose the entire filter comparison in quotes. In other words, this will work:

`c:\>tasklist /fi "status eq Running"`

However, this command will result in an error:

`c:\>tasklist /fi status eq Running`

The following table shows some examples using different operators.

| Filter Name | Valid Operators | Valid Values |
|---|---|---|
| status<br>tasklist /fi "status eq running \| not respond-ing \| unknown "<br>C:\>tasklist /fi "status eq not responding" | eq, ne | You can use a status of running, not responding, or unknown. |
| imagename<br>tasklist /svc /fi "imagename eq *task name*"<br>C:\>tasklist /svc /fi "imagename eq svchost.exe" | eq, ne | The **imagename** is the valid name of a task or image in the list. |
| pid<br>tasklist /fi "pid gt ###"<br>C:\>tasklist /fi "pid gt 100" | eq, ne, gt, lt, ge, le | The process ID (PID) can be any number between 0 and 999,999,999. The actual PID can be identified from the **tasklist** output. |
| session<br>tasklist /fi "session ge #"<br>C:\>tasklist /fi "session ge 1"<br>C:\>tasklist /fi "session eq 0"<br>C:\>tasklist /fi "session eq 1" | eq, ne, gt, lt, ge, le | The number for the session can be used.<br><br>Session 0 is the services session.<br><br>Session 1 is the console session.<br><br>Other sessions are from remote desktop sessions.<br><br>The example will show all non-services sessions. |
| sessionname<br>tasklist /fi "session-name ne *session name*"<br>C:\>tasklist /fi "sessionname ne services"<br>C:\>tasklist /fi "sessionname ne console" | eq, ne | You can enter the session name. Two common session names are services and console. Remote desktop sessions are numbered as RDP-Tcp#x, with the first remote session identified as RDP-Tcp#0. The example will show all non-services sessions. |
| cputime<br>tasklist /fi "cputime gt *HH:MM:SS*"<br>C:\>tasklist /fi "cputime gt 01:00:00" | eq, ne, gt, lt, ge, le | The CPU time is in the format of HH:MM:SS. Hours (HH) can be any positive value. Minutes (MM) and seconds (SS) can be any value between 0 and 59. |

| memusage<br><br>`tasklist /fi "memusage`<br>`gt xxxx"`<br>`C:\>tasklist /fi`<br>`"memusage gt 10240"` | eq, ne, gt, lt, ge, le | The memory usage enables you to view processes using specific amounts of memory expressed in KB. The example will show any processes using more than 10 MB of memory. |
|---|---|---|
| username<br><br>`tasklist /fi "username`<br>`eq username"`<br>`C:\>tasklist /fi`<br>`"username eq darril"`<br>`C:\>tasklist /fi`<br>`"username eq n/a"` | eq, ne | You can view processes being run by specific users with the **username** filter. The **username** value doesn't normally show up unless you use the **/v** switch. In the first example, it will show all the services run by the user darril, and the second example shows the services running without a username. |
| services<br><br>`tasklist /fi "services`<br>`eq servicename"`<br>`C:\>tasklist /fi`<br>`"services eq wsearch"` | eq, ne | You can search for tasks that are running specific services with the **services** filter. The example will show any services that are running the wsearch service (the searchindexer.exe task). |
| modules<br><br>`tasklist /fi "modules eq`<br>`module name"`<br>`C:\>tasklist /fi`<br>`"modules eq ntdll.dll"` | eq, ne | The **modules** filter enables you to search for any tasks using specific modules. The example will list all the services using the ntdll.dll module. |

# Terminating Processes with taskkill

The **taskkill** command can be used to terminate a running process using its process ID (PID) or image name. You can use **taskkill** to terminate processes on the local system or remote system. The basic syntax is

`taskkill /pid processID`

or

`taskkill /im imagename`

> **NOTE:** If there are multiple instances of the process, the command terminates all instances matching the **imagename** parameter in the **/im** switch. However, if the **/pid** switch is used it terminates only the process matching the **processID**. For example, if you have two instances of Notepad running, both will be terminated with **tasklist /im notepad.exe**.

The following table shows how to use some of these switches. An easy process to test these commands is Notepad. You can launch Notepad by entering **notepad** at the command prompt. You can then use the following command to get the details about it:

```
tasklist /fi "imagename eq notepad.exe"
```

You'll see a result similar to the following output. The PID is 1084 in the listing, but you will probably have a different PID.

```
Image Name          PID   Session Name      Session#   Mem Usage
================== ===== =============   =========== ============
notepad.exe        1084  Console           1          4,756 K
```

| Command | Description |
|---|---|
| `/im`<br>`taskkill /im` *task name*<br>`C:\>taskkill /im notepad.exe` | The **/im** switch terminates the process identified by the image name. |
| `/pid`<br>`taskkill /pid` *xxxx*<br>`C:\>taskkill / pid 1084` | The **/pid** switch terminates the process identified by the PID number. |
| `/s`<br>`/u`<br>`/p`<br>`taskkill /s` *system* `/u` *user* `/p`<br>*password* `/im` image name<br>`C:\>taskkill /s dc1 /u pearson\`<br>`administrator /p P@ssw0rd /im`<br>`notepad.exe` | You can use the **/s** switch to run the command on a different computer. You also need to specify the username and password of an account that has permissions on the remote system.<br><br>In the example, the command is run on the computer named dc1 in the pearson domain with the administrator account. |
| `/f`<br>`C:\>taskkill /im notepad.exe /f` | If an application has unsaved data, it will often prompt the user to save the data. You can use the **/f** switch to forcefully terminate the process and override the prompt.<br><br>This parameter is ignored for remote processes; all remote processes are forcefully terminated. |
| `/t`<br>`C:\>taskkill /im notepad.exe /t` | If an application has spawned child processes, you can use the **/t** switch to terminate the process and any child processes that it started. |

**TIP:** You can use the same filters (with the **/fi** switch) in the **taskkill** command as you can use in the **tasklist** command.

## Viewing Installed Drivers with driverquery

The **driverquery** command can be used to view a list of installed device drivers and properties about the drivers. The basic syntax is

```
driverquery
```

You can use some additional switches to modify the output, as shown in the following table.

| Command | Description |
| --- | --- |
| /v<br>C:\>driverquery /v > c:\data\<br>drivers.txt | The **/v** switch is used to provide verbose output. This can be very extensive and isn't very easy to read from the command prompt. If you redirect it to a text file, you can read it using Notepad. |
| /si<br>C:\>driverquery /si | You can view information on both signed and unsigned drivers with the **/si** switch. You can't combine the **/v** and **/si** switches. |
| /fo<br>driverquery /fo table \| list \| csv<br>C:\>driverquery /fo list<br>C:\>driverquery /fo csv > c:\data\<br>drivers.csv | You can use the **/fo** switch to change the format of the output. The default format is **table**. The comma-separated value (**csv**) format can be combined with the redirect symbol (>) to create a file that can easily be viewed using Microsoft Excel. |
| /nh<br>C:\>driverquery /fo csv /nh | The **/nh** switch suppresses headers in the output. It is only valid when used with the **table** or **csv** outputs because the **list** output does not use headers. |
| /s<br>/u<br>/p<br>driverquery /s system /u user /p password<br>C:\>driverquery /s dc1 /u pearson\<br>administrator /p P@ssw0rd | You can use the **/s** switch to run the command on a different computer. You also need to specify the username and password of an account that has permissions on the remote system.<br><br>In the example, the command is run on the computer named dc1 in the pearson domain with the administrator account. |

# CHAPTER 13

# Troubleshooting Network Issues

This chapter provides information and commands concerning the following topics:

- Viewing and manipulating TCP/IP configuration with **ipconfig**
- Viewing the physical address with **getmac**
- Checking connectivity with **ping**
- Viewing the rout er path with **tracert**
- Checking for data loss with **pathping**
- Checking for records in DNS with **nslookup**

## Viewing and Manipulating TCP/IP Configuration with ipconfig

The **ipconfig** command is a very useful command you can use to view and manipulate TCP/IP configuration information. It is most commonly used to view the TCP/IP configuration data for a system. You can do so with this command:

```
ipconfig
```

or

```
ipconfig /all
```

| The Output of ipconfig | Comments |
|---|---|
| `C:\>ipconfig`<br>`Windows IP Configuration` | **ipconfig** without any switches will give basic TCP/IP configuration data for each NIC. This example shows two NICs, named Local Area Connection and Local Area Connection 2. |
| `Ethernet adapter Local Area`<br>`Connection:`<br>`   Connection-specific DNS Suffix`<br>`. :`<br>`   IPv4 Address. . . . . . . . .`<br>`. : 192.168.1.10`<br>`   Subnet Mask . . . . . . . . .`<br>`. : 255.255.255.0`<br>`   Default Gateway . . . . . . .`<br>`: 192.168.1.1` | This is often a good check to see the actual IP address, subnet mask, and default gateway. |

| | |
|---|---|
| `Ethernet adapter Local Area`<br>`Connection 2:`<br>`    Media State . . . . . . . . .`<br>`. : Media disconnected`<br>`    Connection-specific DNS Suffix`<br>`. :` | If a NIC is disconnected at the computer, at the network device (such as a switch), or the cable is broken anywhere in between, it will show "Media disconnected." |

**ipconfig /all** shows much more detailed information, as shown in the following table.

| ipconfig /all Output | Comments |
|---|---|
| `C:\>ipconfig /all`<br>`Windows IP Configuration`<br><br>`    Host Name . . . . . . . . . .`<br>`. : Win7PCG`<br>`    Primary Dns Suffix  . . . . . :`<br>`Pearson.pub`<br>`    Node Type . . . . . . . . . .`<br>`. . : Hybrid`<br>`    IP Routing Enabled. . . . . .`<br>`: No`<br>`    WINS Proxy Enabled. . . . . :`<br>`No`<br>`    DNS Suffix Search List. . . . . :`<br>`Pearson.pub` | The **ipconfig /all** output starts with global information for the system that applies to all network interface cards (NICs).<br><br>The Host Name is the name of the computer. If the computer is joined to a domain, it will be indicated in the Primary Dns Suffix. This will be blank for workgroup computers.<br><br>The Node Type indicates how NetBIOS names will be resolved. Hybrid indicates a WINS server will be queried first (if configured), and then it will broadcast; Mixed indicates it will broadcast first and then query WINS; Broadcast indicating it will broadcast only; Peer-to-peer indicates it will only query a WINS server.<br><br>It's not common to enable IP routing or a WINS proxy on a Windows 7 computer, so IP Routing Enabled and WINS Proxy Enabled will almost always be set to No. If you want hostnames to search additional suffixes beyond the primary DNS suffix (such as training.pearson.pub), you can add those suffixes and they will appear in the search list. |

| | |
|---|---|
| ```
Ethernet adapter Local Area
Connection:
   Connection-specific DNS Suffix
. :
   Description . . . . . . . . . :
Intel 21140-Based PCI Fast Ethernet
Adapter
   Physical Address. . . . . . :
00-03-FF-9C-02-00
   DHCP Enabled. . . . . . . . :
No
   Autoconfiguration Enabled . . .
. : Yes
   Link-local IPv6 Address . . . . .
: fe80::41f0:f763:5451:198a%10
(Preferred)
   IPv4 Address. . . . :
192.168.1.122(Preferred)
   Subnet Mask . . . . . . . . .
. : 255.255.255.0
   Default Gateway . . . . . . .
. : 192.168.1.1
   DNS Servers . . . . . . . . .
. : 192.168.1.10
   NetBIOS over Tcpip. . . . . .
. : Enabled
``` | Each NIC has specific information, starting with the name. The default name of the first NIC is Local Area Connection, but you can change the name of the NICs. The output lists the brand and model of the NIC as a Description.<br><br>The Physical Address is the MAC or Ethernet address.<br><br>When the IP address is statically assigned, DHCP Enabled is No. Autoconfiguration refers to Automatic Private IP Addressing (APIPA). APIPA automatically assigns an IP address in the range of 169.254.$y.z$ to a DHCP client if the DHCP server doesn't respond. It doesn't have any effect for non-DHCP clients, or clients with a statically assigned IP address.<br><br>If a static IPv6 address isn't assigned, a link-local address (with a prefix of fe80) is automatically assigned.<br><br>The default gateway must be on the same subnet. If you're having problems with name resolution, you can ping the IP address of the DNS server as a check. |

In addition to the **/all** switch, you can use several additional switches with **ipconfig**. Some of the switches commonly used with **ipconfig** are listed in the following table.

| ipconfig Switches | Comments |
|---|---|
| `/release`<br>ipconfig **/release** [*adapter*]<br>C:\>**ipconfig /release**<br>C:\>**ipconfig /release "local area connection"**<br>C:\>**ipconfig /release local***  | Releases the DHCP lease for the specified adapters that have DHCP leases. If you don't identify an adapter, it will attempt to release the DHCP lease for all adapters that have DHCP leases.<br><br>You can use the entire name of the connection, or use wildcards. **local\*** represents all connections that start with Local. |
| `/release6`<br>ipconfig **/release6** [*adapter*]<br>C:\>**ipconfig /release6**<br>C:\>**ipconfig /release6 "local area connection"**<br>C:\>**ipconfig /release6 local***  | The **/release6** switch works the same way as **/release** but for IPv6 addresses. |
```

| | |
|---|---|
| `/renew`<br>`ipconfig /renew` *[adapter]*<br>`C:\>ipconfig /renew`<br>`C:\>ipconfig /renew "local area`<br>`connection"`<br>`C:\>ipconfig /renew local*` | You can renew DHCP leases with the **/renew** switch. It attempts to reach a DHCP server and obtain a new DHCP lease or renew the existing lease. The lease will include an IP address and subnet mask at a minimum, but might also include other data such as the default gateway, address of DNS, and domain name. You can identify the adapter the same way you can with the **/release** switch. |
| `/renew6`<br>`ipconfig /renew6` *[adapter]*<br>`C:\>ipconfig /renew6 "local area`<br>`connection"`<br>`C:\>ipconfig /renew6 local*` | The **/renew6** switch works the same way as **/release** but for IPv6 addresses. |
| `/displaydns`<br>`C:\>ipconfig /displaydns` | The DNS cache, or host cache, shows names that have been resolved by DNS and items that are in the Hosts file. You can view the cache with the **/displaydns** switch.<br><br>Items in cache will stay in cache until the Time To Live (TTL) times out. The TTL value is shown in seconds and is provided by DNS when the name is resolved to an IP address.<br><br>**NOTE:** Items in the %windir%\System32\ Drivers\etc\hosts file will automatically be placed in cache. |

```
/displaydns
C:\>ping dc1
pinging dc1.pearson.pub
[192.168.1.10]
with 32 bytes of data:
Reply from 192.168.1.10: bytes=32
time<1ms TTL=128
Reply from 192.168.1.10: bytes=32
time<1ms TTL=128
Reply from 192.168.1.10: bytes=32
time<1ms TTL=128
Reply from 192.168.1.10: bytes=32
time<1ms TTL=128
ping statistics for 192.168.1.10:
    Packets: Sent = 4, Received =
4, Lost = 0 (0% loss),
Approximate round trip times in
milli-seconds:
    Minimum = 0ms, Maximum = 0ms,
Average = 0ms
c:\>ping dc99
ping request could not find host
dc99. Please check the name and
try again.
c:\>ipconfig /displaydns
    dc1.pearson.pub
    ----------------------------
----------
    Record Name . . . . . : dc1.
pearson.pub
    Record Type . . . . . : 1
    Time To Live  . . . . : 3581
    Data Length . . . . . : 4
    Section . . . . . . . : Answer
    A (Host) Record . . . :
192.168.1.10

    Dc99
    ----------------------------
----------
    Name does not exist.
```

In this example, DC1 is pinged within the pearson.pub domain. The first line shows that it was successfully resolved to 192.168.1.10 (underlined for emphasis), and then **ping** sends four echo requests and receives four echo replies.

DC99 is also pinged, but the DNS server doesn't have a record of DC99 and responds with a negative response (underlined).

With some data in the DNS resolver cache, you can now view the cache. Notice that both DC1 and DC99 are in cache but DC1 has an IP address and DC99 simply states that the name doesn't exist.

A TTL of 3581 is close to 60 minutes (3581 seconds divided by 60 = 59.6 minutes). This TTL continuously counts down until it reaches zero and then it is automatically dropped from cache.

If the data is in cache, DNS is not queried again. In other words, if DC1 and DC99 are pinged again, the **ping** will use the data from cache.

Negative responses will stay in cache for 15 minutes unless flushed out of cache using the **ipconfig /flushdns** command.

| | |
|---|---|
| /flushdns<br><br>C:\>ipconfig /flushdns | There are times when you want to remove data from cache without waiting for the TTL to expire. For example, if there is a negative cache entry in cache because DNS didn't have a record for the client, you can purge the DNS cache with the **/flushdns** switch. This will also purge any entries that haven't timed out.<br><br>**NOTE:** Items in the %windir%\system32\ drivers\etc\hosts file will not be purged when you use the **/flushdns** switch. The only way to remove these items from cache is to remove them from the Hosts file. |
| /registerdns<br><br>C:\>ipconfig /registerdns | The **/registerdns** switch initiates manual dynamic registration for the DNS names and IP addresses that are configured at a computer. Dynamic DNS (DDNS) is used within Microsoft domains to dynamically create and update records on DNS servers and it normally occurs when a computer boots. You can use this switch to trouble-shoot a failed DNS name registration or resolve a dynamic update problem between a client and the DNS server with-out rebooting the client computer. |

If you want to see the effect of adding entries in the Hosts file, you can do so with the following steps:

| Steps to Modify Hosts File | Remarks |
|---|---|
| 1. Launch Notepad with elevated permissions. | Click **Start**, type **Notepad** in the Start Search text box, right-click **Notepad**, and select **Run As Administrator**. If prompted by UAC to continue, click **Yes**. |
| 2. Browse to the Hosts file and open it. | Click **File, Open**. Browse to the %windir%\ system32\drivers\etc\ folder. Change **Text Documents (*.txt)** to **All Files** in the Open dialog box. Select the Hosts file and click **Open**. |
| 3. Add a bogus record after the last line in the Hosts file. | Scroll to the bottom of the file and enter the fol-lowing line:<br><br>**192.168.1.2      DC99** |
| 4. Save the Hosts file. | Select **File, Save** to save the file.<br><br>**NOTE:** If you didn't launch Notepad with admin-istrative permissions, you will not be able to save the file. |

| 5. View the cache entry with **ipconfig /displaydns**. | Launch a command prompt and enter **ipconfig /displaydns** to view the entry. |
|---|---|
| 6. Try to purge the Hosts file entry. | Enter **ipconfig /flushdns** to purge all entries. Type in **ipconfig /displaydns** to verify the Hosts entry remains. |
| 7. Return the Hosts file to normal. | Return to Notepad. Delete the line you added (**192.168.1.2      DC99**). Select **File, Save** to save the file. Close Notepad. |

# Viewing the Physical Address with getmac

The **getmac** command is a simple way to view the Media Access Control (MAC) address of a NIC. This is also known as the physical address or Ethernet address. The basic syntax and the output is

```
getmac
```

```
Physical Address   Transport Name

================   ================================================

00-03-FF-9C-02-00 \Device\Tcpip_{496EB04D-3809-4E1B-9307-78AF1FF08CBA}
```

The Transport Name identifies the NIC by the globally unique identifier (GUID).

There are a few switches you can use with the **getmac** command:

| Command | Description |
|---|---|
| `/v`<br>`C:\>getmac /v` | Provides a verbose output. This adds the connection name and network adapter name. |
| `/fo`<br>`getmac /v /fo [table \| list \| csv]`<br>`C:\>getmac /v /fo list` | You can use the **/fo** switch to change the format of the output. The default format is **table**.<br><br>When retrieving verbose output using the **table** format, some of the data is truncated. The **list** format shows the complete output. |
| `/s`<br>`/u`<br>`/p`<br>`getmac /s system /u /p password`<br>`C:\>getmac /s dc1 /u pearson\`<br>`administrator /p P@ssw0rd` | You can use the **/s** switch to run the command on a different computer. You'll also need to specify the username and password of an account that has permissions on the remote system.<br><br>In the example, the command is run on the computer named dc1 in the pearson domain with the administrator account. |

## Checking Connectivity with ping

One of the most valuable troubleshooting tools to check connectivity is **ping**. It can quickly tell you if systems are up and operational and if you are able to resolve names to IP addresses. The basic syntax is

**ping** *hostname*

or

**ping** *IP address*

> **TIP:** If the pinged system responds, you know the system is operational. However, if the pinged system doesn't respond, it doesn't necessarily mean that it is not operational. Its firewall, or a firewall between your system and the remote system, could be blocking ICMP requests.

If you ping the hostname, the first thing that ping does is resolve the name to an IP address. This can be very valuable to determine if name resolution is working. As an example, consider the following **ping** command and its output:

```
c:\>ping dc1
pinging DC1.Pearson.pub [192.168.1.10] with 32 bytes of data:
Reply from 192.168.1.10: bytes=32 time=1ms TTL=128
Reply from 192.168.1.10: bytes=32 time<1ms TTL=128
Reply from 192.168.1.10: bytes=32 time<1ms TTL=128
Reply from 192.168.1.10: bytes=32 time<1ms TTL=128
ping statistics for 192.168.1.10:
    Packets: Sent = 4, Received = 4, Lost = 0 (0% loss),
Approximate round trip times in milli-seconds:
    Minimum = 0ms, Maximum = 1ms, Average = 0ms
```

Notice that the very first line shows that DC1.Pearson.pub has been resolved to 192.168.1.10. In this domain, it is being resolved by DNS, but it could also be resolved from the Hosts file, the lmhosts file, WINS, or broadcasts.

> **TIP:** Because the system is a member of the pearson.pub domain, the pearson.pub suffix is appended to the hostname of dc1, giving a fully qualified domain name (FQDN) of dc1.pearson.pub.

You can get a few different errors from **ping**, which are shown in the following table.

| Error | Example | Description |
|---|---|---|
| Could not find host. | c:\>**ping dc99**<br>Ping request could not find host dc99. Please check the name and try again. | Name resolution methods could not resolve the name to an IP address. This commonly means that the name is not known by the DNS server. |
| Request timed out. | c:\>**ping 192.168.1.1**<br>pinging 192.168.1.1 with 32 bytes of data:<br>Request timed out.<br>Request timed out.<br>Request timed out.<br>Request timed out.<br>ping statistics for 192.168.1.1:<br>    Packets: Sent = 4, Received = 0, Lost = 4 (100% loss), | This indicates that the system is not responding. It could be because the system is not operational. However, the ping might be blocked by the firewall. |
| Destination host unreachable. | c:\>**ping 192.168.3.10**<br>pinging 192.168.3.10 with 32 bytes of data:<br>Reply from 192.168.1.11:<br>Destination host unreachable.<br>Reply from 192.168.1.11:<br>Destination host unreachable.<br>Reply from 192.168.1.11:<br>Destination host unreachable.<br>Reply from 192.168.1.11:<br>Destination host unreachable.<br>ping statistics for 192.168.3.10:<br>    Packets: Sent = 4, Received = 4, Lost = 0 (0% loss), | This often indicates that the default gateway on the local system or the remote system is not configured correctly. The default gateway should be on the same subnet. |

Another error you might read about but rarely (if ever) see is "TTL expired in transit." The TTL value determines the maximum amount of time an IP packet may live in the network without reaching its destination. If you have networking problems with routers and routes on your network, a ping might get caught in a routing loop and expire on the wire.

It's important to reiterate that a "Request timed out" error doesn't necessarily indicate the system is not operational. It could be that the firewall setting is preventing a ping. You can ensure that the firewall is allowing ICMP ping requests with **netsh**, as shown in the following table.

| netsh Commands | Comments |
|---|---|
| `C:\>netsh firewall set icmpsetting 8`<br>`IMPORTANT: Command executed`<br>`successfully.`<br>`However, "netsh firewall" is`<br>`deprecated;`<br>`use "netsh advfirewall firewall"`<br>`instead.` | This enables echo requests.<br><br>However, the **netsh firewall** commands have been deprecated, so the system will complain to you if you use them. |
| `C:\>netsh firewall set icmpsetting 8`<br>`disable` | This disables echo requests. |
| `C:\>netsh advfirewall firewall add`<br>`rule name = "allow icmp incom-`<br>`ing v4 echo request" protocol =`<br>`icmpv4:8,any dir = in action = allow`<br>`Ok.` | You can use the current **netsh advfirewall firewall** command to create a rule. This rule also enables echo requests. |
| `C:\>netsh advfirewall firewall delete`<br>`rule name = "allow icmp incoming v4`<br>`echo request"`<br>`Deleted 1 rule(s).`<br>`Ok.` | You delete the advfirewall rule with this command. |

Ping supports several switches, many of which are shown in the following table.

| ping Switches | Comments |
|---|---|
| `-t`<br>`C:\>ping dc1 -t` | You can use the **-t** switch to have **ping** continue pinging the specified host until you stop it. You can stop it by pressing Ctrl+C.<br><br>While it's running, you can press Ctrl+Break to view statistics. |
| `-n`<br>`ping name or ip -n xx`<br>`C:\>ping 192.168.1.10 -n 10` | You can specify the number of echo requests to send with the **-n** switch. By default, four ping echo requests are sent, but you can give a number such as 10 to send 10 instead. |
| `-a`<br>`C:\>ping 192.168.1.10 -a` | The **-a** switch can be used to resolve addresses to hostnames. This requires a reverse lookup zone and an associated PTR (pointer) record on the DNS server, so it won't always work. |
| `-l`<br>`ping name or ip -l xx`<br>`C:\>ping 192.168.1.10 -l 64` | You can change the size of the ping packet with **-l**. The size is specified in bytes and the default size is 32 bytes. |
| `-i`<br>`ping name or ip -i xxx`<br>`C:\>ping 192.168.1.10 -i 10` | You can modify the TTL with the **-i** switch. The default is 128. |

| | |
|---|---|
| `-4`<br>`ping` *name or IP* `-4`<br>`C:\>ping 192.168.1.10 -4` | You can use the **-4** switch to force **ping** to use IPv4. |
| `-6`<br>`ping` *name or ip* `-6`<br>`C:\>ping 192.168.1.10 -6` | You can use the **-6** switch to force **ping** to use IPv6. |

## Viewing the Router Path with tracert

If you have several routers between your system and the destination computer, you can use the **tracert** command to trace the route. It will list each of the routers by IP address, and if the IP address can be resolved to a name, it will list the name. The basic syntax is

`tracert` *hostname*

or

`tracert` *IP address*

The following example shows the output when using **tracert** to trace the route to a specific server in a network:

| | |
|---|---|
| `C:\>tracert -d dc1.pearson.pub`<br>`Tracing route to dc1.pearson.pub [10.55.99.211]`<br>`over a maximum of 30 hops:`<br>`1    103 ms    79 ms    79 ms    10.174.112.192`<br>`2    75 ms     89 ms     106 ms   10.174.115.255`<br>`3    173 ms    76 ms    74 ms     10.83.27.193`<br>`4    85 ms     89 ms    89 ms     10.83.26.18`<br>`5    117 ms    126 ms   125 ms   10.55.99.211` | **tracert** first resolves the name to an IP address. It then records the time it takes to get to each router and the IP address of the router.<br><br>Without the **-d** command, **tracert** also attempts to resolve the IP address to a name. |

You can use **tracert** in a few other ways, as shown in the following table.

| | |
|---|---|
| `-4`<br>`tracert -4` *host or IP*<br>`C:\>tracert -4 dc1.pearson.pub` | You can force the trace to use IPv4 with the **-4** switch. |
| `-6`<br>`tracert -6` *host or IP*<br>`C:\>tracert -6 dc1.pearson.pub` | You can force the trace to use IPv6 with the **-6** switch. |

## Checking for Data Loss with pathping

Occasionally you might notice that the network response is slow. There are several reasons why the network might be slow, but the **pathping** command can help you narrow down where it's slow.

More specifically, **pathping** traces the route to the destination, just like **tracert**, and then sends 100 echo requests to each router in the path to test for data loss. Anything less than 100 echo replies indicates a percentage of data loss. The pathping usually takes about five minutes to complete. It will finish tracing the route rather quickly, but it takes time to send and receive the 100 pings for each router. The basic syntax of **pathping** is

```
pathping hostname
```

or

```
pathping IP address
```

Additionally, you can use a few switches with **pathping**:

| | |
|---|---|
| `-h`<br>`pathping name or ip -h maximum_hops`<br>`C:\>pathping dc1.pearson.pub -h 15` | The default maximum number of hops, or routers, is 30, but you can modify this number with the **-h** switch. |
| `-n`<br>`C:\>pathping dc1.pearson.pub -n` | **pathping** normally tries to resolve the IP addresses to hostnames, but this can be suppressed with the **-n** switch. |
| `-p`<br>`pathping name or ip -p period`<br>`C:\>pathping dc1.pearson.pub -p 100` | You can cause the system to wait a period of time (specified in milliseconds) between pings with the **-p** switch. |
| `-q`<br>`pathping name or ip -q num_queries`<br>`C:\>pathping dc1.pearson.pub -q 10` | The default number of queries per hop is 100, but you can modify this to a different number with the **-q** switch. |
| `-4`<br>`C:\>pathping dc1.pearson.pub -4` | You can force the trace to use IPv4 with the **-4** switch. |
| `-6`<br>`C:\>pathping dc1.pearson.pub -6` | You can force the trace to use IPv6 with the **-6** switch. |

## Checking for Records in DNS with nslookup

The **nslookup** command can be used to query the Domain Name System (DNS) server and diagnose different issues with DNS. The most common reason to use it with Windows 7 is to check for records. For example, you can use it to determine if an A or Host record exists for a specific hostname. If the record exists, DNS will be able to resolve it to an IP address. The basic syntax is

```
nslookup hostname
```

When **nslookup** is successful, you'll see a response as shown in the following table.

| | |
|---|---|
| `C:\>nslookup dc4` | The basic query will ask DNS if it can resolve the hostname of DC4 to an IP address. |
| `Server:   dc1.pearson.pub`<br>`Address:   192.168.1.10` | The first part of the response is only related to DNS. Because the system is configured with 192.168.1.10 as the IP address of the DNS server, **nslookup** shows that IP address. **nslookup** also tries to do a reverse lookup to determine the name of the system with that IP address.<br><br>If successful, as shown here, **nslookup** displays the name of the DNS server (dc1.pearson.pub in the example). |
| `Name:     dc4.pearson.pub`<br>`Address:   192.168.1.14` | The next part of the response queries DNS for an A or Host record for the host (dc4 in this example). If a record exists, DNS gives the IP address of the host. |

Figure 13-1 shows the DNS console for the pearson.pub domain. Notice that A (Host) records exist for dc4.pearson.pub and dc1.pearson.pub.

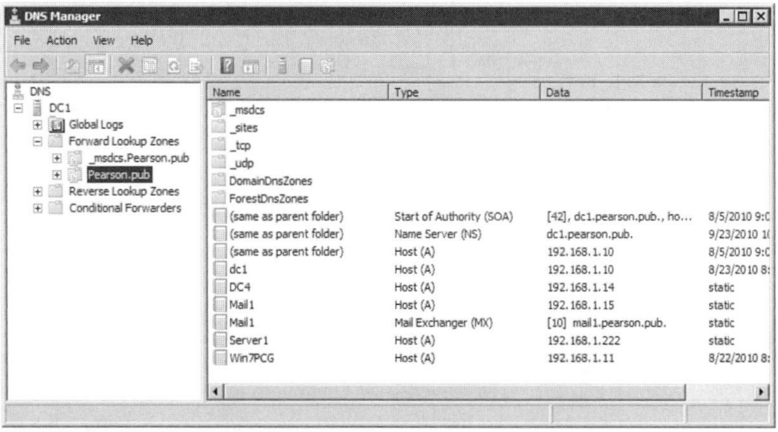

**Figure 13-1** DNS Console Forward Lookup Zone in Pearson.pub

Pointer (PTR) records exist in the reverse lookup zone of a DNS console. Figure 13-2 shows the reverse lookup zone in the pearson.pub domain with the PTR record for dc1.pearson.pub.

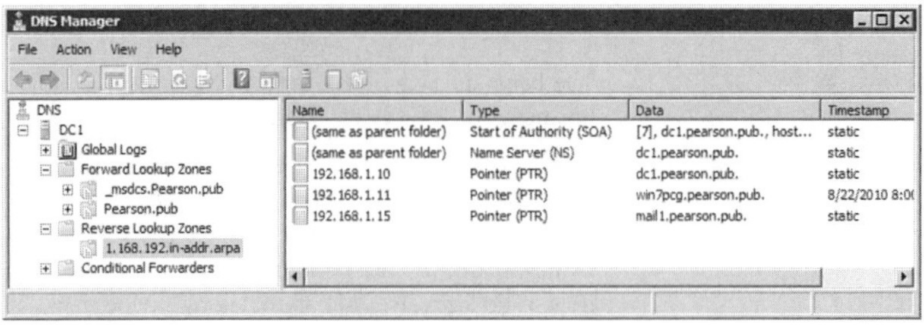

**Figure 13-2** DNS Console Reverse Lookup Zone in Pearson.pub

**NOTE:** Pointer records are optional, and the reverse lookup zone is optional. You'll see different results depending on whether or not the reverse lookup zone exists, and the PTR record exists within the reverse lookup zone.

The following table shows some common examples of different responses you can get from **nslookup**. If you look at Figure 13-1, you'll see that there is not a record for dc99. pearson.pub.

| | |
|---|---|
| `C:\>nslookup dc99`<br>`Server:  dc1.pearson.pub`<br>`Address:  192.168.1.10`<br><br>`*** dc1.pearson.pub can't`<br>`find dc99: Non-existent`<br>`domain` | DNS is being queried for the IP address of dc99, but DNS does not have a record for dc99.<br><br>Notice that the server name and IP address of the DNS server (dc1.pearson.pub and 192.168.1.10) are still shown.<br><br>However, the response shows that a record doesn't exist because dc1 doesn't have a record for dc99. |
| `C:\>nslookup dc4`<br>`Server:  UnKnown`<br>`Address:  192.168.1.10`<br><br>`Name:    dc4.Pearson.pub`<br>`Address:  192.168.1.14` | This shows the result if the PTR record for dc1. pearson.pub is deleted.<br><br>This example shows that the DNS server was able to successfully resolve dc4 to an IP address of 192.168.1.4.<br><br>However, it was unable to resolve the IP address of the DNS server (192.168.1.10) to a name. This is because the DNS server does not have a PTR record for the DNS server.<br><br>If you're focused only on seeing if DNS can resolve dc4 to an IP address, this Unknown response can be ignored. If you're managing the DNS server, you'll probably want to create the PTR record for the DNS server. |

| | |
|---|---|
| `C:\>`**`nslookup dc4`**<br>`DNS request timed out.`<br>`   timeout was 2 seconds.`<br>`Server:  UnKnown`<br>`Address:  192.168.1.10`<br><br>`Name:     dc4.Pearson.pub`<br>`Address:  192.168.1.14` | This shows the result if the reverse lookup zone is deleted.<br><br>This looks like you have serious problems, but it's actually showing the DNS server can successfully resolve dc4 to an IP address.<br><br>The "DNS request timed out" message occurs because DNS does not have a reverse lookup zone. Because reverse lookup zones are optional, this timeout message can be ignored.<br><br>Your system will still have an IP address of the DNS server (192.168.1.10 in the example), but it can't resolve it to a name because the reverse lookup zone (and associated PTR record) do not exist. |

**nslookup** is a shell command with several contexts available to you. If you are managing the DNS server, you'll want to dig into **nslookup** deeper. However, when managing Windows 7 systems, you don't need to go beyond the basics.

This chapter provides information and commands concerning the following topics:

- Manipulating the boot process with **bcdedit**
- Creating a system repair disk with **recdisc**
- Checking and repairing disks with **chkdsk**
- Repairing BitLocker drives with **repair-bde**

## Manipulating the Boot Process with bcdedit

The boot configuration data (BCD) is used to store information that lets the computer know how to boot into Windows 7. Chapter 5, "Manipulating Disks," introduced **bcdedit** in the section that showed how to create a Windows 7 bootable VHD file, "Modifying the BCD Store for the VHD File." This section digs into **bcdedit** a little deeper by showing how you can use it to view and modify the BCD data store. As a reminder, **bcdedit** must be run with elevated privileges.

> **TIP:** The boot.ini file used in Windows XP and previous versions of Windows is not used in Windows 7. All of the boot configuration data is stored in the BCD store. The **bootcfg** command is not used to modify the BCD store.

When looking at the **bcdedit** information and commands, it's useful to understand the boot process. Figure 14-1 shows the overall boot process.

The basic input/output system (BIOS) first launches a Power-On Self Test (POST) process when the computer is turned on. BIOS then uses the master boot record (MBR) to identify the active system partition and starts the NTFS boot code on the MBR. The boot code accesses the Windows Boot Manager from the System BCD store. The Windows Boot Manager then identifies which Windows Boot Loader to load. The Windows Boot Loader can be on the same partition or a different partition.

You can enter **bcdedit** without any switches. It will then display both Windows Boot Manager and Windows Boot Loader information. If you have installed one operating system on your system, you will have one Windows Boot Loader section. However, if you've installed more than one operating system, you'll have a dual-boot or multiboot system and you'll see more than one Windows Boot Loader section.

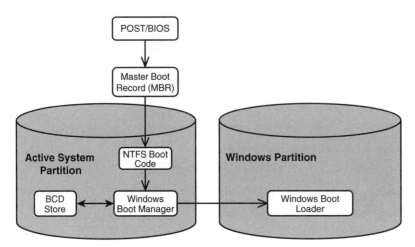

**Figure 14-1**   Windows 7 Boot Process

```
C:\>bcdedit


Windows Boot Manager
--------------------
identifier              {bootmgr}
device                  partition=C:
description             Windows Boot Manager
locale                  en-US
inherit                 {globalsettings}
default                 {current}
resumeobject            {29ae2042-b221-11dd-8baf-86117d7e2179}
displayorder            {current}
                        {923aaeaf-84c0-11de-bac6-00235a33c4ca}
toolsdisplayorder       {memdiag}
timeout                 45


Windows Boot Loader
-------------------
identifier              {current}
```

```
device                partition=C:
path                  \Windows\system32\winload.exe
description           Windows 7
locale                en-US
loadoptions           ddisable_integrity_check
inherit               {bootloadersettings}
recoverysequence      {923aaead-84c0-11de-bac6-00235a33c4ca}
recoveryenabled       Yes
testsigning           No
osdevice              partition=C:
systemroot            \Windows
resumeobject          {29ae2042-b221-11dd-8baf-86117d7e2179}
nx                    OptIn

Windows Boot Loader
-------------------
identifier            {923aaeaf-84c0-11de-bac6-00235a33c4ca}
device                partition=C:
path                  \Windows\system32\winload.exe
description           VHD_Boot
locale                en-US
inherit               {bootloadersettings}
recoverysequence      {923aaead-84c0-11de-bac6-00235a33c4ca}
recoveryenabled       Yes
osdevice              partition=C:
systemroot            \Windows
resumeobject          {29ae2042-b221-11dd-8baf-86117d7e2179}
nx                    OptIn
```

| bcdedit Output | Description |
|---|---|
| `C:\>bcdedit` | If you enter the **bcdedit** command from an elevated prompt, you'll see the boot store contents. In this example, the boot store holds two installations of Windows 7 with one installation in a VHD file. |

```
Windows Boot Manager
--------------------
Identifier        {bootmgr}
Device            partition=c:
Description       Windows Boot Manager
Locale            en-US
Inherit                {globalsettings}
Default           {current}
Resumeobject      {29ae2042-b221-11dd-
8baf-86117d7e2179}
Displayorder      {current} {923aaeaf-
84c0-11de-bac6-00235a33c4ca}
Toolsdisplayorder {memdiag}
Timeout           30
```

The Windows Boot Manager is the first section. It identifies basic information such as the partition (c: in the example).

Because the system is booted into the default, it shows this as {current}. Otherwise, it will identify the operating system based on the globally unique identifier (GUID).

The resumeobject GUID is used when the system restarts from hibernation. If you use the **bcdedit /enum all** command, you'll see the Resume From Hibernate section.

The Displayorder section in the output identifies which operating system will appear first, second, and so on in the Windows boot screen. If there is only one operating system, this will just be {current}.

The Toolsdisplayorder section shows that the user can launch the memory diagnostics (memdiag) from the boot screen.

The Timeout section indicates the system will boot to the default operating system in 30 seconds if the user doesn't take any action.

```
Windows Boot Loader
-------------------
identifier        {current}
device            partition=c:
path                      \Windows\
system32\winload.exe
description       Windows 7
locale            en-US
inherit           {bootloadersettings}
recoverysequence  {923aaead-84c0-
11de-bac6-00235a33c4ca}
recoveryenabled   Yes
osdevice          partition=c:
systemroot        \Windows
resumeobject              {29ae2042-
b221-11dd-8baf-86117d7e2179}
nx                OptIn
```

In this example, the first Windows Boot Loader shows that Windows 7 is the operating system and it's located at c:\Windows\system32\winload.exe.

The recoverysequence setting identifies the GUID for a Windows Recovery Environment (WinRE). This is in another Windows Boot Loader section that can be viewed with the **bcdedit /enum all** command. If the system can't boot into the operating system, it will automatically boot into the recovery sequence GUID and attempt an automatic repair.

```
Windows Boot Loader
-------------------
identifier      {923aaeaf-84c0-11de-
bac6-00235a33c4ca}
device          partition=c:
path                    \Windows\
system32\winload.exe
description     VHD_Boot
locale          en-US
inherit         bootloadersettings}
recoverysequence   {923aaead-84c0-
11de-bac6-00235a33c4ca}
recoveryenabled Yes
osdevice        partition=c:
systemroot      \Windows
resumeobject    {29ae2042-b221-11dd-
8baf-86117d7e2179}
nx              OptIn
```

In this example, a second Windows Boot Loader section is available, indicating the system is a dual-boot system.

The second system is a VHD file, indicated by a description of VHD_Boot.

Notice that the second Windows Boot Loader section has the same GUIDs for the recoverysequence and resumeobject parameters.

**bcdedit** has a much wider range of commands you can use. The commands are divided into several different categories. Some of the categories useful on Windows 7 are

- Commands that operate on a store
- Commands that control output
- Commands that control the Windows Boot Manager
- Commands that operate on entries in the store
- Commands that operate on entry options

When working with these commands, you will often identify the Windows boot loader with the GUID. Remember, you don't have to type in this GUID from scratch. You can cut and paste the GUID from the command line. Check out Chapter 1, "Launching and Using the Command Prompt," if you don't remember how to do this.

> **TIP:** If you're troubleshooting a system that won't boot, you can boot using an installation DVD. When you reach the screen where you select the language, time and currency format, and keyboard or input method, press **Shift+F10**. This will launch the command prompt. You can then access the **bcdedit** tool.

## Commands That Operate on a Store

If you want to manipulate the BCD store, you should first ensure that you have a good backup. That way, no matter what you do, you can always return the store to its original condition. You can back up the store with the **/export** switch and restore it with the **/import** switch, as shown in the following table.

| Command | Description |
|---|---|
| `/export`<br>`bcdedit /export` *path and filename*<br>`C:\>bcdedit /export`<br>`"c:\data\bcdbackup"` | Exporting the store is similar to backing it up. If you've exported it, you can later import it to restore it.<br><br>The command will create a file named bcdbackup in the c:\data folder.<br><br>**NOTE:** If the path and filename has a space, you need to enclose it in quotes, but if it doesn't have spaces, you don't need the quotes. |
| `/import`<br>`bcdedit /import` *path and filename*<br>`C:\>bcdedit /import`<br>`"c:\data\bcdbackup"` | If you've exported the BCD store with the **/export** switch, you can import it with the **/import** switch. You only need to specify the path to the exported fie. |
| `/createstore`<br>`bcdedit /createstore` *path and*<br>*filename*<br>`C:\>bcdedit /createstore c:\data\`<br>`newstore` | You can create a new empty store with the **/createstore** switch. This example shows how to create a new store named newstore.<br><br>**NOTE:** The new store starts completely empty. |
| `/store`<br>`bcdedit /store` *path and filename*<br>`C:\>bcdedit /store`<br>`c:\data\bcdbackup`<br>`C:\>bcdedit /store`<br>`c:\data\newstore` | You can view the contents of any store, including stores that you've exported or created. |

## Commands That Control Output

After you back up the store, you'll want to start taking a look at it. You can view contents of the store using the /v and /enum switches, as shown in the following table.

| Command | Description |
|---|---|
| `/v`<br>`C:\>bcdedit /v` | The **/v** switch enables you to get verbose output with more details. A useful purpose of this switch is to determine the GUID of a Windows Boot Loader.<br><br>**TIP:** The current Windows Boot Loader can be referred to as {current} without the GUID. However, when you use the **/v** switch, it will display the GUID. |

| | |
|---|---|
| ```/enum type```<br>```bcdedit /enum [active | bootapp |```<br>```bootmgr | osloader | resume | all]```<br>```C:\>bcdedit /enum all```<br>```C:\>bcdedit /enum osloader```<br>```C:\>bcdedit /enum resume```<br>```C:\>bcdedit /enum resume /v``` | You can enumerate, or list, the entries in the BCD store with the **/enum** switch followed by the type of entries you want to list.<br><br>**NOTE:** The default type is active, so entering bcdedit is the same as entering bcdedit /enum active.<br><br>Other types are as follows:<br><br>**all**: Lists all entries.<br><br>**osloader**: Lists the operating system entries.<br><br>**resume**: Lists the hibernation entries.<br><br>**bootapp**: Lists all boot environment applications.<br><br>**bootmgr**: Lists only the Boot Manager data.<br><br>Any of the switches can be combined with the **/v** switch to get a little more information. |

## Commands That Control the Boot Manager

Several switches are available that can modify the Boot Manager. This is the first section that appears when you run **bcdedit**. It controls what Boot Loaders are available, their order, and how long to wait before starting the default operating system.

> **TIP:** When entering the GUID in the **bcdedit** command, you need to enclose it within curly braces, **{ }**. In other words, just entering **923aaead-84c0-11de-bac6-00235a33c4ca** will *not* work. It must be entered as **{923aaead-84c0-11de-bac6-00235a33c4ca}**.

| Command | Description |
|---|---|
| `/bootsequence`<br>`bcdedit /bootsequence GUID [`<br>`/addfirst | /addlast | /remove ]`<br>`C:\>bcdedit /bootsequence`<br>`{923aaead-84c0-11de-bac6-`<br>`00235a33c4c } /addfirst`<br>`C:\>bcdedit /bootsequence`<br>`{923aaead-84c0-11de-bac6-`<br>`00235a33c4c } /addlast`<br>`c:\>bcdedit /bootsequence`<br>`{923aaead-84c0-11de-bac6-`<br>`00235a33c4c } /remove` | You change the boot sequence of operating systems for the next boot with the **/bootsequence** switch. This can be useful if you want the system to boot into the recovery operating system on the next boot. After the next boot, the BCD store will revert to the original sequence.<br><br>The example shows how to change the boot sequence with a specified GUID.<br><br>**TIP:** Remember, you can cut and paste the GUID from the command prompt. You don't have to type it in from scratch.<br><br>You can use the **/remove** switch to remove it from the boot sequence. However, it doesn't actually remove the Windows Boot Loader section. The **/delete** switch (shown later in this section) permanently removes the Windows Boot Loader. |
| `/default`<br>`bcdedit /default [GUID]`<br>`C:\>bcdedit /default {18b61673-`<br>`3f06-11de-b3f5-00242106d5b2}` | You can use the **/default** switch to change the default boot operating system. When you install another operating system on an existing system, the newer operating system is usually set as the default. This command enables you to change the default back to the original, or to any other operating system. |
| `/displayorder`<br>`bcdedit /displayorder GUID [ GUID ]`<br>`bcdedit /displayorder GUID /addfirst`<br>`C:\>bcdedit /default`<br>`{923aaeaf-84c0-11de-bac6-`<br>`00235a33c4ca} {18b61673-3f06-11de-`<br>`b3f5-00242106d5b2}`<br>`C:\>bcdedit /default {923aaeaf-`<br>`84c0-11de-bac6-00235a33c4ca}`<br>`/addfirst` | The **/displayorder** switch sets the order in which the Boot Manager displays a multiboot menu. You can enter the GUIDs in the exact order in which you want them displayed, or you can use the **/addfirst** or **/addlast** switches to modify the order.<br><br>You can also use the **/remove** switch to remove a GUID from the display order. Note that the **/remove** GUID doesn't remove the Windows Boot Loader entry, but only removes it from the display order list. You can still view the entry if you use the **bcdedit /enum all** command, and you can return it to the list with either the **/addfirst** or **/addlast** command. |

| `/timeout`<br>`bcdedit /timeout` *xx*<br>`C:\>bcdedit /timeout 15` | The **/timeout** switch is used to set the Boot Manager time-out value. If a user doesn't press a key, the Boot Manager automatically launches the default operations system when the count (given in seconds) is reached. The example changes it to 15 seconds. |
| --- | --- |
| `/toolsdisplayorder`<br>`bcdedit /toolsdisplayorder` *GUID*<br>`bcdedit /toolsdisplayorder` *GUID*<br>`/addfirst \| /addlast`<br>`C:\>bcdedit /toolsdisplayorder`<br>`{123aaeaf-84c0-11de-bac6-00235a33c-`<br>`4ca} /addlast`<br>`C:\>bcdedit /toolsdisplayorder`<br>`{123aaeaf-84c0-11de-bac6-00235a33c-`<br>`4ca} /addfirst` | You can use **/toolsdisplayorder** to add, remove, and modify the order in which tools are displayed. By default, the only tool is the Memory Diagnostic Tool (**memdiag**).<br><br>This works similarly to how the **/displayorder** switch works, except the tools menu is displayed at the bottom of the boot menu. |

You can also use the System Configuration tool (shown in Figure 14-2) to manipulate the BCD store. You don't have as many options, but you can do simple things, such as changing the timeout, from this screen.

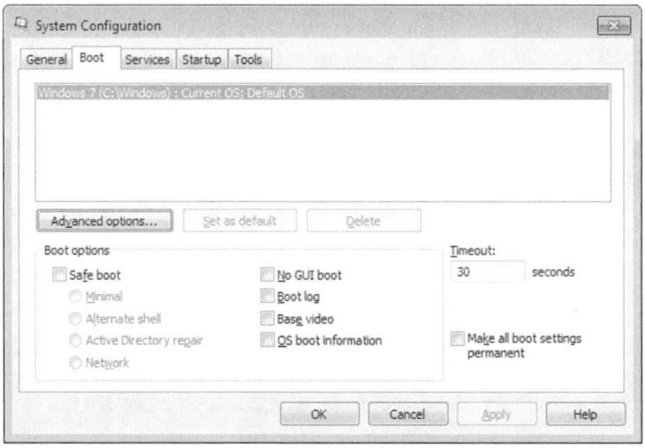

**Figure 14-2**   System Configuration Tool Boot Tab

**TIP:** You can access the System Configuration tool by entering **msconfig** from the command prompt or the Search Programs and Files text box from the Start menu.

## Commands That Operate on Entries in the Store

You might occasionally want to copy or delete Windows Boot Loader entries in the BCD store. For example, you might want to copy an entry, make some changes, and test it before you finalize the changes. If they don't work, you can delete the entry and start over.

| Command | Description |
|---------|-------------|
| /copy<br>bcdedit /copy [GUID] /d "descrip-<br>tion"<br>C:\>bcdedit /copy {current} /d<br>"Copied Windows 7 Boot Loader" | Makes a copy of a Windows Boot Loader entry with the specified description. You can use {current} for the current Boot Loader instead of the GUID. |
| /delete<br>bcdedit /delete [GUID]<br>C:\>bcdedit /delete {820cac52-a49a-<br>11df-bc17-0003ff9c0200} | The **/delete** switch permanently deletes the Windows Boot Loader entry from the store.<br><br>You can use **bcdedit** to retrieve the GUID. |

## Commands That Operate on Entry Options

There might be times when you need to modify individual entries in the Windows Boot Manager and Windows Boot Loader sections. The primary switch you'll use is the **/set** switch.

| Command | Description |
|---------|-------------|
| /set<br>bcdedit /set GUID DATA TYPE VALUE<br>C:\>bcdedit /set {current} device<br>partition=c:<br>C:\>bcdedit /set {4dbbe916-9901-<br>11df-948b-8f16cf2e7b02} descrip-<br>tion "Windows 7 Ultimate" | The **/set** command can be used to set the value of specific data types to specific values. There is a lengthy list of what these data types and values are, but the examples show a couple of values you can set. |

**TIP:** If you want to learn more about available **bcdedit** commands, check out Microsoft's reference document called "BCDedit_reff.docx for Windows Vista and Windows Server 2008." You can find it by searching TechNet (http://technet.micro-soft.com/) with **bcdedit reference**. At this writing, there isn't a version available for Windows 7 and Windows Server 2008 R2, but perhaps when you search there will be updates to the reference.

## Disable Driver Signing

The following table shows how you can disable driver signing checks. This allows you to install unsigned drivers.

| Command | Description |
|---|---|
| /set<br>C:\>bcdedit /set loadoptions<br>disable_integrity_check<br>C:\>bcdedit /set testsigning on | First, set the load options to point to **disable_integrity_check**.<br><br>You then turn it on with the **on** variable. This equates to Disable On. In other words, the check for digital signatures is disabled.<br><br>You can now install unsigned drivers.<br><br>**NOTE:** Some documentation indicates that the disable integrity check option is **ddisable_integrity_check** (with two d's). Both **ddisable_integrity_check** and **disable_integrity_check** work within the command. |
| C:\>bcdedit /set loadoptions<br>disable_integrity_check<br>C:\>bcdedit /set testsigning off | You can turn it off using **off** instead of **on**. This equates to Disable Off, meaning that driver signing is enforced again. |

## Creating a System Repair Disc with recdisc

You can create a recovery disc with the **recdisc** command. You simply enter **recdisc** at the command prompt and a display similar to Figure 14-3 will appear. You might need to select a drive.

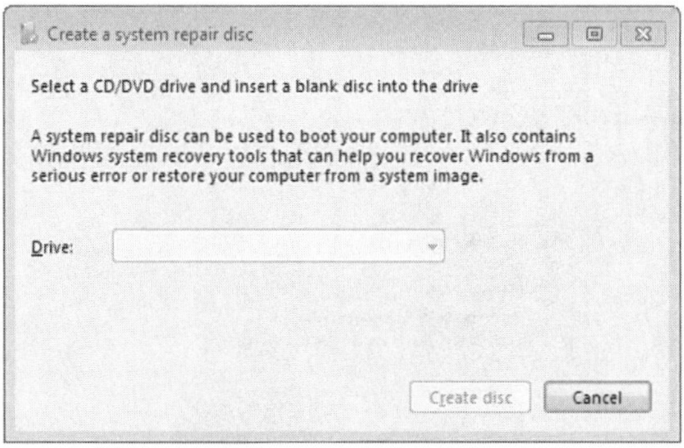

**Figure 14-3**   Creating a System Repair Disc with recdisc

Ensure **Insert** a blank CD into your writeable CD drive and click **Create Disc**. **recdisc** will create a bootable CD with system recovery tools that you can use to recover Windows 7 installations.

If you create a recovery disc while booted into a 64-bit version of Windows 7, **recdisc** will create a 64-bit bootable CD that will work only on 64-bit systems. However, if you create it on a 32-bit version of Windows 7, recdisc will create 32-bit version that will work on both 32- and 64-bit versions.

After you create the CD, you boot into it if you encounter a problem starting Windows. The first screen prompts you to choose your keyboard. Click **Next** and it will search for operating systems on the system and start the recovery procedures. It may automatically locate the problems and prompt you to repair them and restart your computer. Simply click **Repair** and **Restart** and you might be able to boot into your operating system.

> **TIP:** If you're troubleshooting a system that won't boot, you can start a repair manually. First, boot to the installation DVD. When you reach the screen where you select the language, time and currency format, and keyboard or input method, press **Shift+F10**. This will launch the command prompt. You can then run the StartRep.exe application located in the \sources\recovery folder of the installation DVD.

## Checking and Repairing Disks with chkdsk

The **chkdsk** command has been around a long time, but it's still very useful. If you run it from the command prompt, it will check the current volume and report any problems it discovers. You can also run it to fix any problems it discovers. This can be a very valuable tool if you encounter a drive on its last legs. You can often fix the problems and back up the drive before it's gone for good.

You can also launch the Check Disk tool from Windows Explorer, as shown in Figure 14-4. You can access this tool by opening Windows Explorer, right-clicking a drive, selecting **Properties**, and then selecting the **Tools** tab. If you click **Check Now**, the Check Disk dialog box appears.

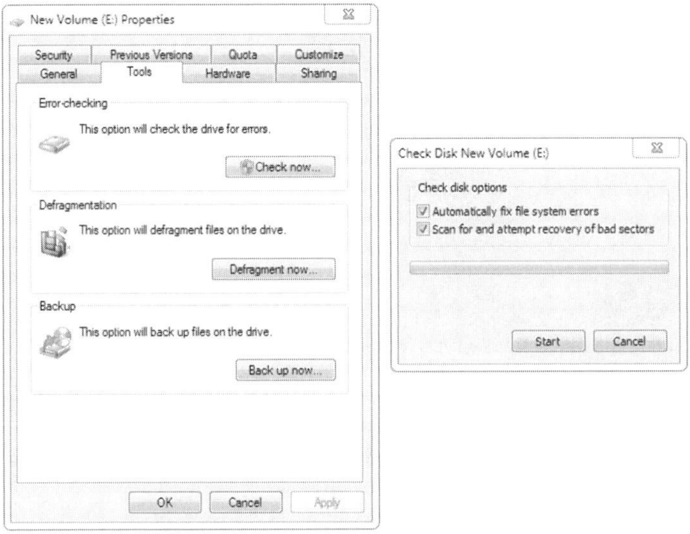

**Figure 14-4**   Checking Disks with Windows Explorer

If you run the tool from the command line, you'll be able to immediately see the results of the scan as it checks the drive. The following table shows these results from a successful scan.

| Command | Description |
|---|---|
| `C:\>chkdsk`<br>`The type of the file system is NTFS.`<br>`WARNING!  F parameter not specified.`<br>`Running CHKDSK in read-only mode.` | **chkdsk** can be run without any parameters on the current drive. It first identifies the file system. It will usually be NTFS, except on USB drives. The F parameter (or **/f** switch) will fix problems, but without the **/f** switch, **chkdsk** will only check the system and report problems, not fix them. |
| `CHKDSK is verifying files (stage 1`<br>`of 3)...`<br>`   55552 file records processed.`<br>`File verification completed.`<br>`   36 large file records processed.`<br>`   0 bad file records processed.`<br>`   2 EA records processed.`<br>`   44 reparse records processed.` | The first stage of **chkdsk** verifies files.<br><br>A report indicating 0 bad files is good. |
| `CHKDSK is verifying indexes (stage 2`<br>`of 3)...`<br>`   75680 index entries processed.`<br>`Index verification completed.`<br>`   0 unindexed files scanned.`<br>`   0 unindexed files recovered.` | The second stage verifies indexes. If any problems are discovered, they are reported here. |
| `CHKDSK is verifying security de-`<br>`scriptors (stage 3 of 3)...`<br>`   55552 file SDs/SIDs processed.`<br>`Security descriptor verification`<br>`completed.`<br>`   10065 data files processed.`<br>`CHKDSK is verifying Usn Journal...`<br>`   34575008 USN bytes processed.`<br>`Usn Journal verification completed.` | In the third stage, **chkdsk** verifies security descriptors (such as access control lists) and the Usn Journal.<br><br>The Usn Journal is a persistent log of all changes made on the drive. It works similarly to a database log for a database. When changes are made to the drive, they are first recorded to the Usn Journal and then later committed to the hard drive. NTFS is better able to survive surprise power losses without the system shifting into blue screen mode where it just won't boot. |

| | |
|---|---|
| `Windows has checked the file system`<br>`and found no problems.`<br>`  92102655 KB total disk space.`<br>`  13104516 KB in 35341 files.`<br>`    26656 KB in 10066 indexes.`<br>`        0 KB in bad sectors.`<br>`   158283 KB in use by the system.`<br>`    65536 KB occupied by the log`<br>`file.`<br>`   78813200 KB available on disk.`<br>`      4096 bytes in each allocation`<br>`unit.`<br>`   23025663 total allocation units on`<br>`disk.`<br>`   19703300 allocation units avail-`<br>`able on disk.` | **chkdsk** then summarizes its findings. In this example, no problems were discovered. |

There are several switches you can use with **chkdsk**. The most important switch is the **/f** switch, which actually fixes problems that are discovered on a drive.

| Command | Description |
|---|---|
| `/f`<br>`E:\>chkdsk /f` | Fixes any errors that are discovered on the disk. |
| `/v`<br>`E:\>chkdsk /f /v` | Verbose mode works differently on FAT/FAT32 drives and NTFS drives. On NTFS drives, it displays cleanup messages if any cleanup is done. On FAT/FAT32 drives, it displays the full path and name of every file on the disk. |
| `/x`<br>`E:\>chkdsk /f /x` | You can use the **/x** switch to force a check of the drive even if it's being held by other processes. This implies the **/f** switch because you can check the drives in read-only mode even if other processes have them locked.<br><br>This will not override a check of the boot or system partition. You must schedule these to be checked and fixed on the next boot.<br><br>If a drive cannot be accessed because it's held by a different process, you'll see an error similar to this:<br><br>`Chkdsk cannot run because the volume is in use by`<br>`another process. Chkdsk may run if this volume is`<br>`dismounted first.`<br>`ALL OPENED HANDLES TO THIS VOLUME WOULD THEN BE`<br>`INVALID.`<br>`Would you like to force a dismount on this volume?`<br>`(Y/N)` |

| | |
|---|---|
| | If you press **N** for No, you'll then see this message:<br><br>`Chkdsk cannot run because the volume is in use by`<br>`another process. Would you like to schedule this`<br>`volume to be checked the next time the system re-`<br>`starts? (Y/N)`<br>You can press **Y** to schedule it. |
| /r<br>`E:\>chkdsk /r` | Locates bad sectors and recovers readable information. This switch implies **/f**, meaning it will fix the problems that it finds. |
| /1:*size*<br>`chkdsk /1:xxxx`<br>`E:\>chkdsk /1:8192`<br>`e:\>chkdsk /1` | You can use the **/l** switch to change the log file size for NTFS volumes. The size is entered in KB. Without a number, it displays information on the current log file size. |
| /i<br>`E:\>chkdsk /i` | This performs a check of index entries. It doesn't take as long as a full check. You can combine it with the **/f** switch to fix any problems that are discovered. |
| /b<br>`E:\>chkdsk /b` | When a hard disk is first formatted, clusters are checked and marked as bad. This assumes that a quick format has not been done, which skips this check.<br><br>You can use the **/b** switch to check the disk for bad clusters and mark any bad clusters it discovers. |

# Repairing BitLocker Drives with repair-bde

The **repair-bde** command can be used to repair damaged BitLocker encrypted drives as long as you have the recovery key or recovery password.

**repair-bde** is unable to repair a drive that failed during the encryption or decryption process. It assumes that if any of the drive is encrypted, all of it is encrypted. If BitLocker failed during an encryption or decryption process, you'll need to restore the data from your backup. Of course, this brings up an important point.

> **TIP:** You should encrypt a drive only after backing up all the important data. While the mass majority of encryption processes complete without incident, encryption does have the potential to render the drive unreadable if the process is somehow interrupted prior to completion.

The general syntax of **repair-bde** is

`repair-bde` *source drive destination drive* `-rk` | `-rp`

| Command | Description |
|---|---|
| `-rk` *filename and path*<br>`repair-bde` *source destination* `-rk`<br>*filename and path*<br>`D:\>repair-bde c: d: -rk`<br>`f:\reckey.bek` | You can specify a recovery key from a recovery key file using the filename and path of the recovery key file.<br><br>This example will recover the c: drive to the D: drive using the recovery key stored in the F:\reckey.bek file. |
| `-rp` *recovery password*<br>`repair-bde` *source destination* `-rp`<br>*recovery password*<br>`D:\>repair-bde c: d: -rp 111111-`<br>`222222-333333-444444-555555-666666-`<br>`777777-888888` | The recovery password switch (**-rp**) enables you to enter the recovery password at the command line.<br><br>This example will recover the c: drive to the D: drive using the recovery key stored in the F:\reckey.bek file. |
| `-f` *filename and path*<br>`D:\>repair-bde c: d: -rk`<br>`f:\reckey.bek /f` | The **-f** switch forces a volume to be dismounted even if it cannot be locked. |
| `-lf` *log file path and name*<br>`repair-bde c: d: -rk f:\reckey.bek`<br>`-lf` *log file path and name*<br>`D:\>repair-bde c: d: -rk`<br>`f:\reckey.bek -lf d:\rbdelog.txt` | You can log the results to a log file with the **-lf** switch. |

**TIP:** If you don't have the recovery password or recovery key, you won't be able to recover a drive with **repair-bde**. This might be a good time to review the procedures used to store BitLocker recovery data. For example, if you're in a domain, you can store it in Active Directory and then easily view it using the BitLocker Recovery Password Viewer for Active Directory. Check out these TechNet articles for more information: "Backing Up BitLocker and TPM Recovery Information to AD DS" (http://technet.microsoft.com/dd875529.aspx) and "BitLocker Recovery Password Viewer for Active Directory" (http://technet.microsoft.com/dd875531.aspx).

This chapter provides information and commands concerning the following topics:

- Configuring Windows 7 for remote administration
- Connecting to remote systems with **mstsc**
- Configuring Windows Remote Management with **winrm**
- Executing commands remotely with **winrs**

## Configuring Windows 7 for Remote Administration

Before you can remotely administer a Windows 7 system, it needs to be configured.
There are different ways of doing this depending on what you're trying to accomplish.

| Goal | Method to Enable It |
|------|---------------------|
| Connect to a remote system with Remote Desktop Connection (RDC). | Enable Remote Desktop via the System Properties dialog box. |
| Connect to a remote system using an MMC snap-in such as Event Viewer. | Enable the firewall. |
| Connect to a remote system to execute **winrs** commands. | Enable with **winrm quickconfig**. |

These three tasks are described in more depth in the following sections.

### Configuring System for Remote Desktop Connection (RDC)

Remote Desktop Connection enables you to connect to a system and control the desktop.
However, this is not enabled by default. You can access the screen to enable RDC by
clicking **Start**, right-clicking **Computer**, clicking **Properties**, and clicking the **Remote**
tab. You'll see a screen similar to Figure 15-1.

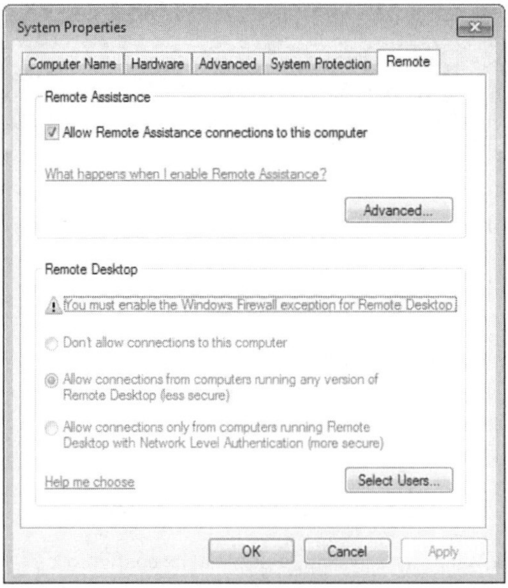

**Figure 15-1**  Enabling Remote Desktop

There are three possible settings, as described in the following table.

| Setting | Description |
|---|---|
| Don't allow connections to this computer | Remote Desktop connections are blocked. |
| Allow connections from computers running any version of Remote Desktop (less secure) | Remote Desktop connections are allowed from any computer running the Remote Desktop protocol. |
| Allow connections only from computers running Remote Desktop with Network Level Authentication (more secure) | Older computers such as Windows XP do not natively support Network Level Authentication (NLA) so they will be blocked from connecting. |

**TIP:** You can use any version of Windows 7 to connect to another host with RDC. However, only Windows 7 Professional and greater allow you to run RDC as a host and accept connections. Other versions won't have settings to allow you to enable Remote Desktop.

Figure 15-1 shows that the computer is enabled for Remote Desktop from any computer that supports the Remote Desktop protocol.

However, the warning shows that the Windows Firewall exception is not enabled. You can enable it by clicking the Warning link.. In some situations, you might need to manually configure the exception. You can enable the Windows Firewall exception with the following steps:

**Step 1.** Click **You Must Enable the Windows Firewall Exception for Remote Desktop**.

**Step 2.** Review the information in the Help and Support topic and select **Click to Open Windows Firewall**.

**Step 3.** Select **Allow a Program or Feature Through Windows Firewall**, as shown in Figure 15-2.

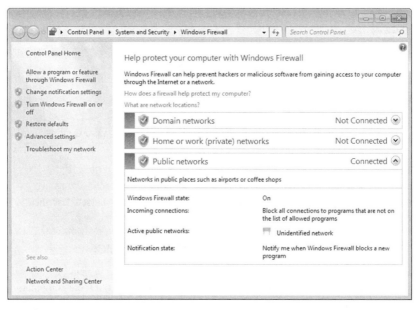

**Figure 15-2** Accessing the Windows Firewall

**Step 4.** Click the Change Settings button.

**Step 5.** Scroll to the Remote Desktop settings. Check the Remote Desktop check box for the desired profile(s). Figure 15-3 shows the Remote Desktop exception enabled for the Domain profile and for the Home/Work (Private) profile, but not for the Public profile.

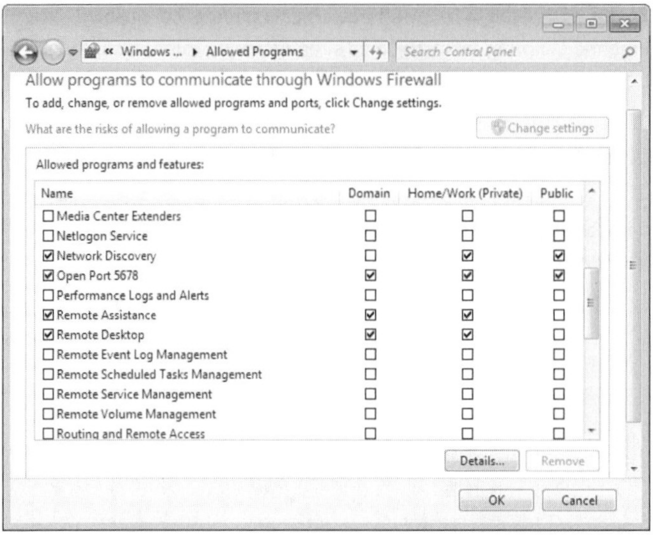

**Figure 15-3** Adding the Remote Desktop Exception to the Firewall

**Step 6.**  Click OK in the Windows Firewall Allowed Programs window and close other open windows.

At this point, the Windows 7 system is configured to allow remote connections using RDC. The upcoming section "Connecting to Remote Systems with **mstsc**" describes how to connect using RDC.

## Configuring System for Remote Access Using an MMC

You can use most Microsoft Management Console (MMC) snap-ins to manage the local computer or remote computers. However, if you want to manage the remote computer, the remote computer must first be configured to accept the connection.

> **TIP:** If you try to connect to the remote snap-in but receive the error message "The RPC server is unavailable," the primary thing to check is the firewall on the remote system. Ensure that the appropriate rules allow the access. An easy way to verify this is to temporarily disable Windows Firewall with Advanced Security for the profile you're using (Domain, Private, or Public). If you can connect after disabling the firewall, you know that you just need to identify the inbound rule to enable.

Different snap-ins have different Windows Firewall inbound rules that need to be enabled. Figure 15-4 shows Windows Firewall with Advanced Security. If you want to manage the Event Viewer remotely, you need to enable the Remote Event Log Management rules for the appropriate profile.

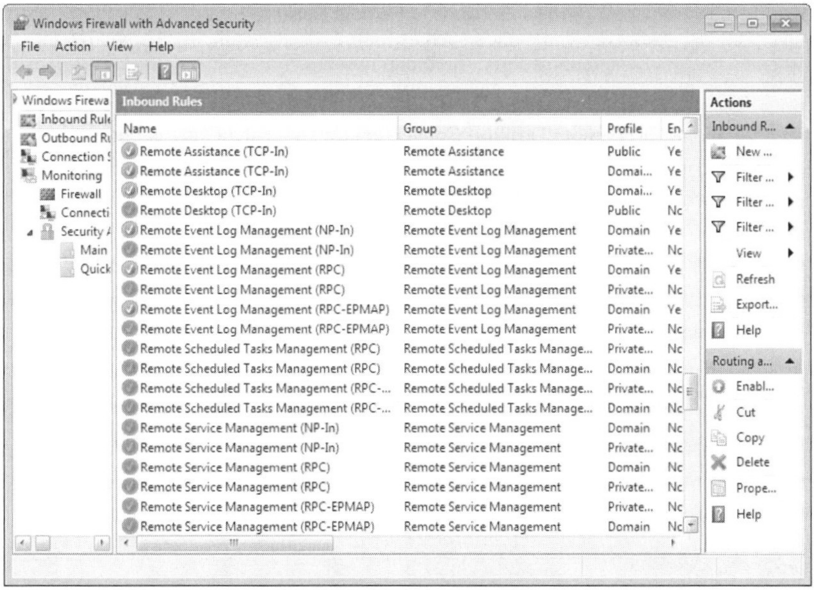

**Figure 15-4**   Viewing the Windows Firewall with Advanced Security Inbound Rules

The following table identifies the different inbound rules to enable for remote administration of the different MMCs.

| Snap-in | Firewall Exception |
|---|---|
| Event Viewer | Remote Event Log Management |
| Task Scheduler | Remote Scheduled Tasks Management |
| Services | Remote Service Management |
| Disks | Remote Volume Management |
| Other MMCs (such as Computer Management) | File and Printer Sharing |

**NOTE:** You need to enable the rule only for the profile you're using. For example, if
the remote computer is in a domain, enable the rule for the Domain profile. Otherwise,
enable it for the Private profile. It's unlikely you'll be enabling the exception for the
Public profile.

# Connecting to Remote Systems with mstsc

You can launch Remote Desktop Connection from the command line with the **mstsc**
command. This command name is short for Microsoft Terminal Services Connection.
You can enter it from the command prompt or the Search box after clicking Start.

> **TIP:** Microsoft renamed Terminal Services to Remote Desktop Services in Windows Server 2008 R2. However, commands such as **mstsc** will still work. In other words, the command has not been renamed from **mstsc** to **msrdsc**.

Figure 15-5 shows the Remote Desktop Connection tool after the Options button in the lower-left corner has been clicked. You can also access this by choosing **Start, All Programs, Accessories, Remote Desktop Connection**.

**Figure 15-5**  Remote Desktop Connection

At this point, you can enter the computer name and click **Connect**. You'll be prompted to enter the credentials of a user that has permission to log on remotely.

> **NOTE:** You can configure the settings you want for the connection in any of the tabs and then click **Save As** to save the settings as an .rdp configuration file. You can then use this file to connect.

Some of the switches you can use with **mstsc** are shown in the following table.

| Switch | Description |
|---|---|
| Using a connection file:<br><br>**mstsc** *file path and name*<br>C:\>**mstsc c:\data\dc1.rdp** | If you have an .rdp file that includes the connection information, you can use it with **mstsc**. You won't need to reconfigure all the settings each time you connect to a server. |

| | |
|---|---|
| `/v:server[:port]`<br>`C:\>mstsc /v:dc1`<br>`C:\>mstsc /v:dc1:5678` | The **/v** switch enables you to specify which server to connect to and specify the port.<br><br>The default port is 3389 but it can be changed. For example, if the port was changed to 5678, you could use the example command. |
| `/admin`<br>`C:\>mstsc /admin /v:dc1` | Connects to one of the two administrator sessions. This is the default as long as the remote server is not running Remote Desktop Services as a Session Host server. In other words, as long as the remote server is not hosting RDS desktops or applications, the **/admin** switch is not needed.<br><br>**NOTE:** Microsoft recommends using this instead of the **/console** switch to connect to Windows Server 2003 servers from Windows 7 or Windows Server 2008 servers. |
| `/console`<br>`C:\>mstsc /console`<br>`The preferred method is:`<br>`C:\>mstsc /admin /v:dc1` | This was used to connect to the console session for Windows Server 2003 computers. However, it has been deprecated and will cause errors in certain situations, so it should be replaced with the **/admin** switch. It is ignored when connecting to a Windows Server 2008 or Windows Server 2008 R2 server. |
| `/f`<br>`C:\>mstsc /f /v:dc1` | Connect in full screen mode. |
| `/w:number`<br>`mstsc /w:number`<br>`c:\>mstsc /w:800 /v:dc1` | Specifies the width of the screen in pixels. This directly affects the displayed resolution. |
| `/h:number`<br>`mstsc /h: number`<br>`C:\>mstsc /h:600 /w:800 /v:dc1` | Specifies the height of the screen in pixels. This directly affects the displayed resolution.<br><br>The example specifies a screen size of 800 by 600 pixels. |
| `/span`<br>`C:\>mstsc /span /v:dc1` | Allows spanning across multiple monitors if the local computer is using multiple monitors.<br><br>Matches the Remote Desktop width and height with the local virtual desktop. |
| `/multimon`<br>`C:\>mstsc /multimon /v:dc1` | Configures the Remote Desktop session monitor layout to be identical to the current client-side configuration. |
| `/public`<br>`C:\>mstsc /public /v:dc1` | Runs RDC without caching the passwords and bitmaps. |

| | |
|---|---|
| `/edit file path and name`<br>`C:\>mstsc /edit c:\data\dc1.rdp` | This command opens the RDC console. You can then edit the settings and save over the original .rdp file by clicking Save.<br><br>**TIP:** The .rdp file is a simple text file. It's also possible to view and/or edit the file in Notepad by entering **notepad** *file path and name*. |

**NOTE**: Windows Server 2008 and Windows Server 2008 R2 servers are limited to only two remote administrator connections at a time. In Windows Server 2003, you could connect to the console remotely giving you access to three sessions. However, the console session is not available for remote connectivity in Windows Server 2008 and Windows Server 2008 R2.

## Configuring Windows Remote Management with winrm

Windows Remote Management (**winrm**) is Microsoft's implementation of the WS-Management Protocol. This is used to execute commands from the command line on one computer to view or manipulate the configuration on another computer. However, before you can execute **winrs** commands (discussed in the next section), you must first configure the remote system. The command is

`winrm quickconfig`

The system will respond with

```
WinRM is not set up to receive requests on this machine.
The following changes must be made:


Set the WinRM service type to delayed auto start.
Start the WinRM service.


Make these changes [y/n]?
```

If you run this on a computer that is not in a domain, you'll also see this as one of the items to be changed:

```
Configure LocalAccountTokenFilterPolicy to grant administrative rights
remotely to local users.
```

If you press **Y** to make the changes, it will then respond with

```
WinRM has been updated to receive requests.
WinRM service type changed successfully.
WinRM service started.
WinRM is not set up to allow remote access to this machine for manage-
ment.
```

The following changes must be made:

Create a WinRM listener on HTTP://* to accept WS-Man requests to any IP
on this machine.
Enable the WinRM firewall exception.

Make these changes [y/n]?

> **TIP:** If you are trying to configure a domain computer and get an Access Denied error
> with the code WSMANFault -2147024891, it indicates you are logged on locally. The
> local administrator account doesn't have permission to make this change if the com-
> puter is a member of the domain.

If you press **Y** to make the changes, it will then respond with

WinRM has been updated for remote management.
Created a WinRM listener on HTTP://* to accept WS-Man requests to any IP
on this machine.
WinRM firewall exception enabled.

At this point, you can begin executing remote commands against the system by using
**winrs**.

> **NOTE:** The **winrm** tool includes many other commands you can enter. However, these
> tools are rarely used on desktop computers.

## Executing Commands Remotely with winrs

**winrs** is a command-line tool you can use to execute commands on remote systems. The
basic syntax is

```
winrs -r:system command
```

You specify the name of the remote system using its hostname, and then you can execute just about any command that you can execute from the local command prompt.

For example, if you simply wanted to view what is in the DNS cache of a remote system
named win7pcg, you could use this command:

```
winrs -r:win7pcg ipconfig /displaydns
```

Other switches you can use with **winrs** are shown in the following table.

| Switch | Description |
| --- | --- |
| -u username<br>C:\>winrs -r:win7pcg<br>-u:pearson\administrator<br>ipconfig /displaydns | You can specify a username with the -u switch.<br><br>This example will prompt you for a password. |

| `-u username -p password`<br>`C:\>winrs -r:win7pcg`<br>`-u:pearson\administrator`<br>`-p:P@ssw0rd ipconfig`<br>`/displaydns` | If you use the **-u** switch for a username, you can also include the **-p** switch with the password to avoid the prompt for a password. |
|---|---|
| `-d directory path`<br>`C:\>winrs -r:win7pcg -d:c:`<br>`\data ipconfig /displaydns` | Specify the starting directory for the remote shell. It will normally start in the user profile of the user account executing the command.<br><br>This is identified by %userprofile% and is c:\ users\*username* on most systems. |
| `-nop`<br>`C:\>winrs -r:win7pcg -nop`<br>`ipconfig /displaydns` | Specifies that the user's profiles should not be loaded to the remote system. |

This chapter provides information and commands concerning the following topics:

- Understanding **wmic**
- Configuring the firewall to allow **wmic**
- Running **wmic**
- Modifying the format with the **/format** switch
- Retrieving help from **wmic**
- Understanding aliases
- Using verbs

## Understanding wmic

**wmic** is the command-line implementation of Windows Management Instrumentation (WMI). It extends WMI so that you can execute many WMI commands without a full understanding of the underlying details.

WMI is a group of technologies that allows different applications to interact with the Windows operating system. It is based on the Web-Based Enterprise Management (WBEM) standard and it's a full-blown scripting tool. Administrators use WMI scripting to perform a wide variety of administrative tasks, and WMI scripting is included in many third-party vendor tools.

> **NOTE:** Creating scripts with WMI is beyond the scope of this book. However, the scripting pros at Microsoft have an active website with a lot of rich content on WMI. Check it out here: http://technet.microsoft.com/dd742341.aspx.

Some of the most valuable commands and switches are summarized in the following table.

| Command | Description |
|---------|-------------|
| `wmic alias list brief`<br>`C:\>wmic alias list brief` | Retrieves a list of all aliases. |
| `wmic aliasname list full`<br>`C:\>wmic computersystem list full` | Retrieves a list of all properties and known values for any alias. |
| `wmic aliasname get /?`<br>`C:\>wmic computersystem get /?` | Retrieves a list of properties for an alias, including the data type and available operations. |
| `wmic aliasname set /?`<br>`C:\>wmic computersystem set /?` | Retrieves a list of properties for an alias that can be modified. The list includes the data type and available operations. |
| `/output:target`<br>`C:\>wmic /output:c:\data\cpu.txt`<br>`computersystem list full` | Redirects the output to a file. You can redirect the output to the Clipboard by using **/output:clipboard**. |
| `delete (a process)`<br>`wmic process where (name =`<br>`process-name) delete`<br>`C:\>wmic process where (name =`<br>`'notepad.exe') delete` | Deletes an instance of a running process. |

## Configuring the Firewall to Allow wmic

If you want to run **wmic** commands on remote computers, you may need to enable the firewall on the remote connections. The primary error you'll see that indicates that wmic commands are prevented by the firewall is "The RPC server is unavailable."

> **TIP:** You'll also see the error "The RPC server is unavailable" if the remote system is unreachable. You can try the **ping** command to determine if the remote system is operational and verify you're using the correct hostname.

You can configure the firewall to allow **wmic** commands by allowing the WMI program through the firewall in the proper profile. Figure 16-1 shows the window for doing so, which you can reach by starting the Control Panel, entering **Firewall** in the Search Control Panel text box, and selecting **Allowing a Program Through Windows Firewall**.

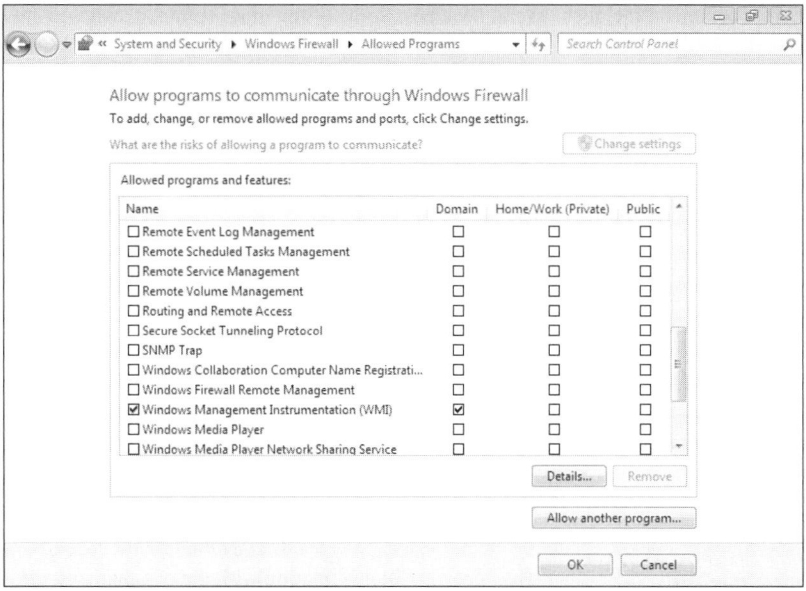

**Figure 16-1** Enabling Windows Management Instrumentation in the Firewall

# Running wmic

**wmic** is a shell command similar to **netsh**, covered in Chapter 11, "Configuring Windows 7 with netsh." You can enter **wmic** from the command prompt to enter the wmic shell. The wmic shell prompt starts in the root\cli name space, from which you can then enter commands. For example, if you want to get detailed information on the computer, you can use the **computersystem list full** command:

```
C:\>wmic
wmic:root\cli>computersystem list full
```

You can also enter the full **wmic** command from the command prompt by preceding it with **wmic**. For example, the following command provides the same output as the previous command:

```
C:\>wmic computersystem list full
```

If you were writing this within WMI (not **wmic**), you would have to understand the query language, and the query would look something like this:

```
Select * from Win32_ComputerSystem
```

However, thanks to the **wmic** built-in aliases, you don't have to learn the query language to use **wmic**.

The **wmic** command includes several switches. Some of the more common switches are listed in the following table.

**TIP:** Some commands don't recognize the switch unless it is entered before the command (right after **wmic**) rather than after the command (at the end of the **wmic** command string).

| Switch | Description |
|---|---|
| /? [:brief \| :full]<br>C:\>wmic /?<br>C:\>wmic /?:full | Shows the syntax of all global switches and aliases.<br><br>The default listing is **brief**, but you can also specify **full** to get a more verbose listing of help. |
| /node:*remotecomputer*<br>**wmic /node:***remotecomputer command*<br>C:\>**wmic /node:win7pcg** computersystem<br>C:\>**wmic /node:win7pcg** printer list brief | You can use the **/node** switch to retrieve information from any remote computers.<br><br>The first example retrieves information with the computersystem alias, and the second example uses the printer alias. |
| /user:*username*<br>**wmic /node:***remotecomputer* **/user:***username*<br>*command*<br>C:\>**wmic /node:win7pcg /user:pearson**<br>\administrator computersystem | Provides the username to be used during the session or for the command. You will be prompted to enter a password.<br><br>This is useful when connecting to remote systems, but it can't be used to change the credentials on the local system. |
| /password:*password*<br>**wmic /node:***remotecomputer* **/user:***username*<br>**/password:***password command*<br>C:\>**wmic /node:win7pcg /user:pearson**<br>\administrator /password:P@ssw0rd<br>computersystem | Provides the password to be used with the specified user. This command must be used with a username. |

| /output:*target* [**stdout** \| **clipboard** \| *file path and name*]<br>**wmic** /**node**:*remotecomputer* /**output**:*target command*<br>C:\>**wmic** /**node:win7pcg** /**output:clipboard computersystem**<br>C:\>**wmic** /**node:win7pcg** /**output:filename computersystem**<br>C:\>**wmic** /**node:win7pcg** /**output:c:\ scripts\test.txt computersystem** | Identifies where to redirect the output. The output is normally sent to the screen but can be sent to the Clipboard or to a file. The **/output** switch needs to go before the alias.<br><br>When sending it to a file, the path must exist or the command will fail with an "Invalid file name" error.<br><br>**TIP:** The normal redirect symbol (**>**) can also be used, as in the following example:<br><br>C:\>**wmic** /**node:win7pcg computersystem > c:\scripts\ test.txt** |
|---|---|
| /append:*target* [**stdout** \| **clipboard** \| *file path and name*]<br>C:\>**wmic** /**node**:*remotecomputer* /**append**:*filename command*<br>C:\>**wmic** /**node:win7pcg** /**append:c: \scripts\test.txt computersystem** | Identifies where to redirect the output.<br><br>If the file doesn't exist, it will be created. If it does exist, the output is appended to the file.<br><br>When sending it to a file, the path must exist or the command will fail with an "Invalid file name" error.<br><br>**NOTE:** The **/append** switch sends the data to the file and to the screen. |

## Modifying the Format with the /format Switch

The **/format** switch has a few more options that you might find useful. It can be very useful when you combine it with the **/output** switch to send the data to a file in a specific format.

> **TIP:** Each of these commands uses the **computersystem** alias. However, the format of the command is the same with any alias.

| Format Switch | Description |
|---|---|
| table<br>/format:table<br>C:\>wmic computersystem list full /<br>format:table | Formats the output as a table with headers. |
| list<br>/format:list<br>C:\>wmic computersystem list full /<br>format:list | Formats the output as a list of each property followed by the value. |
| csv<br>/format:csv<br>C:\>wmic computersystem list full /<br>format:csv<br>C:\>wmic /output:c:\data\test.csv<br>computersystem list full /format:csv | Formats the output as comma-separated values. The header is displayed first separated by commas. The data is then displayed separated by commas.<br><br>CSV files are easily read in Microsoft Excel, so it's common to use the output switch to send this data to a file.<br><br>**NOTE:** When you use the output switch, it needs go before the alias. |
| xml<br>/format:xml<br>C:\>wmic computersystem list full /<br>format:xml<br>C:\>wmic /output:c:\data\test.xml<br>computersystem list full /format:xml | Formats the output in Extensible Markup Language (XML) format.<br><br>If you enter the path to the XML file (such as C:\data\test.xml), the file opens in your web browser. |
| hform<br>C:\>wmic computersystem list full /<br>format:hform<br>C:\>wmic /output:c:\data\test.html<br>computersystem list full /format:hform | Formats the output as an HTML document. This is useful to display all the properties of an object on a separate row.<br><br>If you enter the path to the HTML file (such as C:\data\test.html), the file opens in your web browser.<br><br>Figure 16-2 shows the output of this command. |
| htable<br>C:\>wmic computersystem list brief<br>/format:htable<br>C:\>wmic /output:c:\data\test3.html<br>useraccount list brief /format:htable | Formats the output as an HTML document. In the table format, each object is a single row.<br><br>Figure 16-3 shows the output of this command. |

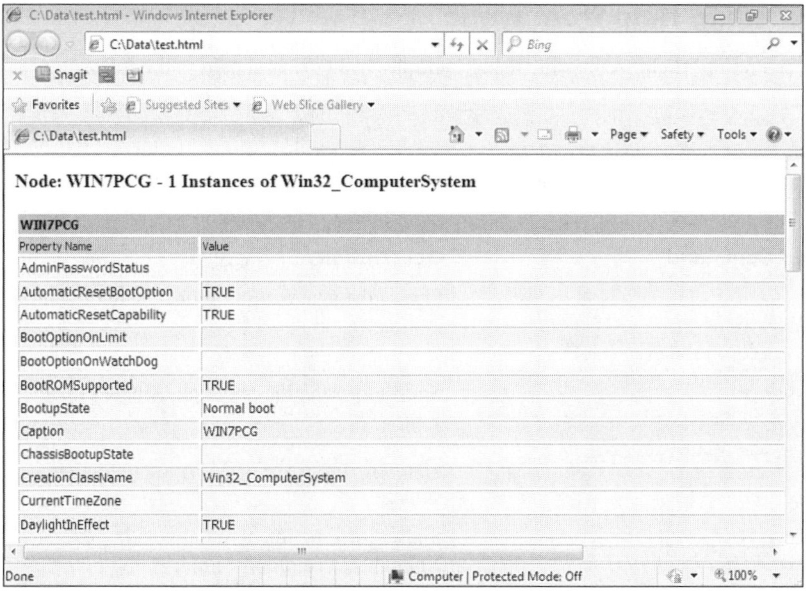

**Figure 16-2** Viewing the Output of **wmic** in Internet Explorer in hform Format

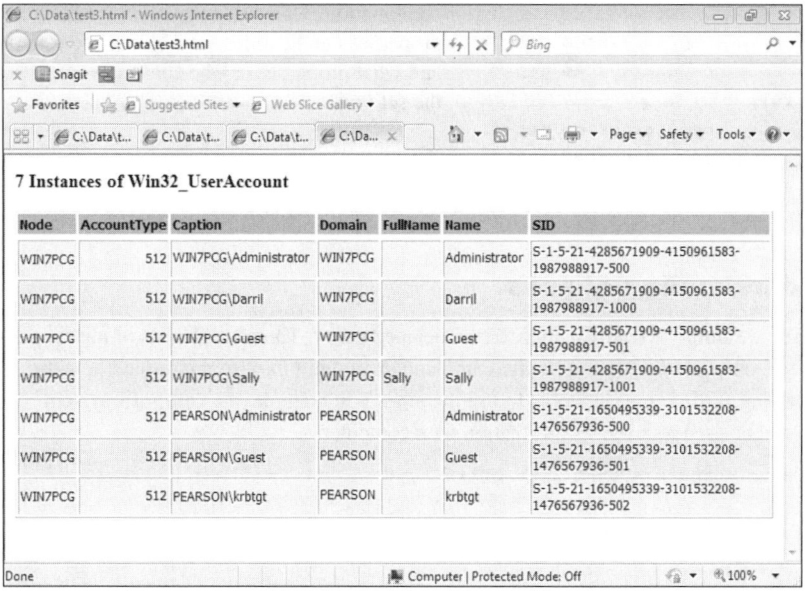

**Figure 16-3** Viewing the Output of **wmic** in Internet Explorer in htable Format

# Retrieving Help from wmic

You can retrieve help from **wmic** using multiple methods, as shown in the following table.

> **TIP:** Each of these help commands supports the **/?:full** clause. This sometimes provides more verbose output, but other times it doesn't provide any extra information.

| Help Command | Description |
|---|---|
| `/?`<br>`C:\>wmic /?`<br>`C:\>wmic /?:full` | Shows the syntax of all global switches and aliases. |
| `switch /?`<br>`/switch_name /?`<br>`C:\>wmic /output /?` | Shows information about any single global switch.<br><br>The example will show help on the output switch. |
| `alias /?`<br>`wmic alias /?`<br>`C:\>wmic computersystem /?` | Shows information about aliases in general when the word **alias** is used. If you give the name of an actual alias, it provides information on the alias. |
| `alias verb /?`<br>`wmic alias verb /?`<br>`C:\>wmic computersystem get /?`<br>`C:\>wmic computersystem get /?:full`<br>`C:\>wmic computersystem set /?`<br>`C:\>wmic computersystem set /?:full` | Shows information about one alias and verb combination. This can let you know what properties can be retrieved with the **get** verb and what properties can be configured with the **set** verb. |

# Understanding Aliases

Aliases are simply friendly names for the detailed query. There are dozens of aliases that you can enter instead of a full **wmic** command. You don't have to understand how the underlying WMI language works to use the alias. For example, the **computersystem** alias can be used to retrieve information on a computer:

```
C:\>wmic computersystem list brief
Domain        Manufacturer        Model          Name
PrimaryOwnerName  TotalPhysicalMemory


Pearson.pub  Microsoft Corporation  Virtual Machine  WIN7PCG
Darril            1610145792

C:\>wmic /node:dc1 computersystem list brief /format:list
```

```
Domain=Pearson.pub
Manufacturer=Microsoft Corporation
Model=Virtual Machine
Name=DC1
PrimaryOwnerName=Windows User
TotalPhysicalMemory=1610063872
```

The **/format:list** switch sends the output as a list instead of a table, which sometimes can be harder to read. The **list brief** clause is used to show some basic details. You can retrieve a much fuller output by using the **list full** clause:

> **TIP:** The **list full** clause sends the output in the list format by default, so this clause is not needed here.

```
C:\>wmic computersystem list full

AdminPasswordStatus=3
AutomaticResetBootOption=TRUE
.  .  .
Description=AT/AT COMPATIBLE
Domain=Pearson.pub
DomainRole=1
.  .  .
EnableDaylightSavingsTime=TRUE
.  .  .
Manufacturer=Microsoft Corporation
Model=Virtual Machine
Name=WIN7PCG
.  .  .
ThermalState=1
TotalPhysicalMemory=1610145792
UserName=PEARSON\Administrator
WakeUpType=6
Workgroup=
```

> **NOTE:** The entire output for **computersystem list full** spans multiple pages and thus is not listed in its entirety here.

The following tables show many of the aliases that are available. The first column shows the alias friendly name with a short description and its usage. The second column shows the Pwhere usage. If the alias will list multiple items, such as multiple services, you can retrieve data on a single item. WMI uses the Pwhere clause, but with **wmic** you only need to include the name between two single apostrophes. The third column shows the underlying WMI query that is executed.

**NOTE:** Some items have only a single instance, so a Pwhere clause is not defined within the alias.

## Operating System Aliases

The following table shows some aliases that can retrieve data on the operating system.

| Alias Friendly Name and Usage | Pwhere Format | WMI Query |
|---|---|---|
| computersystem<br><br>Details on installed operating system and settings<br><br>`C:\>wmic computersystem list brief` | Not defined | `Select * from Win32_ComputerSystem` |
| os<br><br>Operating system details<br><br>`C:\>wmic os list brief` | Not defined | `Select * from Win32_OperatingSystem` |
| environment<br><br>Listing of environment variables<br><br>`C:\>wmic environment list brief` | Not defined | `Select * from Win32_Environment` |
| sysdriver<br><br>Installed services and drivers and current state<br><br>`C:\>wmic sysdriver list brief` | Where Name='#'<br><br>`C:\>wmic sysdriver 'disk' list brief` | `Select * from Win32_SystemDriver` |
| service<br><br>System services<br><br>`C:\>wmic service list brief` | Where Name='#'<br><br>`C:\>wmic service 'winrm' list full` | `Select * from Win32_Service` |
| process<br><br>Running processes<br><br>`C:\>wmic process list brief` | Where ProcessId='#'<br><br>`C:\>wmic process '6668' list brief` | `Select * from Win32_Process` |
| startup<br><br>Identify startup programs<br><br>`C:\>wmic startup list brief` | Where Caption='#'<br><br>`C:\>wmic startup 'sidebar' list brief` | `Select * from Win32_StartupCommand` |
| registry<br><br>Information on registry<br><br>`C:\>wmic registry list full` | Not defined | `Select * from Win32_Registry` |

| qfe | Not defined | Select * from Win32_ |
|---|---|---|
| Quick fix engineering (hot-fixes) | | QuickFixEngineering |
| `C:\>wmic qfe list brief` | | |
| nteventlog | Where | Select * from Win32_ |
| Event logs | LogfileName='#' | NTEventlogFile |
| `C:\>wmic nteventlog list brief` | `C:\>wmic ntevent-log 'application' list brief` | |
| timezone | Not defined | Select * from Win32_ |
| Time zone data | | TimeZone |
| `C:\>wmic timezone list full` | | |
| bootconfig | Not defined | Select * from Win32_ |
| Boot configuration data | | BootConfiguration |
| `C:\>wmic bootconfig list full` | | |
| recoveros | Not defined | Select * from Win32_ |
| Location of recovery OS | | OSRecoveryConfiguration |
| `C:\>wmic recoveros list brief` | | |
| wmiset | Not defined | Select * from Win32_ |
| WMI settings, including whether it's enabled or not | | WMISetting |
| `C:\>wmic wmiset list brief` | | |

## Disk Drive Aliases

These aliases can be used to retrieve information related to disks.

| Alias Friendly Name and Usage | Pwhere Format | WMI Query |
|---|---|---|
| diskdrive | Where Index='#' | Select * from Win32_ |
| Details on dis3k drive | `C:\>wmic diskdrive '1' list brief` | DiskDrive |
| `C:\>wmic diskdrive list full` | | |
| logicaldisk | Where Name='#' | Select * from Win32_ |
| Drive data | `C:\>wmic logicaldisk 'c:' list brief` | LogicalDisk |
| `C:\>wmic logicaldisk list full` | | |

| partition<br>Information on disk partitions or volumes<br>`C:\>wmic partition list brief` | Where Index='#'<br>`C:\>wmic partition '0' list full` | `Select * from Win32_ DiskPartition` |
|---|---|---|
| diskquota<br>Disk quota settings<br>`C:\>wmic diskquota list full` | Not defined | `Select * from Win32_ DiskQuota` |
| quotasetting<br>Disk quota settings<br>`C:\>wmic quotasetting list brief` | Not defined | `Select * from Win32_ QuotaSetting` |
| pagefile<br>Details on paging file(s)<br>`C:\>wmic pagefile list brief` | Not defined | `Select * from Win32_ PageFileUsage` |
| share<br>Network shares<br>`C:\>wmic share list brief` | Where Name='#'<br>`C:\>wmic share 'c$' list full` | `Select * from Win32_ Share` |
| idecontroller<br>IDE disk controllers<br>`C:\>wmic idecontroller list brief` | Not defined | `Select * from Win32_ IDEController` |
| cdrom<br>CD- and DVD-ROM drives<br>`C:\>wmic cdrom list brief` | Where Drive='#'<br>`C:\>wmic cdrom 'd:' list brief` | `Select * from Win32_ CDROMDrive` |

## System Hardware Aliases

These aliases can be used to retrieve information on different hardware within the system.

| Alias Friendly Name and Usage | Pwhere Format | WMI Query |
|---|---|---|
| csproduct<br>Computer system model<br>`C:\>wmic csproduct list full` | Not defined | `Select * from Win32_ ComputerSystemProduct` |

| | | |
|---|---|---|
| `cpu`<br>Processor information<br>`C:\>wmic cpu list full` | Where DeviceID='#'<br>`C:\>wmic cpu 'cpu0' list brief` | `Select * from WIN32_ PROCESSOR` |
| `systemslot`<br>Information on expansion slots<br>`C:\>wmic systemslot list brief` | Not defined | `Select * from Win32_ SystemSlot` |
| `memorychip`<br>Memory sticks<br>`C:\>wmic memorychip list full` | Where Tag = '#'<br>`C:\>wmic memorychip ' physical memory 0 ' list brief` | `Select * from Win32_ PhysicalMemory` |
| `memphysical`<br>Memory totals<br>`C:\>wmic memphysical list full` | Not defined | `Select * from Win32_ PhysicalMemoryArray` |
| `bios`<br>Details on BIOS<br>`C:\>wmic bios list full` | Not defined | `Select * from Win32_BIOS` |
| `desktopmonitor`<br>Display monitor<br>`C:\>wmic desktopmoni-tor list full` | Where DeviceID='#'<br>`C:\>wmic desktop-monitor 'desktop-monitor1' list full` | `Select * from WIN32_ DESKTOPMONITOR` |
| `nicconfig`<br>Configuration of network interface cards (NICs)<br>`C:\>wmic nicconfig list brief` | Where Index='#'<br>`C:\>wmic nicconfig '1' list brief` | `Select * from Win32_ NetworkAdapter Configuration` |
| `nic`<br>NICs<br>`C:\>wmic nic list brief` | Where DeviceID='#'<br>`C:\>wmic nic '1' list brief` | `Select * from Win32_ NetworkAdapter` |
| `printer`<br>Installed printers<br>`C:\>wmic printer list brief` | Where Name='#'<br>`C:\>wmic printer 'Microsoft xps document writer' list full` | `Select * from Win32_ Printer` |

## User, Group, and Domain Aliases

You can use these aliases to get information on objects such as users and groups.

| Alias Friendly name and Usage | Pwhere Format | WMI Query |
|---|---|---|
| useraccount<br><br>User account details<br><br>`C:\>wmic useraccount list brief` | Not defined | `Select * from Win32_UserAccount` |
| group<br><br>User groups<br><br>`C:\>wmic group list brief` | Not defined | `Select * from Win32_Group` |
| sysaccount<br><br>Detailed information on all user and groups, including all the built-in accounts<br><br>`C:\>wmic sysaccount list brief` | Where Name='#'<br><br>`C:\>wmic sysaccount 'everyone' list brief` | `Select * from Win32_SystemAccount` |
| ntdomain<br><br>Information on domain (if joined)<br><br>`C:\>wmic ntdomain list brief` | Where DomainName='#'<br><br>`C:\>wmic service 'pearson' list full` | `Select * from Win32_NTDomain` |

**TIP:** These lists of aliases are not complete. If you want to retrieve a full list of all the available aliases, use the command **wmic alias list brief**.

# Using Verbs

There are several verbs that can be used with aliases. In simplest terms, the verbs are commands that you can use to work with the aliases.

| Verbs (Commands) | Description |
|---|---|
| where<br>where (*property* = "*value*")<br>wmic alias where (*property* = "*value*") list full<br>`C:\>wmic useraccount where (name = "guest") list full` | Use to filter the output. The value must be enclosed in double quotes.<br><br>Only valid properties of the alias can be used in a **where** clause. You can view all valid properties of any alias with the following command:<br><br>`wmic alias list full` |

| | |
|---|---|
| ```get```<br>```get property```<br>```wmic /node:remotecomputer alias```<br>```get property```<br>```C:\>wmic /node:win7pcg```<br>```computersystem get username```<br>```C:\>wmic /node:win7pcg```<br>```computersystem get username,```<br>```domain, totalphysicalmemory```<br>```C:\>wmic useraccount where (name =```<br>```"sally") get```<br>```C:\>wmic useraccount where (name =```<br>```"sally") get disabled``` | You can use the **get** command to retrieve one or more properties of any alias. If you want to retrieve multiple properties, you separate each with a comma.<br><br>**TIP:** You can identify all the properties you can retrieve from an alias by using the command **wmic alias list full**. You can identify all the properties that can be retrieved with the **wmic alias get /?** command.<br><br>The first example to the left gets the username of a logged-in user on a remote system of a remote computer. The second example gets the username, the domain, and the amount of physical memory installed on the remote computer.<br><br>You can also use a **where** clause to filter the data. In the last two examples, a **where** clause is used to retrieve properties on a user account named Sally, and then only the value of the disabled property. |
| ```set```<br>```set property = "value"```<br>```wmic /node:remotecomputer alias```<br>```set property = "value"```<br>```wmic /node:remotecomputer alias```<br>```set property```<br>```C:\>wmic /node:win7pcg useraccount```<br>```where (name = "guest") set```<br>```disabled = "true"``` | The **set** command allows you to set some alias properties.<br><br>The example combines the **set** command with the **where** clause to disable the guest account on a remote system. The value must be specified in double quotes.<br><br>**TIP:** You can't set all properties. For example, the memphysical alias reports what physical memory is installed, but you can't change these properties with the **set** command. You can identify all the properties that can be configured with the **wmic alias set /?** command. |
| ```delete```<br>```wmic alias where (property =```<br>```value) delete```<br>```C:\>wmic process where (name =```<br>```'notepad.exe') delete``` | Deletes an instance.<br><br>You can use this to terminate processes. The example terminates a running instance of Notepad. |

| | |
|---|---|
| `assoc`<br>`wmic` *`alias`* `assoc`<br>`C:\>wmic os assoc`<br>`wmic alias where (`*`property`* `=`<br>`'`*`value`*`') assoc`<br>`C:\>wmic group where (name =`<br>`'administrators') assoc` | **assoc** shows the associations with an object. In the first example, it displays information about the operating system alias.<br><br>The second example shows all WMI objects that are associated with the Administrators group by adding a **where** clause. |

This chapter provides information and commands concerning the following topics:

- Understanding WIM files
- Using Windows Deployment Services and images
- Comparing boot and install images
- Comparing thick and thin images

## Understanding WIM Files

Windows 7 uses the Windows Imaging Format (WIM) file-based disk image format for installations. A WIM file includes all of the files that are needed for an installation.

**NOTE:** Older images were sector based instead of file based. Deploying a sector-based image onto a system would remove the entire contents of the drive where the image was deployed. A file-based image only installs the files and can preserve the existing structure of the system, including existing files.

Image files can include multiple images. For example, the install.wim image file on many Windows 7 installation DVDs includes all of the images needed for the following operating systems:

- Windows 7 Starter
- Windows 7 Home Basic
- Windows 7 Home Premium
- Windows 7 Professional
- Windows 7 Ultimate

IT professionals can also create their own images using different tools. Just as the install.wim image file holds multiple images, image files created by IT professionals can include multiple images. Some of the tools used to create, manage, and deploy images are identified in the following table.

| Tool | Description |
|------|-------------|
| **imagex** | A command-line tool that is part of the Windows Automated Installation Kit (WAIK), which is a free download. **imagex** can be used to capture and deploy images from the command line. |
| **dism** | A command-line tool that is part of the WAIK. **dism** is used to perform offline servicing of images. |
| Windows Deployment Services (WDS) | A role that can be added to Windows Server 2008 or Windows Server 2008 R2 servers. WDS can automate the deployment of images to multiple images at the same time using multicasting. |
| System Center Configuration Manager (SCCM) | An advanced server add-on product that can be used to deploy images. SCCM includes all the benefits of the free WDS role and includes many additional tools. It can also be used to schedule and deploy patches, and schedule and deploy applications. |
| Microsoft Deployment Toolkit (MDT) | A free download that can be used to enhance the capabilities of WDS and/or SCCM when deploying Windows 7. |

**NOTE:** Chapter 19, "Installing the Windows Automated Installation Kit," presents the Windows Automated Installation Kit (WAIK), Chapter 20, "Using imagex," shows many of the useful **imagex** commands, and Chapter 21, "Using the Deployment Image Service and Management (DISM) Tool," shows many of the useful **dism** commands.

Figure 17-1 shows the process when capturing and deploying an image with **imagex**. You start by installing Windows 7 on a reference computer. You can then configure the computer and add any desired applications. When the computer is ready, you prepare it by running the System Preparation Tool (**sysprep**). You can then capture the image using tools such as **imagex** or WDS.

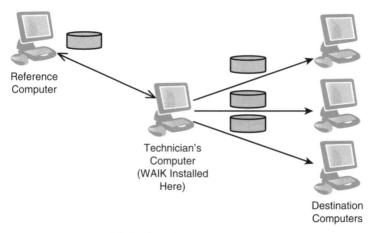

Reference
Computer

Technician's
Computer
(WAIK Installed
Here)

Destination
Computers

**Figure 17-1** Using WAIK Tools to Capture and Deploy Images

You can then use tools on the technician's computer to manage and deploy the image. For example, you can create bootable DVDs or bootable USBs to deploy the image to any individual system, and you can use **dism** to service the image offline.

## Using Windows Deployment Services and Images

Windows Deployment Services (WDS) is commonly used to capture and deploy Windows 7 images in small to medium-sized organizations. It is a free server role available in Windows Server 2008 and Server 2008 R2.

Figure 17-2 shows the WDS console on a Windows Server 2008 server. The WDS server holds both install and boot images. After it's configured, an administrator can configure multicast transmissions of images to clients.

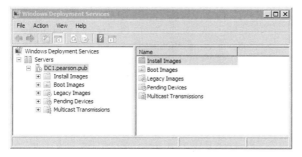

**Figure 17-2**  WDS Console

Figure 17-3 shows the overall process of capturing and deploying images with WDS. After a reference computer is prepared, you can capture the image with WDS. You can then deploy images to multiple clients at a time by using multicasting.

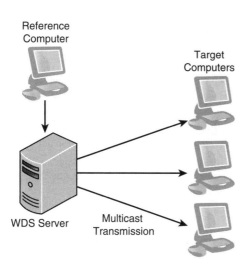

**Figure 17-3**  WDS Used to Capture and Deploy Images

**TIP:** Images stored on the WDS server can also be serviced by **dism**. This enables you to add and remove components without starting over on the reference computer.

WDS has several requirements. If you're running a domain, you probably already have these components running. The network requirements for WDS are given in the following table.

| Network Requirements for WDS | Comments |
|---|---|
| Domain controller | WDS needs Active Directory Domain Services (AD DS) hosted on a domain controller. |
| Domain Name System (DNS) | DNS is required in any Microsoft domain. DNS resolves names to IP addresses and is also used to locate domain controllers within a domain. |
| Dynamic Host Configuration Protocol (DHCP) server | DHCP is required by WDS to provide TCP/IP configuration information to the clients, and then direct the clients to the WDS server. |
| WDS server | The WDS server captures, hosts, and deploys the images. |

**TIP:** A significant feature of images deployed by WDS is dynamic driver provisioning. You can reduce the size of images by centrally storing drivers on a server. Clients can then download only the drivers that Plug and Play detects are needed. This also reduces the number of potential driver conflicts.

There are multiple steps involved when using WDS to capture and deploy images. The following two tables outline the overall steps for each process.

| WDS Capture Steps | Remarks |
|---|---|
| 1. Install Windows 7 on a reference computer. Install applications and configure the computer. | This must be a clean installation. An upgraded computer can't be captured with WDS. |
| 2. Prepare the system for imaging with the System Preparation (sysprep) tool. | Sysprep removes the system-unique settings. WDS won't capture an image unless it has been sysprepped.<br><br>**NOTE:** Chapter 18, "Preparing a System to be Imaged with Sysprep," covers the **sysprep** commands. |
| 3. Boot the reference computer using pre-boot execution environment (PXE, pronounced "pixie") boot to connect with WDS. | The administrator presses F12 to start the PXE boot and then presses F12 again to connect to WDS. The administrator then selects a capture image.<br><br>**NOTE:** The capture image is derived from the boot.wim boot image and provides access to the Windows Preinstallation Environment (WinPE). |

| 4. Capture the image with WDS. | The administrator follows the onscreen prompts and then WDS captures the image. The image is stored locally on the reference computer. The WDS capture process can also be configured to copy the image over the network to the WDS server after it is captured. |
|---|---|

Images stored on the WDS server can be deployed to clients. The following steps show the overall process.

**NOTE:** WDS can deploy thin images to the client without capturing specialized images. For example, the installation DVD includes thin images in the install.wim file. These images can be imported into WDS and multicast to clients without any modification.

| WDS Deployment Steps | Remarks |
|---|---|
| 1. Configure the WDS server to deploy images. | This encompasses many steps such as creating image groups, configuring permissions, and configuring casting of specific images. |
| 2. Boot the target system using PXE boot to connect with WDS. | The user presses F12 during the boot process to start the PXE boot and then presses F12 again to connect to a WDS server on the network. |
| 3. User logs on and is presented with a selection of images based on permissions. | Only images that a user has permission to select are shown. The user can then select the appropriate image. |
| 4. Image is cast to the system. | WDS begins sending the image. |

**NOTE:** WDS can be configured to send an image as soon as a client connects, after a preset number of clients connect, or at a specific time.

## Comparing Boot and Install Images

All images aren't created equal. There are important distinctions between the boot and install images.

| Image Type | Description |
|---|---|
| Boot images | A boot image boots into the WinPE. Its primary purpose is to load a minimal operating system so that the full operating system can be loaded, or to perform troubleshooting. Boot images can be modified to additional command-line tools, but the WinPE doesn't support the installation of full applications. The boot.wim file on the installation DVD includes a single boot image.<br><br>**NOTE:** The Windows Recovery Environment (WinRE) is a form of the boot image and only boots into the preinstallation environment. |

| Install images | Install images are used to install the full Windows 7 operating system. Install images can include applications and operating system configuration changes. The install.wim file on the installation DVD includes several install images. |

The **dism /get-wiminfo** command shows the different images that are available in the install.wim image file.

> **TIP:** The following commands are run from the Deployment Tools Command Prompt of the Windows Automated Installation Kit (WAIK). The install.wim and boot.wim files were copied from the sources folder of an installation DVD to the c:\images folder.

```
C:\>dism /get-wiminfo /wimfile:c:\images\install.wim

Deployment Image Servicing and Management tool
Version: 6.1.7600.16385

Details for image : c:\images\install.wim

Index : 1
Name : Windows 7 STARTER
Description : Windows 7 STARTER
Size : 7,936,340,784 bytes

Index : 2
Name : Windows 7 HOMEBASIC
Description : Windows 7 HOMEBASIC
Size : 7,992,394,907 bytes

Index : 3
Name : Windows 7 HOMEPREMIUM
Description : Windows 7 HOMEPREMIUM
Size : 8,432,859,356 bytes

Index : 4
Name : Windows 7 PROFESSIONAL
Description : Windows 7 PROFESSIONAL
Size : 8,313,318,889 bytes

Index : 5
Name : Windows 7 ULTIMATE
Description : Windows 7 ULTIMATE
Size : 8,471,060,645 bytes

The operation completed successfully.
```

Similarly, you can use the **dism** command to show the contents of the boot.wim file.

> **NOTE:** The boot.wim file available on the installation DVD holds only one image. This boots into the WinPE.

```
C:\>dism /get-wiminfo /wimfile:c:\images\boot.wim

Deployment Image Servicing and Management tool
Version: 6.1.7600.16385

Details for image : c:\images\boot.wim

Index : 1
Name : <undefined>
Description : <undefined>
Size : 1,147,673,833 bytes

The operation completed successfully.
```

Similarly, you can use the **imagex** command to retrieve more detailed information on the images within a WIM file.

> **NOTE:** Some of the duplicate information in the following output was cut to conserve space. However, the XML nodes for each of the images are similar.

> **TIP:** All of the images in the image file must use the same compression method. Images commonly use LZX compression, the same compression method used in Microsoft's cabinet (.cab) files. You can see the compression used in the WIM Information header from the **imagex** output.

```
C:\>imagex /info c:\images\install.wim

ImageX Tool for Windows
Copyright (C) Microsoft Corp. All rights reserved.
Version: 6.1.7600.16385

WIM Information:
----------------
Path:        c:\images\install.wim
GUID:        {4db440bc-7222-4651-9192-1798c4b29bcb}
Image Count: 5
Compression: LZX
Part Number: 1/1
Attributes:  0xc
             Integrity info
             Relative path junction
```

```
Available Image Choices:
-----------------------
<WIM>
  <TOTALBYTES>2188572852</TOTALBYTES>
  <IMAGE INDEX="1">
    <DIRCOUNT>9044</DIRCOUNT>
    <FILECOUNT>45608</FILECOUNT>
    <TOTALBYTES>7936340784</TOTALBYTES>
    <CREATIONTIME>
      <HIGHPART>0x01CA0443</HIGHPART>
      <LOWPART>0x6568BDF8</LOWPART>
    </CREATIONTIME>
    <LASTMODIFICATIONTIME>
      <HIGHPART>0x01CA045F</HIGHPART>
      <LOWPART>0x905A47C2</LOWPART>
    </LASTMODIFICATIONTIME>
    <WINDOWS>
      <ARCH>0</ARCH>
      <PRODUCTNAME>Microsoftr Windowsr Operating System</PRODUCTNAME>
      <EDITIONID>Starter</EDITIONID>
      <INSTALLATIONTYPE>Client</INSTALLATIONTYPE>
      <HAL>acpiapic</HAL>
      <PRODUCTTYPE>WinNT</PRODUCTTYPE>
      <PRODUCTSUITE>Terminal Server</PRODUCTSUITE>
      <LANGUAGES>
        <LANGUAGE>en-US</LANGUAGE>
        <DEFAULT>en-US</DEFAULT>
      </LANGUAGES>
      <VERSION>
        <MAJOR>6</MAJOR>
        <MINOR>1</MINOR>
        <BUILD>7600</BUILD>
        <SPBUILD>16385</SPBUILD>
        <SPLEVEL>0</SPLEVEL>
      </VERSION>
      <SYSTEMROOT>WINDOWS</SYSTEMROOT>
    </WINDOWS>
    <NAME>Windows 7 STARTER</NAME>
    <DESCRIPTION>Windows 7 STARTER</DESCRIPTION>
    <FLAGS>Starter</FLAGS>
    <HARDLINKBYTES>3070770507</HARDLINKBYTES>
    <DISPLAYNAME>Windows 7 Starter</DISPLAYNAME>
```

```
    <DISPLAYDESCRIPTION>Windows 7 Starter</DISPLAYDESCRIPTION>
  </IMAGE>
. . .
  <IMAGE INDEX="5">
    <DIRCOUNT>9384</DIRCOUNT>
    <FILECOUNT>47447</FILECOUNT>
    <TOTALBYTES>8471060645</TOTALBYTES>
    <CREATIONTIME>
      <HIGHPART>0x01CA0443</HIGHPART>
      <LOWPART>0x6568BDF8</LOWPART>
    </CREATIONTIME>
    <LASTMODIFICATIONTIME>
      <HIGHPART>0x01CA045F</HIGHPART>
      <LOWPART>0xD8F30230</LOWPART>
    </LASTMODIFICATIONTIME>
    <WINDOWS>
      <ARCH>0</ARCH>
      <PRODUCTNAME>Microsoftr Windowsr Operating System</PRODUCTNAME>
      <EDITIONID>Ultimate</EDITIONID>
      <INSTALLATIONTYPE>Client</INSTALLATIONTYPE>
      <HAL>acpiapic</HAL>
      <PRODUCTTYPE>WinNT</PRODUCTTYPE>
      <PRODUCTSUITE>Terminal Server</PRODUCTSUITE>
      <LANGUAGES>
        <LANGUAGE>en-US</LANGUAGE>
        <DEFAULT>en-US</DEFAULT>
      </LANGUAGES>
      <VERSION>
        <MAJOR>6</MAJOR>
        <MINOR>1</MINOR>
        <BUILD>7600</BUILD>
        <SPBUILD>16385</SPBUILD>
        <SPLEVEL>0</SPLEVEL>
      </VERSION>
      <SYSTEMROOT>WINDOWS</SYSTEMROOT>
    </WINDOWS>
    <NAME>Windows 7 ULTIMATE</NAME>
    <DESCRIPTION>Windows 7 ULTIMATE</DESCRIPTION>
    <FLAGS>Ultimate</FLAGS>
    <HARDLINKBYTES>3504554899</HARDLINKBYTES>
    <DISPLAYNAME>Windows 7 Ultimate</DISPLAYNAME>
    <DISPLAYDESCRIPTION>Windows 7 Ultimate</DISPLAYDESCRIPTION>
  </IMAGE>
</WIM>
```

**NOTE:** Notice the size of these images. Image 1 has 7,936,340,784 total bytes (about 8 GB), and image 5 has 8,471,060,645 total bytes (a little more than 8 GB). The other three images (not shown in the output) are also about 8 GB. However, the total size of the install.wim file is only 2,188,587,580 (about 2 GB). In other words, one 2-GB file is storing five 8-GB images. The file is compressed and it also uses single file instance storage to conserve space.

The following output shows the details on the boot.wim file from **imagex**:

```
C:\>imagex /info c:\images\boot.wim

ImageX Tool for Windows
Copyright (C) Microsoft Corp. All rights reserved.
Version: 6.1.7600.16385


WIM Information:
----------------
Path:        c:\images\boot.wim
GUID:        {7eef1171-f5e1-4de4-9ded-50569a1f85c5}
Image Count: 1
Compression: LZX
Part Number: 1/1
Boot Index:  1
Attributes:  0xc
             Integrity info
             Relative path junction


Available Image Choices:
------------------------
<WIM>
  <TOTALBYTES>210718503</TOTALBYTES>
  <IMAGE INDEX="1">
    <DIRCOUNT>2222</DIRCOUNT>
    <FILECOUNT>9804</FILECOUNT>
    <TOTALBYTES>1147673833</TOTALBYTES>
    <CREATIONTIME>
      <HIGHPART>0x01C9A155</HIGHPART>
      <LOWPART>0xB20996BE</LOWPART>
    </CREATIONTIME>
    <LASTMODIFICATIONTIME>
      <HIGHPART>0x01C9A155</HIGHPART>
      <LOWPART>0xB20996BE</LOWPART>
    </LASTMODIFICATIONTIME>
  </IMAGE>
</WIM>
```

# Comparing Thick and Thin Images

Although you can use the install images provided by Microsoft, you can also customize your images. You start by creating a reference computer. You can then configure this computer exactly as you want it for the end user and install any applications that are needed by the end user.

Customized images are referred to as thin, thick, or hybrid images, as described in the following table.

**NOTE:** Chapter 19 discusses the installation of the WAIK, and Chapters 20 and 21 provide command-line examples of the **imagex** and **dism** WAIK tools, respectively.

| Image Type | Description |
|---|---|
| Thin image | Only the operating system is installed. A thin image includes very few extras. Applications can be installed using other methods after the deployment of the operating system. For example, Group Policy or System Center Configuration Manager (SCCM) can deploy needed applications. |
| Thick image | The operating system and all needed applications are installed. This is used in smaller organizations where all users have identical configuration. It is also used in some situations where the computer won't necessarily have connectivity to the network. For example, laptop computers that will be issued to mobile workers often benefit from a thick image. |
| Hybrid image | A cross between thin and thick images. A hybrid starts as a thin image and then includes all the applications that are needed by all users in the organization. For example, all users may use Microsoft Office, so this can be included. Other applications can be targeted to individual systems by tools such as Group Policy or SCCM. |

Automated installations with images are referred to as lite-touch installations (LTI) or zero-touch installations (ZTI).

| Installation Method | Description |
|---|---|
| Lite-touch | Windows Deployment Services (WDS) and/or the Microsoft Deployment Toolkit (MDT) can be used to provide some automation to the installation. Users could perform actions such as pressing the F12 key to start the process, logging on, and selecting an image to deploy. WDS and MDT can then automate the rest of the installation. WDS supports multicast transmissions. |
| Zero-touch | Microsoft System Center Configuration Manager (SCCM) can be used to completely automate the deployment with no intervention. SCCM can be configured to discover the systems and then deploy the operating system without any user action. SCCM supports multicast transmissions. |

**NOTE:** Both lite-touch and zero-touch are formal terms defined by Microsoft. Full-touch installation isn't a formal term, but it implies installing the operating system manually.

This chapter provides information and commands concerning the following topics:

- Understanding sysprep
- Running the sysprep GUI
- Running sysprep from the command line

## Understanding Sysprep

The System Preparation (**sysprep**) tool is used to remove the unique information on a Windows 7 computer. It removes a wide variety of computer- and user-specific settings on a Windows 7 computer, including the system's security identifier (SID).

> **TIP:** The SID needs to be unique in a domain. If multiple computers have the same SID, you'll end up with significant problems that can be difficult to troubleshoot.

Figure 18-1 shows how **sysprep** fits into the overall process of capturing and deploying images. The reference computer is a new installation of Windows 7 that includes all of the desired settings and applications. **sysprep** removes the unique settings on this reference computer to prepare it for imaging.

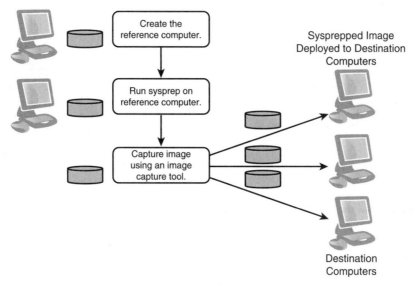

**Figure 18-1**   Sysprep in the Image Capture Process

After **sysprep** is run, an image capture tool such as **imagex** or WDS is used to capture the image. This captured image can then be deployed to multiple systems in the network.

> **TIP:** If an image is not prepared with **sysprep**, WDS will not be able to capture it. While **imagex** may be able capture images without running **sysprep**, this is not a supported use and may violate the license agreement.

You can run **sysprep** only on a new installation of Windows 7. It will not run if you attempt to run it on a system that has been upgraded. Additionally, it resets the activation on the system, and the activation can be reset only three times. In other words, it should not be run on systems that are in production.

## Running the Sysprep GUI

You can run **sysprep** either from the graphical user interface (GUI) or from the command prompt. Figure 18-2 shows the sysprep GUI with the typical settings selected. This file is located in the C:\Windows\System32\Sysprep folder by default. You can launch the GUI with this command:

```
C:\windows\system32\sysprep\sysprep
```

> **NOTE:** The path to the sysprep GUI is not known by default, so you must include the full path.

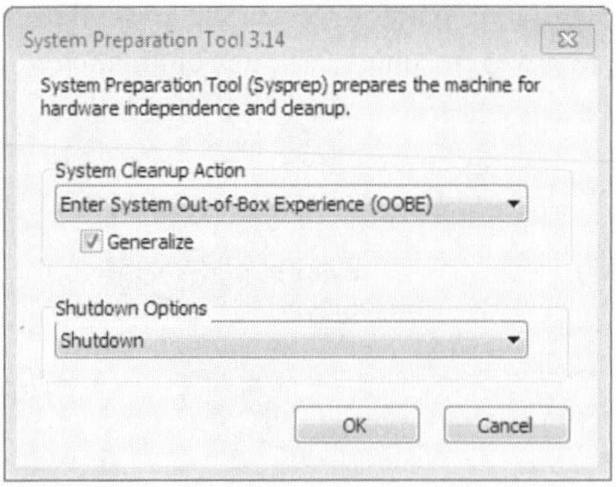

**Figure 18-2**  Running the Sysprep GUI

The figure shows two sections, System Cleanup Action, which includes the Generalize check box, and Shutdown Options. The following tables describe these settings.

| System Cleanup Action Selection | Description |
| --- | --- |
| Enter System Out-of-Box Experience (OOBE) | This is used to prepare the computer to be delivered to the user. It causes the system to enter the Windows Welcome phase when it reboots.<br><br>**NOTE:** Windows Welcome is also called Machine OOBE. |

| Generalize | When checked, the Generalize check box resets the user- and computer-specific settings, including the SID and the activation data. |
|---|---|
| Enter System Audit Mode | Audit mode bypasses the Windows Welcome phase and is used to add additional devices or applications to an installation. Audit mode is primarily used by original equipment manufacturers (OEMs) and some large organizations to add additional customization settings.<br><br>**NOTE:** Because audit mode bypasses the Windows Welcome phase of the installation, it can't be used to deploy an operating system to an end user. You still must select OOBE after booting into audit mode. |

You have several choices of what **sysprep** will do after it runs. The most common choice is Shutdown. The following table shows these choices.

| Shutdown Option | Description |
|---|---|
| Shutdown | The system will shut down. The image is now ready to be captured. When you're ready to capture the image, you turn the system on and follow the procedures based on the image capture tool you're using. |
| Reboot | If you are ready to capture the image immediately, you can select Reboot. This setting is also commonly used with the Audit mode by OEMs. |
| Quit | This simply quits the **sysprep** application. You can shut it down later. |

**TIP:** If the system reboots before the image is captured, it will enter the Windows Welcome phase. You'll need to rerun **sysprep** to prepare the system before imaging it.

# Running Sysprep from the Command Line

**sysprep** can also be run from the command line. The most commonly used command is

```
C:\windows\system32\sysprep\sysprep /generalize /oobe
```

**TIP:** The path to the **sysprep** folder is not known by default, so you must either modify the path or include the path when executing the command.

The following table shows the different switches available with **sysprep**.

| sysprep Switch | Description |
| --- | --- |
| `/?`<br>`C:\>c:\windows\system32\sysprep\sysprep /?` | Retrieves dialog boxes that show help. |
| `/generalize`<br>`C:\>c:\windows\system32\sysprep\sysprep /generalize /oobe` | This option removes all unique system information from the Windows installation. It resets the SID, clears system restore points, and deletes event logs.<br><br>**NOTE:** A new SID is created during the specialize configuration pass when the system is rebooted. Windows activation also resets (as long as activation hasn't already been reset three times). |
| `/oobe`<br>`C:\>c:\windows\system32\sysprep\sysprep /generalize /oobe` | The out-of-box experience (**oobe**) switch ensures the system enters the Windows Welcome mode when it restarts. Either an answer file can be used to answer the installation GUI's questions, or users can answer the questions in the Windows Welcome mode. |
| `/quiet`<br>`C:\>c:\windows\system32\sysprep\sysprep /generalize /oobe /quiet` | Onscreen confirmation messages are suppressed. This option is useful if you are automating **sysprep**. |
| `/audit` | Audit mode is used by OEMs, but is rarely used by organizations. It enables you to boot into the system and add additional devices or applications. |
| `/shutdown`<br>`C:\>c:\windows\system32\sysprep\sysprep /generalize /oobe /shutdown` | Shuts down the computer after **sysprep** completes. |
| `/reboot`<br>`C:\>c:\windows\system32\sysprep\sysprep /generalize /audit /reboot` | Reboots the computer after running **sysprep**. Use this option to audit the computer and to verify that the first-run experience operates correctly. |

| | |
|---|---|
| `/quit`<br>`C:\>c:\windows\system32\sysprep\sysprep`<br>`/generalize /oobe /quit` | Closes **sysprep** after running the specified commands. |
| `/unattend:filename`<br>`C:\>c:\windows\system32\sysprep\sys-`<br>`prep /generalize /oobe /shutdown`<br>`/unattend:answer.xml` | This applies settings from the specified answer file to Windows during an unattended installation.<br><br>You can create the answer file with the Windows System Image Manager (WSIM) included with the Windows Automated Installation Kit (WAIK). |

**NOTE:** You can view the full **sysprep** technical reference pages at http://technet. microsoft.com/library/dd744263.aspx.

This chapter provides information and commands concerning the following topics:

- Downloading the WAIK
- Installing the WAIK
- Viewing the WAIK tools

## Downloading the WAIK

The Windows Automated Installation Kit (WAIK) has gone through several changes over the years. The current edition is Windows Automated Installation Kit for Windows 7. It provides tools to help you install, customize, and deploy both Windows 7 and Windows Server 2008 R2 operating systems.

You can get a free copy by following these steps.

| Step | Remarks |
|------|---------|
| 1. Go to Microsoft's download center at http://www.microsoft.com/downloads. | Most Microsoft downloads are available through this central location. |
| 2. Enter **WAIK** in the search box. | This will show a listing of several available downloads. |
| 3. Select **Windows AIK for Windows 7.** | This will likely be at the top of the list. |
| 4. Click **Download** to download the file. | The file is named KB3AIK-EN.iso. This is a DVD .iso image that can be burned to DVD. Download the file to a location on your system. |
| 5. Place a DVD in your DVD burner. Right-click the .iso file and select **Burn Disc Image**. | This will create a DVD you can use to install the WAIK. |

## Installing the WAIK

After you have a CD, the installation is fairly simple. Put the CD into your drive and wait for AutoPlay to launch the installation program automatically. If AutoPlay doesn't launch it, browse to the CD and double-click **StartCD.exe** to launch the installation wizard.

Figure 19-1 shows the WAIK installation screen, and the following table lists its components.

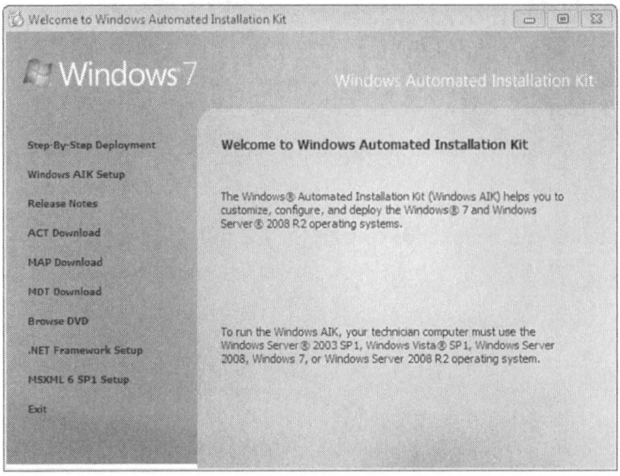

**Figure 19-1**  Installing the WAIK

| WAIK CD Contents | Description |
| --- | --- |
| Step-by-Step Deployment | This is an .htm file that includes detailed steps to perform the following tasks:<br><br>1. Build an answer file.<br><br>2. Build a reference installation.<br><br>3. Create bootable Windows PE media.<br><br>4. Capture the installation onto a network share.<br><br>5. Deploy from a network share. |
| Windows AIK Setup | This launches an installation wizard you can use to install the WAIK. |
| Release Notes | This launches a readme.htm file that contains additional information available at release time. |
| ACT Download | This is a link to download the Microsoft Application Compatibility Toolkit (ACT). |
| MAP Download | This is a link to download the Microsoft Assessment and Planning Toolkit (MAP). |
| MDT Download | This is a link to download the Microsoft Deployment Toolkit (MDT). |
| Browse DVD | Launch Windows Explorer to view the CD contents. |
| .NET Framework Setup | Windows AIK requires .NET Framework 2.0. If you're installing this on an older operating system such as Windows XP, you can use this link to install it. |
| MSXML 6 SP1 Setup | Windows AIK requires MSXML 6 SP1 Setup. If you're installing this on an older operating system, you can use this link to install it. |

Click **Windows AIK Setup** and follow the onscreen wizard to complete the installation. When the installation is complete, you'll have several tools available to you, listed and described in the following table.

| WAIK Tool | Description |
| --- | --- |
| Deployment Tools Command Prompt<br><br>Choose **Start, All Programs, Microsoft Windows AIK, Deployment Tools Command Prompt** | This temporarily updates the path to provide easy access to **dism, imagex,** and **oscdimg.** |
| Windows System Image Manager (WSIM)<br><br>Choose **Start, All Programs, Microsoft Windows AIK, Windows System Image Manager** | WSIM can be used to create unattended answer files. |
| Documentation folder<br><br>Choose **Start, All Programs, Microsoft Windows AIK, Documentation** | This includes links to the following help files:<br><br>Step-by-Step – Basic Windows Deployment for IT Pros<br><br>Unattended Windows Setup Reference<br><br>Windows Automated Installation Kit User's Guide<br><br>Windows PE User's Guide<br><br>Software Development Kit (SDK) folder |
| VAMT 1.2 folder<br><br>Choose **Start, All Programs, Microsoft Windows AIK, VAMT 1.2** | The following two tools are available here:<br><br>Volume Activation Management Tool Help<br><br>Volume Activation Management Tool |
| Help files<br><br>Use Windows Explorer and browse to<br><br>**C:\Program Files\Windows aik\Docs\chms** | This folder includes several help files, including the USMT help file (showing help on **scanstate** and **loadstate**), and the WinPE help file. |
| White papers<br><br>Use Windows Explorer and browse to<br><br>**C:\Program Files\Windows aik\Docs\ Whitepapers** | The single document here is the Step-by-Step: Basic Windows Deployment for IT Professionals .htm file. |
| Samples<br><br>Use Windows Explorer and browse to<br><br>**C:\Program Files\Windows aik\Samples** | This folder includes several sample files and folders. Of particular note are several sample unattend.xml files. |

| Software development kit files<br><br>Use Windows Explorer and browse to<br><br>**C:\Program Files\Windows aik\sdks** | Software developers have additional folders from the software development kit (SDK). |
|---|---|
| Tools<br><br>Use Windows Explorer and browse to<br><br>**C:\Program Files\Windows aik\Tools** | The Tools folder includes several folders of tools used to create and manage images. For example, the USMT folder holds both 32-bit and 64-bit versions of **loadstate** and **scanstate** tools. |

**NOTE:** Chapter 24. "Capturing User Data with **scanstate**," reviews **scanstate** commands and Chapter 25, "Restoring User Data with **loadstate**," reviews **loadstate** commands.

## Viewing the WAIK Tools

You can launch the Deployment Tools Command Prompt by choosing **Start, All Programs, Microsoft Windows AIK, Deployment Tools Command Prompt**.

Figure 19-2 shows the Deployment Tools Command Prompt and a command prompt launched with administrative permissions. The Deployment Tools Command Prompt ensures you have access to **dism**, **oscdimg**, and **imagex**. Notice that the path to the **imagex** tool is not in the path from the normal command prompt, so if you try to run it from a command prompt without the full path, it will fail.

**TIP:** The **dism** command will run from a command prompt run with administrative permissions because a copy of the **dism** file is located in the c:\windows\system32 folder by default. However, this is not the same version of **dism** that is available from the Deployment Tools Command Prompt. The version available from the Deployment Tools Command Prompt is larger, and presumably has additional features.

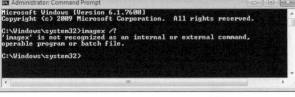

**Figure 19-2** Deployment Tools Command Prompt

**NOTE:** Chapter 20, "Using imagex," reviews **imagex** commands and Chapter 21, "Using the Deployment Image Service and Management (DISN) Tool," reviews **dism** commands. The **oscdimg** command is used to create an .iso image containing specified files and folders. The .iso image can then be burned to CD.

Figure 19-3 shows the User State Migration Tool (USMT) 4.0 User's Guide. This is an invaluable file when mastering the **scanstate** and **loadstate** commands. A shortcut to this file is not available on the Start menu. Instead, you need to launch it using Windows Explorer from here: C:\Program Files\Windows aik\Docs\chms.

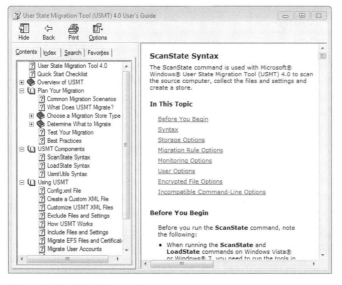

**Figure 19-3**   USMT User's Guide

You can create full unattended answer files using the Windows System Image Manager (WSIM), but there are sample answer files available. Figure 19-4 shows the autounattend_sample.xml file that is available in the c:\program files\windows aik\ samples folder.

**TIP:** You can use this answer file as a template. One way is to rename it to autounattend.xml and place it in the root of a USB flash drive. Put the USB in the system and then boot the system using the system installation DVD. The installation will automatically use the autounattend.xml file from the USB flash drive.

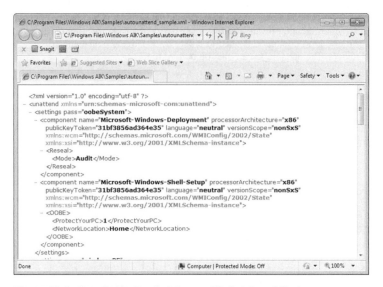

**Figure 19-4**   Sample Unattended Answer File in Internet Explorer

**NOTE:** The sample unattended answer file was created for an x86-based (32-bit) image. If you plan on using it for a 64-bit installation, you need to create a new answer file using the amd64-based (64-bit) settings.

You can create and modify answer files using WSIM. Figure 19-5 shows WSIM with the autounattend_sample.xml answer file opened. You can modify the file, and save it with a different name, such as autounattend.xml.

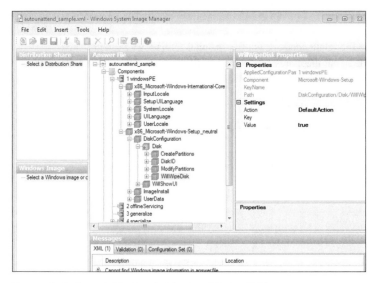

**Figure 19-5**   Sample Unattended Answer File in WSIM

This chapter provides information and commands concerning the following topics:

- Creating WinPE on a bootable USB
- Capturing images with **imagex**
- Appending images with **imagex**
- Deleting images with **imagex**
- Deploying images with **imagex**

## Creating WinPE on a Bootable USB

The **imagex** tool can be used to capture an image from a reference computer. As a reminder, the following steps (shown in Figure 20-1) must be taken first:

| Imaging Steps | Remarks |
|---|---|
| 1. Create a reference computer. | This must be a clean installation (not an upgrade). |
| 2. Configure the reference computer. | Modify the configuration of the system based on the organization's needs. Install any needed applications. |
| 3. Run **sysprep**. | Prepare the computer by running **sysprep** and shutting the system down. At this point the computer is ready to be imaged. |

You now need to boot the system without booting into the sysprepped image. One method is to create a bootable USB drive. You can use the steps in the following table to create a bootable USB drive that includes the **imagex** tool.

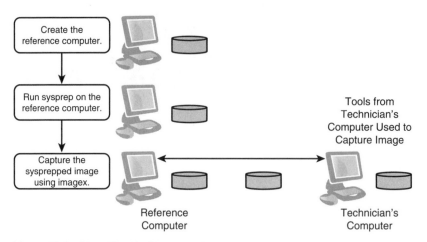

**Figure 20-1** Steps Used to Prepare and Capture an Image

**NOTE:** These steps should be performed on the technician's computer (described in Chapter 17, "Understanding Images") that has the WAIK installed.

**TIP:** You can create a bootable USB drive for a 32-bit system (x86) or a 64-bit system (amd64). The steps for each are slightly different. Steps for both are listed here.

| Steps to Create a Bootable USB Flash Drive | Remarks |
|---|---|
| 1. Launch the Deployment Tools Command Prompt on the technician's computer with administrative permissions. | This is located at **Start, All Programs, Microsoft Windows AIK**. Right-click **Deployment Tools Command Prompt** and select **Run As Administrator**. |
| 2. Copy the contents of the Windows Preinstallation Environment (WinPE) into a folder on your system.<br><br>Enter the following command for a 32-bit system:<br><br>`C:\>copype x86 c:\win7pe_x86`<br><br>Enter the following command for a 64-bit system:<br><br>`C:\>copype amd64 c:\win7pe_x64` | The format of this command is **copype. cmd** *arch destination*, where *arch* is the architecture (either **x86** or **amd64**) and you can specify a different destination if desired.<br><br>When complete, multiple files and folders will be copied into the win7pe_x## folder. |

| | |
|---|---|
| 3. Copy winpe.wim into the appropriate folder and rename it **boot.wim**.<br><br>Enter the following command for a 32-bit system:<br><br>`C:\>copy c:\win7pe_x86\winpe.wim c:\win7pe_x86\iso\sources\boot.wim`<br><br>Enter the following command for a 64-bit system:<br><br>`C:\>copy c:\win7pe_x64\winpe.wim c:\win7pe_x64\iso\sources\boot.wim` | The winpe.wim file is the actual WinPE boot file. When it is copied and renamed as boot.wim, media created with these folders will boot to the WinPE. |
| 4. Add the **imagex** tool.<br><br>Enter the following command for a 32-bit system:<br><br>`C:\>copy "c:\program files\ windows aik\tools\x86\imagex.exe" c:\win7pe_x86\iso`<br><br>Enter the following command for a 64-bit system:<br><br>`C:\>copy "c:\program files\windows aik\tools\amd64\imagex.exe" c:\ win7pe_x64\iso` | The **imagex** tool is needed to capture the image. By copying it into the iso folder, it will be included on the bootable USB flash drive. |
| 5. Insert a USB drive into the system. | **CAUTION:** All data on this drive will be erased. |
| 6. Launch diskpart by entering the following command:<br><br>`C:\>diskpart` | This enters the command-line disk partition tool. |
| 7. Identify the disk number of the USB drive with the following command:<br><br>`DISKPART>list disk` | All of the disks in your system will be listed. Identify the disk number of the USB flash drive. You can usually identify it based on the size. |
| 8. Select the USB flash drive with the **select disk** command:<br><br>`DISKPART>select disk 6` | All subsequent commands will execute on the selected disk.<br><br>**CAUTION:** Ensure that you enter the disk number of the disk that is your USB drive. If you select the wrong drive, the following steps will delete data on the wrong drive. |
| 9. Enter the following command to delete all the data on this disk:<br><br>`DISKPART>clean` | The **clean** command sets all bytes and sectors on the disk to zero, effectively deleting all data. |

| 10. Use this command to create a primary partition:<br><br>`DISKPART>create partition primary` | This creates a single primary partition on the disk. |
|---|---|
| 11. Select the partition:<br><br>`DISKPART>select partition 1` | This selects the partition. |
| 12. Set the partition as an active partition:<br><br>`DISKPART>active` | The **active** command sets the selected partition as an active partition. When set to active, BIOS understands this as a valid system partition (which is bootable). |
| 13. Format the partition:<br><br>`DISKPART>format quick fs=fat32` | You can also format the drive as NTFS with the following command:<br><br>`format quick fs=ntfs`<br><br>**TIP:** If you want to copy files larger than 2 GB to the USB drive, you need to format it as NTFS. A drive formatted as FAT32 cannot copy these larger files and reports that there is not enough disk space. |
| 14. Assign a drive letter:<br><br>`DISKPART>assign` | This assigns a drive letter to the selected partition. At this point, the drive is ready to accept the WinPE files. |
| 15. Leave diskpart:<br><br>`DISKPART>exit` | This exits diskpart. |
| 16. Copy the WinPE files onto the USB.<br><br>Enter the following command for a 32-bit system:<br><br>`C:\>xcopy c:\win7pe_86\iso\*.* /e g:\`<br><br>Enter the following command for a 64-bit system:<br><br>`C:\>xcopy c:\win7pe_64\iso\*.* /e g:\` | Substitute the letter *g* with the actual letter assigned to your USB drive.<br><br>At this point, you have a bootable USB flash drive. It will boot into WinPE and it has **imagex** available. |

You can also build on these steps to create a bootable CD. The only additional steps you need to take are to create an .iso image and burn the image to the CD, as described in the following table.

**TIP:** These steps assume you have completed all the steps in the previous table up to adding the **imagex** tool. It's not necessary to create a bootable USB prior to creating a bootable CD.

| Steps to Create a Bootable CD with WinPE | Remarks |
|---|---|
| 1. Ensure that the deployment tools have been launched from the command prompt, the WinPE folders have been created, and imagex has been added to the folders. | These steps were performed in the previous table. |
| 2. Create an .iso image.<br><br>Enter the following command for a 32-bit system:<br><br>`C:\>oscdimg -n -bC:\win7pe_x86\etfs-boot.com C:\win7pe_x86\ISO C:\win7pe_x86\winpe_x86.iso`<br><br>Enter the following command for a 64-bit system:<br><br>`C:\>oscdimg -n -bC:\win7pe_x64\etfs-boot.com C:\win7pe_x64\ISO C:\win7pe_x64\winpe_x64.iso` | These commands create an .iso image called winpe_x86.iso (for a 32-bit system) or winpe_x64.iso (for a 64-bit system).<br><br>The **-n** switch enables long file-names. The **-b** switch identifies the location of the etfsboot.com file.<br><br>**TIP:** There is no space between **-b** and the path and filename of the etfsboot.com file. This will not work:<br><br>`C:\>oscdimg -n -b  C:\win7pe_x86\etfsboot.com C:\win7pe_x86\ISO C:\win7pe_x86\winpe_x86.iso` |
| 3. Burn the CD.<br><br>Use Windows Explorer to browse to the location of the .iso file (C:\win7pe_x86\ or C:\win7pe_x64\).<br><br>Right-click the .iso file and select **Burn Disk Image**. | The .iso files are named winpe_x86.iso and winpe_x64.iso.<br><br>When complete, you will have a bootable CD that will boot into the WinPE. Because it has the **imagex** file, it can also be used to capture images. |

# Capturing Images with imagex

The **imagex** command can be used to capture an image to a new .wim file. The basic syntax is

```
imagex /capture /flags "edition" image_path image_filename "image_name"
["description"] [switches]
```

For example, the following command can be used to capture a Windows 7 Enterprise installation on the C: drive of a system and store it at the following location: E:\images\win7wim. The name is given as "Win 7 Sales".

**TIP:** The **capture** command captures the command to a new .wim file. If you want to add an image to an existing file, use the **/append** switch.

```
imagex /capture /flags "enterprise" c: e:\images\win7.wim "Win7 Sales"
```

The following table shows the different elements used with the **/capture** switch.

| imagex /capture Commands | Description |
|---|---|
| /flags "*edition*"<br>/flags "enterprise" \| "professional"<br>\| "ultimate"<br>C:\>imagex /capture /flags "enter-prise" c: e:\images\win7sales.wim<br>"Win 7 Sales" | The **/flags** switch can be used to specify which edition you are capturing. Although this isn't needed if you're deploying the image with **imagex**, it is needed when using other tools to deploy the image. Valid parameters for the **/flags** switch are **"enterprise"**, **"professional"**, or **"ultimate"**.<br><br>**NOTE:** Quotes are required around these values. |
| *image_path*<br>C:\>imagex /capture /flags "enter-prise" c: e:\images\win7sales.wim<br>"Win 7 Sales" | Specifies the path of the drive to capture as an image.<br><br>In the example, the c: drive is being captured. |
| *image_filename*<br>C:\>imagex /capture /flags "enter-prise" c: e:\images\win7sales.wim<br>"Win 7 Sales" | Specifies the name and the location of the new .wim file. In the example, the image filename is E:\images\win7sales.wim. |
| "*image_name*"<br>C:\>imagex /capture /flags "enter-prise" c: e:\images\win7sales.wim<br>"Win 7 Sales" | This is the name of the image and can be used to identify it in a .wim file that includes multiple images. The image name must be enclosed in quotes.<br><br>In this example, the image name is "Win 7 Sales".<br><br>**TIP:** Because the image name has spaces, it must be enclosed in quotes. It's common to always use quotes even if the name doesn't include spaces.<br><br>**NOTE:** Images can also be identified by their assigned index number. The first image in the file will be assigned the index number of 1. |
| "*description*"<br>C:\>imagex /capture /flags "enter-prise" c: e:\images\win7sales.wim<br>"Win 7 Sales" "Windows 7 Image for Sales personnel" | Provides a description of the image. The description is optional. If included, it must be enclosed in quotes.<br><br>In this example, the description is "Windows 7 Image for Sales personnel".<br><br>**TIP:** Because the description has spaces, it must be enclosed in quotes. |

| | |
|---|---|
| /check<br>C:\>imagex /capture /flags "enter-<br>prise" c: e:\images\win7sales.wim<br>"Win 7 Sales" /check | Checks the integrity of the .wim file. |
| /verify<br>C:\>imagex /capture /flags "enter-<br>prise" c: e:\images\win7sales.wim<br>"Win 7 Sales" /verify | Enables file resource verification by checking for errors and file duplication. |
| /logfile *file.log*<br>C:\>imagex /capture /flags "enter-<br>prise" c: e:\images\win7sales.wim<br>"Win 7 Sales 1" /verify /logfile<br>d:\imagexappend.log | This will create a plain text file that stores **imagex** command events. |

> **TIP:** You can view the contents of any image using the **imagex /info** *imagefile* command. The section "Comparing Boot and Install Images" in Chapter 17 shows how to view the contents of an image using either **imagex** or **dism**.

## Appending Images with imagex

The .wim files can hold multiple images. If you already have a .wim file and you want to add additional images to it, you can use the **/append** switch when capturing the image. The basic syntax is

```
imagex /append /flags "edition" image_path image_file "image_name"
["description"] [switches]
```

For example, the following command can be used to capture a Windows 7 Enterprise installation on the C: drive of a system and store it at E:\images\win7wim:

```
imagex /append /flags "enterprise" c: e:\images\win7.wim "Win 7 sales"
```

> **TIP:** The primary benefit of appending an image is that duplicate files are not stored more than once. **imagex** compares the files to capture against existing resources and ensures that the same files are not duplicated.

| imagex /append Commands | Description |
|---|---|
| /flags *"edition"*<br>/flags "enterprise" \| "professional"<br>\| "ultimate"<br>C:\>imagex /append /flags "enter-<br>prise" c: e:\images\win7sales.wim<br>"Win 7 Sales" | The **/flags** switch can be used to specify which edition you are appending. This isn't needed if you're deploying the image with **imagex**, but it is needed when using other tools to deploy the image. Valid parameters for the **/flags** switch are **"enterprise"**, **"professional"**, or **"ultimate"**. |

| | |
|---|---|
| *image_path*<br>`C:\>imagex /append /flags "enter-`<br>`prise" c: e:\images\win7sales.wim`<br>`"Win 7 Sales"` | Specifies the path of the drive to append as an image.<br><br>In the example, the C: drive is being appended. |
| *image_file*<br>`C:\>imagex /append /flags "enter-`<br>`prise" c: e:\images\win7sales.wim`<br>`"Win 7 Sales"` | Specifies the name and the location of the existing .wim file to append.<br><br>In the example, the image file is E:\images\win7sales.wim.<br><br>**CAUTION:** Ensure there is enough room on the target drive. If the append operation fails due to not enough space, the appended .wim file might become corrupt. |
| `"`*image_name*`"`<br>`C:\>imagex /append /flags "enter-`<br>`prise" c: e:\images\win7sales.wim`<br>`"Win 7 Sales"` | This is the name of the image and can be used to identify it in a .wim file that includes multiple images. The image name must be enclosed in quotes because it has spaces in it. In this example, the image name is "Win 7 Sales".<br><br>Images can also be identified by their assigned index number. An appended image will automatically be assigned the next available number. For example, if the .wim file has two images and you append a third image to it, it will be assigned the index value of 3. |
| `"`*description*`"`<br>`C:\>imagex /append /flags "enter-`<br>`prise" c: e:\images\win7sales.wim`<br>`"Win 7 Sales" "Windows 7 Image for`<br>`Sales personnel"` | Provides a description of the image. The description is optional. If included, it must be enclosed in quotes.<br><br>In this example, the description is "Windows 7 Image for Sales personnel". |
| `/verify`<br>`C:\>imagex /append /flags "enter-`<br>`prise" c: e:\images\win7sales.wim`<br>`"Windows 7 Image for Sales`<br>`personnel" /verify` | Enables file resource verification by checking for errors and file duplication. |
| `/logfile` *file.log*<br>`C:\>imagex /append /flags "enter-`<br>`prise" c: e:\images\win7sales.wim`<br>`"Windows 7 Image for Sales`<br>`personnel" /verify /logfile`<br>`d:\imagexappend.log` | This will create a plain text file that stores **imagex** command events. |

## Deleting Images with imagex

Occasionally, you'll want to delete an image from an image file. For example, you might have an image file with multiple images, one of which has become obsolete. Instead of keeping it in the file, you can delete it to conserve space, while still keeping the other images intact. The basic syntax is

```
imagex /delete image_file "image_name" | image_number
```

The following table shows the syntax for the **/delete** switch.

| imagex /delete Switch | Description |
|---|---|
| image_file<br>C:\>imagex /delete e:\images<br>\win7sales.wim "Win 7 Sales" | Specifies the name and the location of the existing .wim file to delete.<br><br>In this example, the path and name of the image file is E:\images\win7sales.wim. |
| "image_name"<br>C:\>imagex /delete e:\images<br>\win7sales.wim "Win 7 Sales" | Provides the name of the image within the image file to be deleted.<br><br>In this example, the name of the image is "Win 7 Sales". |
| image_number<br>C:\>imagex /delete e:\images<br>\win7sales.wim 3 | The image can also be deleted using the index number. You can view a listing of the images in the image file with the **/info** switch:<br><br>imagex /info E:\images<br>\win7sales.wim<br><br>The output identifies the image names and their index numbers. |

## Deploying Images with imagex

Images can be deployed to a system using the **imagex** command and the **/apply** switch. The basic syntax is

```
imagex /apply image_file {"image_name" | image_number} image_path
```

For example, if you want to apply the first image in the E:\images\win7.wim file to the C: drive of a system, you could use the following command:

```
imagex /apply e:\images\win7.wim 1 c:
```

You can also apply the image based on the name, as follows:

```
imagex /apply e:\images\win7.wim "Win 7 Sales" c:
```

| imagex /apply Switch | Description |
|---|---|
| *image_file*<br>`C:\>imagex /apply e:\images\`<br>`win7.wim 1 c:` | Specifies the name and the location of the volume image to apply.<br><br>In the example, e:\images\win7sales.wim represents *image_file*. |
| `"`*image_name*`"`<br>`C:\>imagex /apply e:\images\`<br>`win7.wim "Win7 Sales" c:` | Specifies the name of the image in the .wim file. You can use this or the image number.<br><br>**NOTE:** The name needs to be enclosed in quotes. |
| *image_number*<br>`C:\>imagex /apply e:\images\`<br>`win7.wim 1 c:` | Specifies the number of the specific volume within the .wim file. Wim files can hold multiple images, and the first one is numbered 1.<br><br>You can view a listing of the images in the image file with one of the following commands:<br><br>`imagex /info e:\images\win7.wim`<br><br>or<br><br>`dism /get-wiminfo /wimfile:e:`<br>`\images\win7.wim`<br><br>The example uses the first image in the file. |
| *image_path*<br>`C:\>imagex /apply e:\images\`<br>`win7.wim 1 c:` | Specifies the file path where the image will be applied. In the example, the image will be applied to the C: drive. |

This chapter provides information and commands concerning the following topics:

- Online servicing versus offline servicing
- Mounting images
- Getting information about mounted images
- Modifying images
- Saving images

## Online Servicing Versus Offline Servicing

You can use the Deployment Image Service and Management (**dism**) tool to service images offline. In other words, you can service images without having the image booted into the operating system. The following table describes online and offline servicing methods.

| Image Servicing Method | Description |
|---|---|
| Online servicing | The computer is booted into the operating system. The image of the computer must be recaptured to save any changes. |
| Offline servicing | The image is extracted from a .wim file and fully expanded in a process known as mounting the image. |

As a reminder, Figure 21-1 shows how **dism** fits into the overall picture of image management. First, Windows 7 is installed and configured on a reference computer with any additional applications desired. The system is prepared with sysprep and then the image is captured. Chapter 20, "Using imagex," provided details on how the image is captured with **imagex**, but it could just as easily be captured with another tool such as Windows Deployment Services (WDS). The captured image can then be serviced offline with dism on the technician's computer.

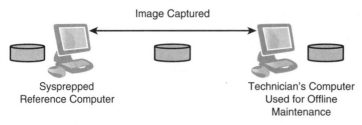

Image Captured

Sysprepped
Reference Computer

Technician's Computer
Used for Offline
Maintenance

**Figure 21-1**   A Windows 7 Image Mounted for Offline Servicing

## Mounting Images

**dism** is used to mount images for offline servicing. After the image is mounted, you can service it. The basic syntax of the command to mount an image is

```
dism /mount-wim /wimfile:path /index:number /mountdir:path
```

For example, if you wanted to mount into the c:\mountdir folder the first image in the win7.wim file located in the c:\images folder, you would use this command:

```
dism /mount-wim /wimfile:c:\images\win7.wim /index:1 /mountdir:c:
\mountdir
```

Figure 21-2 shows the output as an image is mounted with **dism**. Mounting an image can take a few minutes, but **dism** provides a dynamic status bar showing progress as it mounts the image.

**Figure 21-2**   Mounting an Image with **dism**

When using the **dism** command to work with images, you need to know how to use some key switches. These include the **/wimfile**, **/index**, and **/mountdir** switches.

| Basic dism Switch | Description |
|---|---|
| `/wimfile:`*path and filename*<br>`/wimfile:h:\images\install.wim`<br>`/wimfile:h:\images\install.wim`<br>`/index:1 /wimfile:c:\mountdir` | This points to the location of the source .wim file. In the example, the install.wim file is being used and it's located in the h:\images folder. |
| `/index:`*number*<br>`/index:1`<br>`/wimfile:h:\images\install.wim`<br>`/index:1 /wimfile:c:\mountdir` | This is the index number of the image within the .wim file.<br><br>**TIP:** You can retrieve a listing of the images within the .wim file with the following command:<br><br>`dism /get-wiminfo /wimfile:h:`<br>`\images\install.wim` |
| `/mountdir`<br>`/wimfile:h:\images\install.wim`<br>`/index:1 /wimfile:c:\mountdir` | This identifies the path of an existing folder that will be used to mount the image.<br><br>**NOTE:** If the folder doesn't exist, the command will fail. |

Figure 21-3 shows what a mounted image looks like in Windows Explorer (in the c:\mountdir folder). Notice that it looks just like any other folder in Windows Explorer. You can add and remove files here and use other dism tools to add and remove drivers, features, applications, and more.

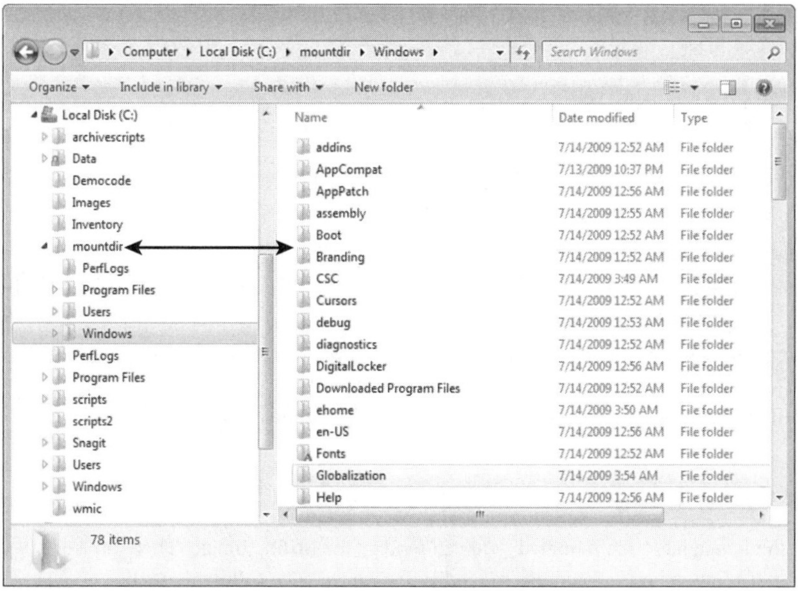

**Figure 21-3** Windows 7 Image Mounted for Offline Servicing

The following table shows how the basic switches are used in full **dism** commands.

| Basic dism Command | Description |
|---|---|
| `/mount-wim`<br>`dism /mount-wim /wimfile:`*path and*<br>*filename* `/index:`*number* `/mountdir:`*path*<br>`C:\>dism /mount-wim /wimfile:c:\images\`<br>`win7.wim /index:1 /mountdir:c:\mountdir` | The **/mount-wim** switch extracts the contents of an image file into a folder.<br><br>**NOTE:** Changes to the image are not saved until the image is committed. |
| `/read-only`<br>`C:\>dism /mount-wim /wimfile:c:\images\`<br>`win7.wim /index:1 /mountdir:c:\mountdir`<br>`/read-only` | You can use the **/read-only** switch to mount the image with read-only permissions. This enables you to browse the image without making changes. |

## Getting Information About Mounted Images

You can view information about mounted images with the **/get-mountedwiminfo** switch. It doesn't require any other information. The command is shown in the following code snippet. The output shows you which image is mounted, and where it is mounted.

```
C:\>dism /get-mountedwiminfo

Deployment Image Servicing and Management tool
Version: 6.1.7600.16385

Mounted images:

Mount Dir : c:\mountwim
Image File : c:\images\win7.wim
Image Index : 5
Mounted Read/Write : Yes
Status : Ok

The operation completed successfully.
```

If no images are mounted, the command outputs "No mounted images found."

## Modifying Images

After the image has been mounted, you can modify the offline image. There are several categories of switches you can use to modify the image. The following sections cover

- Working with drivers
- Working with packages and features
- Miscellaneous image modifications

## Working with Drivers

You can use **dism** to identify drivers installed in an image and add and remove drivers from an image.

| dism Switches for Drivers | Description |
|---|---|
| Get drivers<br><br>`/get-drivers [/all] [/format:table \| /format:list]`<br>`C:\>dism /image:c:\mountdir /get-drivers`<br>`C:\>dism /image:c:\mountdir /get-drivers /all`<br>`C:\>dism /image:c:\mountdir /get-drivers /all /format:table`<br>`C:\>dism /image:c:\mountdir /get-drivers /all /format:table > drivers.txt` | Retrieves a listing of all driver packages in the image.<br><br>The **/all** switch specifies that all drivers (not just third-party drivers) should be retrieved. The default format is **list**, but you can also retrieve the data in a table format.<br><br>**TIP:** Third-party drivers are given a published name in the format of oem#.inf, starting with zero. For example, the first driver is oem0.inf, the second is oem1.inf, and so on. You can use this name to get detailed information about the driver. |
| Get information about a specific driver<br><br>`/get-driverinfo /driver:drivername.inf`<br>`C:\>dism /image:c:\mountdir /get-driverinfo /driver:oem0.inf`<br>`C:\>dism /image:c:\mountdir /get-driverinfo /driver:1394.inf` | Retrieves information about a specific driver.<br><br>The first example retrieves detailed information about the first third-party driver (oem0.inf). The second example provides detailed information about the Windows USB driver (1394.inf). |
| Add a driver<br><br>`/add-driver /driver:path`<br>`C:\>dism /image:c:\mountdir /add-driver /driver:c:\drivers \dell2335dnprinter` | The **/add-driver** switch needs the **/driver** switch to specify the location of the driver package. This is simply the folder where the driver package is located.<br><br>**NOTE:** This command will not work if the driver is in the cabinet file format. It must be extracted from the cabinet file first. |
| Remove a driver<br><br>`/remove-driver /driver:publishedname`<br>`C:\>dism /image:c:\mountdir /remove-driver /driver:oem1.inf` | The **/remove-driver** switch requires the **/driver** switch to identify the driver using the published name.<br><br>**NOTE:** You can retrieve a listing of the drivers (including the drivers published names) with the **/get-drivers** switch, as follows:<br><br>`dism /image:c:\mountdir /get-drivers` |

**TIP:** You can search for and retrieve Windows 7 drivers from the Microsoft catalog site: http://catalog.update.microsoft.com/. You can enter "Windows 7" (or any search term) in the search box to retrieve drivers for Windows 7. Then, add drivers to your basket and download them. The drivers are downloaded as cabinet files. You can extract them to a folder, and then just point to the folder when using the **/add-driver** command. **dism** determines which drivers from the folder to install to match the operating system.

## Working with Packages and Features

**dism** provides several tools that you can use to add and remove both packages and features. *Packages* are applications that can come in the form of cabinet files or Microsoft update files. *Features* are built-in features of Windows 7 that you can enable or disable with **dism**. The following two tables show the syntax for the package and feature switches.

**TIP:** Package names must be entered using the exact case. If the exact case is not used, the commands will fail.

| dism Switches for Packages | Description |
|---|---|
| Get packages<br><br>`/get-packages [/all] [/format:table`<br>`| /format:list]`<br>`C:\>dism /image:c:\mountdir`<br>`/get-packages`<br>`C:\>dism /image:c:\mountdir`<br>`/get-packages /format:table`<br>`C:\>dism /image:c:\mountdir`<br>`/get- packages /format:table >`<br>`packages.txt` | You can retrieve a list of packages that are currently available in the image with the **/get-packages** switch. This switch has similar options to those of the **/get-drivers** switch.<br><br>**TIP:** Packages are identified with the Package Identity property. These identities can be very long, as the following example shows:<br><br>Package Identity : Microsoft-Windows-LocalPack-US-Package~31bf3856ad364 e35~x86~~6.1.7600.16385<br><br>When using them, you can cut them from the deployment tools command prompt to use in other commands. Make sure you use the exact case for the package name. |
| Get package information<br><br>`/get-packageinfo`<br>`/packagename:package identity`<br>`C:\>dism /image:c:\mountdir`<br>`/get-packageinfo`<br>`/packagename:Microsoft-Windows-`<br>`LocalPack-ZA-Package~`<br>`31bf3856ad364e35~x86~~6.1.7600.16385` | You can retrieve detailed information about packages that are installed in the image, or packages.<br><br>You can retrieve information about installed packages with the **/packagename** switch. Make sure you use the exact case for the package name. |

| Get application patch information<br><br>`/get-apppatchinfo`<br>`C:\>dism /image:c:\mountdir`<br>`/get-apppatchinfo` | You can check to see if any patches have been applied to applications within the system with the **/get-apppatchinfo** switch. |
|---|---|
| Get patch information<br><br>`/get-apppatches /productcode:{guid}`<br>`C:\>dism /image:c:\mountdir`<br>`/get-apppatches /productcode:`<br>`{7764DEFC-C5D1-413C-8428-`<br>`2AA903BF6DAA}` | If application patches have been applied, you can retrieve detailed information about any single patch by adding the **/productcode** switch to **the /get-apppatches** switch. |
| Add packages<br><br>`/add-package /packagepath:path and`<br>`package file name`<br>`C:\>dism /image:c:\mountdir`<br>`/add-package /packagepath:c:`<br>`\downloads\x86fre_grmrsat_msu.msu` | The **/add-package** switch requires the **/package-path** switch to identify the path and name of the package file. Package files can be cabinet files (.cab) or Microsoft update files (.msu).<br><br>The example installs the Remote Server Administration Tools (RSAT) into the Windows 7 installation. |
| Remove packages<br><br>`/remove-package`<br>`/packagename:package name`<br>`C:\>dism /image:c:\mountdir`<br>`/remove-package`<br>`/packagename:Microsoft-Windows-`<br>`LocalPack-ZA-Package~`<br>`31bf3856ad364e35~x86~~6.1.7600.16385` | You can remove any package installed in the image with the **/remove-package** switch.<br><br>The package name is the package identity property. The package identity property is included when you retrieve a list of packages with the **/get-packages** switch. Make sure you use the exact case for the package name. |

**TIP:** Feature names must be entered using the exact case. If the exact case is not used, the commands will fail. In other words if you're trying to disable all games and you use **inboxgames** instead of **InboxGames**, the command will fail.

| dism Switches for Features | Description |
|---|---|
| Get features<br><br>`/get-features [/all]`<br>`[/format:table | /format:list]`<br>`C:\>dism /image:c:\mountdir`<br>`/get-features`<br>`C:\>dism /image:c:\mountdir`<br>`/get-features /format:table`<br>`C:\>dism /image:c:\mountdir`<br>`/get-features /format:table >`<br>`features.txt` | You can retrieve a list of features that are currently available in the image with the **/get-features** switch. This switch has similar options to those of the **/get-drivers** switch, described earlier in the chapter. |

| Get feature information<br><br>`/get-featureinfo`<br>`/feature-name:`*`featurename`*<br>`C:\>dism /image:c:\mountdir`<br>`/get-featureinfo /featurename:`<br>`RemoteServerAdministrationTools` | You can retrieve specific information about any feature with the **/get-featureinfo** switch. This switch requires the name of the feature, identified with the **/featurename** switch. Make sure you use the exact case for the feature name.<br><br>**TIP:** The **/get-features** switch provides a list of all features and includes the feature name property needed for the **/get-featureinfo** switch.<br><br>This example assumes RSAT was installed as a package. |
|---|---|
| Enable a feature<br><br>`/enable-feature`<br>`/feature-name:`*`featurename`*<br>`C:\>dism /image:c:\mountdir`<br>`/enable-feature /featurename:`<br>`RemoteServerAdministrationTools`<br>`C:\>dism /image:c:`<br>`\mountdir /enable-feature`<br>`/featurename:InboxGames` | The **/enable-feature** switch requires the **/feature-name** switch. Make sure you use the exact case for the feature name.<br><br>The first example enables the RSAT features and assumes that the RSAT package has been installed.<br><br>The second example enables games. |
| Disable a feature<br><br>`/disable-feature`<br>`/featurename:`*`featurename`*<br>`C:\>dism /image:c:\mountdir`<br>`/disable-feature /featurename:R`<br>`emoteServerAdministrationTools`<br>`C:\>dism /image:c:`<br>`\mountdir /disable-feature`<br>`/featurename:InboxGames` | The **/disable-feature** switch requires the **/feature-name** switch. Make sure you use the exact case for the feature name.<br><br>The first example disables the RSAT features and assumes that the RSAT package has been installed.<br><br>The second example disables games. |

## Miscellaneous Image Modifications

Sometimes you might want to identify the current edition of an image or even modify the edition or the product key within an image. The following table shows the commands to do so.

| Miscellaneous Switches | Description |
|---|---|
| Get current edition<br><br>`/get-currentedition`<br>`C:\>dism /image:c:\mountdir`<br>`/get-currentedition` | Identify the current edition in the mounted image. |

| Get target editions<br><br>`C:\>dism /image:c:\mountdir`<br>`/get-targeteditions` | Identify editions that the current edition can be changed to. For example, if the current edition is Professional, it can be upgraded to Ultimate. |
|---|---|
| Set edition<br><br>`C:\>dism /image:c:\mountdir`<br>`/set-edition:ultimate` | Change the edition from the current edition to the specified edition.<br><br>**NOTE:** You can only change to a higher edition. You cannot change to a lower edition. |
| Set a product key<br><br>`C:\>dism /image:c:\mountdir`<br>`/set-product-`<br>`key:12345-12345-12345-12345-12345` | If you change the edition, you might need to set a new product key. You must use a valid product key for the edition. The key is validated with this command, though the image is not activated. |

# Saving Images

After you have completed servicing the image offline, you need to save the changes. The following table shows some of the commands used to unmount the image and either save the changes or discard the changes.

| Committing and Unmounting Images | Description |
|---|---|
| Commit the changes<br><br>`/commit-wim /mountdir:`*`path`*<br>`C:\>dism /commit-wim /mountdir:c:`<br>`\mountdir` | This applies the changes made offline to the image. The image is then saved back to its original location. You cannot commit the changes if the image was mounted in read-only mode.<br><br>**NOTE:** The image remains mounted until the **unmount-wim** command is executed. |
| Unmount the image and save the changes<br><br>`/unmount-wim /mountdir:`*`path`*` {/commit`<br>`| /discard }`<br>`C:\>dism /unmount-wim /mountdir:c:`<br>`\mountdir /commit` | The **unmount** command releases all the resources dedicated to tracking the mounted images.<br><br>You need to either commit or discard the changes.<br><br>**NOTE:** When the unmount operation is complete, the files in the mounted folder will be deleted. Additionally, if you execute **dism /get-mountedwiminfo**, it will show that the image is no longer mounted. |

| Unmount the image and discard the changes<br><br>`/unmount-wim /mountdir:path {/commit`<br>`| /discard}`<br>`C:\>dism /unmount-wim /mountdir:c:`<br>`\mountdir /discard` | When combined with the **/discard** switch, the image is unmounted, but the changes are not saved to the original image. |
|---|---|

Figure 21-4 shows the progress of the **dism unmount** command. Notice that it completes the command in two steps. The first step saves the image, and the second step unmounts the image. After the image is unmounted, the contents of the mount folder are deleted.

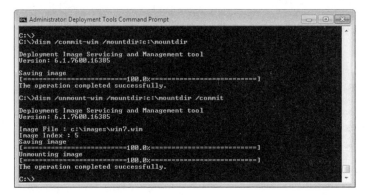

**Figure 21-4**   Committing and Unmounting an Image

This chapter provides information and commands concerning the following topics:

- Add drivers to WinPE with **drvload**
- Run commands within WinPE with **wpeutil**

## Add Drivers to WinPE with drvload

Occasionally, you might want to add drivers to a booted Windows Preinstallation Environment (WinPE). For example, you might need a specific driver loaded to access an external drive or to enable a network interface card (NIC). You can do so with the **drvload** command. The **drvload** command is available in WinPE, but it is not available in a regular operating system. The basic syntax is

```
drvload inf_path
```

A setup information file (.inf) includes multiple sections with the instructions needed to install the driver. The folder holding the .inf file usually holds several more files that are part of the drive package.

> **TIP:** You can load drivers to offline images using **dism**, covered in Chapter 21, "Using the Deployment Image Service and Management (dism) Tool." The same commands used to service offline installation images work with offline boot images such as a WinPE image.

| drvload Command | Description |
| --- | --- |
| Load a single driver<br><br>X:\>drvload c:\data\drivera\abc.inf | You need to specify the full path to the driver's .inf file. Supporting files referenced by the .inf file should be in the same folder. In the example, the driver's .inf file is located in the C:\data\drivera\ folder.<br><br>**NOTE: drvload** starts on a RAM disk on the X: drive. |
| Load multiple drivers<br><br>X:\>drvload c:\data\drivera\abc.inf c:\data\driverx\xyz.inf | You can load multiple drivers in a single command by separating the paths with a space. |

> **TIP:** After loading a disk driver, you might need to force a rescan to ensure it's recognized. If you are loading a disk driver, you can use the **diskpart rescan** command from the command prompt.

## Run Commands Within WinPE with wpeutil

The Windows PE utility (**wpeutil**) is a command-line tool you can use in WinPE. The basic syntax is

```
wpeutil command [argument]
```

For example, if you wanted to reboot the WinPE, you could use the following command:

```
wpeutil reboot
```

Figure 22-1 shows the **wpeutil** command executing various commands in WinPE, and the following table lists the commonly used commands.

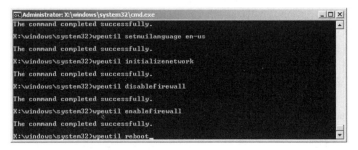

**Figure 22-1**   Executing **wpeutil** in the WinPE Environment

> **NOTE:** The **wpeutil** command is not available when you are booted into Windows 7 normally.

| Commonly Used wpeutil Command | Description |
|---|---|
| X:\>**wpeutil shutdown** | Shuts down the current WinPE session. |
| X:\>**wpeutil reboot** | Reboots the current WinPE session. |
| X:\>**wpeutil initializenetwork** | Initializes network components and drivers. Network drivers must be available to load. |
| X:\>**wpeutil enablefirewall** | Enables the firewall. |
| X:\>**wpeutil disablefirewall** | Disables the firewall. |

| | |
|---|---|
| `X:\>wpeutil setmuilanguage en-us` | Sets the language. The multilingual user interface (MUI) allows multiple languages, and if you're using a CD from a different country, you can set the language to English with the example command. |
| `X:\>wpeutil listkeyboardlayouts 1033` | Lists available keyboard layouts with their IDs. The ID can be used to modify the keyboard layout. For example, the standard U.S. keyboard ID is 0409:00000409, and the Dvorak U.S. keyboard ID is 0409:00010409. |
| `X:\>wpeutil setkeyboardlayout`<br>`0409:00000409` | Sets the keyboard to the standard U.S. keyboard. |

This chapter provides information and commands concerning the following topics:

- Installing Windows 7 with **setup**
- Using the autounattend.xml file
- Using **slmgr**

## Installing Windows 7 with setup

In addition to installing Windows 7 using **imagex** (covered in Chapter 20, "Using imagex"), you can also install Windows 7 from the command line using the **setup** application. Setup.exe is located at the root of the installation DVD. The basic syntax is

```
setup [options]
```

> **TIP:** If AutoPlay is enabled, the **setup** application automatically starts when you insert the installation DVD.

The following table shows the common **setup** options.

> **NOTE:** You don't have to run setup from the installation DVD. You can also copy the contents of the installation DVD to a network share and run **setup** from the network share.

| setup Option | Description |
|---|---|
| Use an answer file<br><br>`setup /unattend:filename`<br>`E:\>setup`<br>`/unattend:\\file1\win7\unattend.xml`<br>`E:\>setup /unattend:e:\unattend.xml` | You can use either a local path or a UNC path (\\*servername\sharename*) for the filename.<br><br>**NOTE:** These examples assume the DVD-ROM drive is the E: drive and the path has been changed to E:. |

| Use a different installation environment<br><br>`setup /intallfrom:`*`path`*<br>`E:\>setup`<br>`/intallfrom:e:\64\install.wim` | Specifies a different install.wim file to use. By default, the install.wim file in the \sources\ folder is used. This is useful if you want to install an image with a different architecture. For example, the installation DVD may include 32-bit images, but you might want to use a 64-bit image located elsewhere. |
|---|---|
| Use WDS server discover mode<br><br>`E:\>setup /wdsdiscover` | The client will search for a Windows Deployment Services (WDS) server. |
| Specify the WDS server to use<br><br>`setup  /wdsdiscover  /`<br>`wdsserver:`*`server-name`*<br>`E:\>setup  /wdsdiscover`<br>`/wdsserver:wds1` | The client will search for the named WDS server. The **/wdsdiscover** switch is required when using the **/wdsserver** switch. |
| `setup /tempdrive:`*`driveletter`*<br>`setup /tempdrive:d` | Identifies an alternative drive to use for temporary files. Temporary files will be copied to the root of the specified drive instead of to the installation partition during the installation.<br><br>**NOTE:** The colon (:) is not needed after the drive letter. |

# Using the Autounattend.xml File

You can complete a semiautomated installation of Windows 7 using the installation DVD. This method allows you to boot to the installation DVD and have the autounattend.xml file provide all the answers for the installation.

> **TIP:** Answer files are named unattend.xml by default. However, Windows will not automatically use an answer file named unattend.xml file. This prevents an accidental repartitioning of the disk. If you want Windows to use the answer file automatically, it must be renamed autounattend.xml. The setup program searches for this autounattend.xml file on the root of a USB flash drive when it starts.

One method of using the autounattend.xml file uses these steps:

| Installation Step | Remarks |
|---|---|
| 1. Create an answer file and rename it autounattend.xml. | You can use one of the samples in the C:\Program Files\Windows AIK\Samples folder as a template, or create an answer file using the Windows System Image Manager (WSIM) to create an answer file. |
| 2. Copy the autounattend.xml file to the root of a USB drive. | The name of the file must be autounattend.xml. |

| 3. Boot the system using the installation DVD. | If necessary, configure the BIOS to ensure you can boot to the DVD. |
| 4. As soon as the boot process starts from the installation DVD, insert the USB flash drive. | The installation will recognize the autounattend.xml file at the root of the USB drive and use it for the installation. |

The Windows 7 installation will also look in other locations for an XML file. The following table shows the order of precedence for answer files during the installation.

**NOTE:** Some locations (such as removable media) require the answer file to be named autounattend.xml, while other locations provide more flexibility.

| Search Order for an XML File | Description |
| --- | --- |
| Registry<br><br>HKEYLocalMachine\System\Setup \| UnattendFile *key* | The value of the UnattendFile key can point to the location of the .xml file. It doesn't have to be named autounattend.xml or unattend.xml. |
| %windir$\Panther\unattend | The name of the file must be either autounattend.xml or unattend.xml. |
| %windir$\Panther | A cached copy of the answer file is stored here during the setup process. This file should not be used, modified, or deleted during the Windows setup process. Also, because it is modified by the Windows Setup program, it should not be used after the installation has completed. |
| Removable read/write media (such as a USB flash drive)<br><br>In order of the drives (A:, B:, and so on) | The name of the answer file must be autounattend.xml and it must be in the root of the drive. |
| Removable read-only media (such as a CD or DVD)<br><br>In order of the drives (A:, B:, and so on) | The name of the answer file must be autounattend.xml and it must be in the root of the drive. |

# Using slmgr

The software licensing manager (slmgr) tool is a VBScript script that you can use to modify many different license settings. The basic syntax is

```
slmgr options
```

**TIP:** Some documentation indicates that **slmgr** uses a dash (-) for switches, whereas other documentation indicates a forward slash (/) is needed. Both work equally well.

This section is divided into the different uses of the slmgr tool as follows:

- Basic **slmgr** commands
- **lmgr** activation commands
- **lmgr** commands used for KMS clients
- **lmgr** switches used for token-based activation

## Basic **slmgr** Commands

You can use the **slmgr** tool to reset the activation grace period and view the licensing information, as shown in the following table.

| Basic slmgr Command | Description |
|---|---|
| Reset the grace period<br><br>`/rearm`<br>`C:\>slmgr /rearm` | The grace period is the time when Windows 7 will run normally without being activated, and is 30 days by default.<br><br>You can reset the grace period up to three times. |
| Retrieve license information<br><br>`/dli [activation-id \| all]`<br>`C:\>slmgr /dli`<br>`C:\>slmgr /dli all` | This returns information on the current license by default.<br><br>You can use **all** to view all licenses, or specify an activation ID to view a specific license.<br><br>**NOTE:** The activation IDs are shown with the **/dlv** switch. |
| Retrieve license information in verbose mode<br><br>`/dlv [activation-id \| all]`<br>`C:\>slmgr /dlv`<br>`C:\>slmgr /dlv all` | This works just like **/dli** but provides more detailed information about the licenses.<br><br>Figure 23-1 shows the output from this command. |
| Display expiration status<br><br>`/xpr [activation-id]`<br>`C:\>slmgr /xpr` | This displays the expiration status for the current license. During and after the grace period, this indicates Notification mode. Once activated, it indicates the system is "permanently activated."<br><br>If a KMS server has issued a temporary license, it will indicate the grace period end date. |

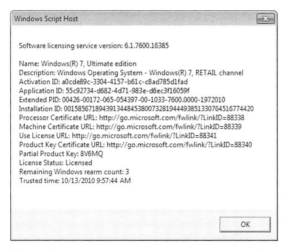

**Figure 23-1**    Viewing Detailed Information About the Default License

## slmgr Activation Commands

The **slmgr** tool also includes several commands you can use for activation, as shown in the following table.

| slmgr Activation Command | Description |
|---|---|
| Activate Windows 7<br><br>`/ato [activation-id]`<br>`C:\>slmgr /ato`<br>`C:\>slmgr /ato 12345-12345-`<br>`2345-12345` | Activate Windows now. You can use the current activation ID (by not specifying one, as in the first example), or activate Windows with a different activation ID (as shown in the second example).<br><br>This is useful if a computer is being configured in an online environment but will be deployed in an isolated environment without Internet access.<br><br>**NOTE:** Activation normally doesn't occur until three days after the installation. |
| Change the product key<br><br>`/ipk product key`<br>`slmgr /ipk 12345-12345-2345-`<br>`12345` | The **/ipk** switch installs the product key or replaces the existing key with the specified key. |

| Clear the product key<br><br>`/cpky`<br>`C:\>slmgr /cpky` | Remove the product key from the registry. This can be done to prevent disclosure attacks trying to discover the enterprise volume license key. |
|---|---|
| Uninstall the product key<br><br>`/upk`<br>`C:\>slmgr /upk` | Uninstall the product key. |
| Install the system license<br><br>`/ilc` *License file*<br>`C:\>slmgr /ilc vamt.xml` | License files are received from the Volume Activation Management Tool (VAMT). |
| Reinstall system license files<br><br>`/rilc`<br>`C:\>slmgr /rilc` | Existing license files are reinstalled. |
| Display the activation ID<br><br>`/dti`<br>`C:\>slmgr /dti` | You can use this for offline activation. |

## slmgr Commands Used for KMS Clients

Many organizations use a Key Management Server (KMS) with volume license keys. The following table shows some switches that can be used for the KMS clients.

| slmgr KMS Client Command | Description |
|---|---|
| Identify the KMS server<br><br>`/skms` *servername*<br>`C:\>slmgr /skms server1` | You can name the KMS server that the KMS client should use. The name should be resolvable via DNS. |
| Modify the default KMS port<br><br>`/skms` *servername:port*<br>`C:\>slmgr /skms server1:1689` | The default port for the KMS server is 1688. If it's changed on the KMS server, you need to change it on the KMS client. |
| Clear the KMS server and port information<br><br>`/ckms`<br>`C:\>slmgr /ckms` | Clears any previously configured KMS server and port settings. |
| Enable KMS host caching<br><br>`/skhc`<br>`C:\>slmgr /skhc` | When the KMS client activates with a KMS server, it will cache the name of the server and connect to it when it needs to reactivate. KMS host caching is enabled by default. |
| Disable KMS host caching<br><br>`/ckhc`<br>`C:\>slmgr /ckhc` | Clearing the KMS host cache causes the client to use discovery with DNS to locate the KMS server. |

## slmgr Commands Used for Token-Based Activation

Some organizations use token-based activation for Windows 7. The following table shows many of the **slmgr** switches used with token-based activation.

| slmgr KMS Client Command | Description |
|---|---|
| List installed token-based activation licenses<br><br>`/lil`<br>`C:\>slmgr /lil` | This will be blank if token-based activation is not used. |
| Remove installed token-based activation licenses<br><br>`/ril [ilid]`<br>`C:\>slmgr /ril` | You can remove all licenses, or only a specific license identified by the installed license ID shown with the **/lil** switch. The example removes all licenses. |
| Clear the token-based activation-only flag<br><br>`/ctao`<br>`C:\>slmgr /ctao` | When cleared, token-based activation is not used. The flag is cleared by default. |
| Set the token-based activation-only flag<br><br>`/stao`<br>`C:\>slmgr /stao` | When set, token-based activation is used. |
| List token-based activation certificates<br><br>`/ltc`<br>`C:\>slmgr /ltc` | Provides a listing of any installed activation certificates. |

This chapter provides information and commands concerning the following topics:

- Understanding migration stores
- Reviewing migration paths
- Understanding hard-link migration stores
- Capturing migration data with **scanstate**

## Understanding Migration Stores

A *migration store* is a database of user files and settings. It doesn't include any applications, but it does include the settings for the applications. For example, if the same version of Microsoft Word is installed on the original computer and the new computer, the configurable settings for Microsoft Word will be transferred over. However, if Word is not installed on the new computer, migrating the store will not install it.

Migration data includes the following.

| Migration Data | Description |
|---|---|
| User accounts | You can migrate all user accounts, or pick which user accounts to migrate. The migrated data for the user accounts includes the users' profiles. |
| E-mail | E-mail files such as Outlook .pst files are migrated. |
| Multimedia such as music, pictures, and video | Multimedia files are migrated, and you can choose which files to include or omit. |
| Web browser settings | This includes settings such as favorites and the home page. |
| Other data | Other non-Windows folders are analyzed for data. You can choose what data to include or omit. |

## Reviewing Migration Paths

The two primary migration methods are described in the following table.

| Migration Method | Description |
|---|---|
| Windows Easy Transfer<br><br>■ Transfer data with Windows Easy Transfer cable or network connection<br><br>■ Transfer data to an external hard drive or USB flash drive | This is a wizard to transfer files and settings. This can be done for single systems, but it is very time consuming so it isn't used often in large organizations. Figure 24-1 shows the Windows Easy Transfer tool, and Figure 24-2 shows the process.<br><br>TIP: You must use the Windows 7 version of the Windows Easy Transfer tool on both computers. It is available as a free download from Microsoft's download site (www.microsoft.com/downloads). |
| Migrate with User State Migration Tool (USMT)<br><br>Capture data with **scanstate**<br><br>Restore data with **loadstate** | **scanstate** and **loadstate** tools are part of the USMT installed with the Windows Automated Installation Kit (WAIK).<br><br>NOTE: This chapter includes scanstate commands. Chapter 25, "Restoring User Data with loadstate," includes loadstate commands. |

TIP: Windows Easy Transfer is a manual method used for single computers. USMT methods can be automated and used for multiple computers.

**Figure 24-1** Windows Easy Transfer Tool

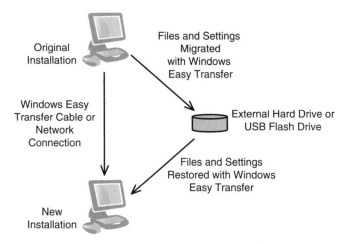

**Figure 24-2** Transferring Data with Windows Easy Transfer Tool

**TIP:** Windows XP can't be upgraded to Windows 7. Smaller organizations that may have performed upgrades to help users keep their data and settings are now forced to do new installations. This makes mastering migration techniques much more important.

When using the USMT tools, there are two primary scenarios to consider. One is a PC *refresh*, where the same hardware is used but Windows 7 replaces the current operating system. The second is a PC *replacement*, where the hardware and the operating system are replaced.

**TIP:** Most large organizations bypass upgrades. Instead, they save the users' migration data, install the new operating system through automation, and then transfer the migration store.

Figure 24-3 shows the how **scanstate** and **loadstate** fit into these scenarios. In each, **scanstate** is used to capture the migration data and **loadstate** restores it. Migration data can be stored on the internal hard drive, an external hard drive, or a network share.

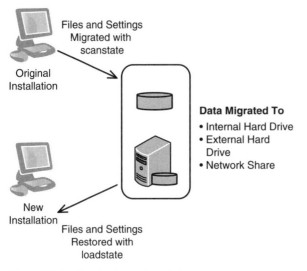

Files and Settings
Migrated with
scanstate

Original
Installation

**Data Migrated To**
• Internal Hard Drive
• External Hard
  Drive
• Network Share

New
Installation
Files and Settings
Restored with
loadstate

**Figure 24-3**   Transferring Data with USMT Tools

**TIP:** Whenever possible, the migration data should be stored locally. The amount of data that needs to be transferred can be significant and might seriously degrade network performance if transferred to and from a network share.

There are several possible PC refresh scenarios.

| PC Refresh Scenario (Same Hardware) | Description |
|---|---|
| PC refresh with compressed migration store | 1. **scanstate** captures the migration store from the original installation and stores it in a compressed state. The store can be stored locally or on a network share.<br><br>**NOTE:** Compression is required if you want to encrypt the migration store, but it can't be used for hard-link migrations.<br><br>2. Windows 7 is installed on the system.<br><br>3. **loadstate** restores the migrated data. |
| PC refresh using hard-link migration store | 1. **scanstate** captures the migrated data as a hard-link migration store on the local system.<br><br>**NOTE:** Hard-link migration stores cannot be compressed.<br><br>2. Windows 7 is installed on the system.<br><br>3. **loadstate** restores the migration data using the hard-link option. |

| PC refresh using Windows.old and hard-link migration store | 1. **scanstate** captures the migrated data as a hard-link migration store. |
|---|---|
| | 2. Windows 7 is installed on the system without modifying the existing partitions. |
| | **NOTE:** Windows 7 will create a folder named Windows.old during a clean installation if it detects an existing operating system on the system. **scanstate** can retrieve data from Windows.old even if **scanstate** wasn't run before Windows 7 was installed. |
| | 3. **scanstate** captures migrated data from the Windows.old folder after the installation. This can be done instead of step 1, or in addition to step 1. |
| | 4. **loadstate** restores the migration data from the Windows.old folder and the hard-link store. |

If the computers are replaced, you have two PC replacement scenarios.

| PC Replacement Scenario (New Hardware) | Description |
|---|---|
| PC replacement using manual network migration | 1. **scanstate** captures the migrated data on the original computer and stores it on the network.<br><br>2. **loadstate** restores the migrated data onto the new computers. |
| PC replacement using managed network migration | 1. Automated tools such as scripts or System Center Configuration Manager (SCCM) run **scanstate** on existing computers.<br><br>2. Automated tools run **loadstate** on the new computers. |

# Understanding Hard-Link Migration Stores

A hard-link migration store doesn't actually hold any data. Instead, it provides an additional link (a hard link) to existing files. When the hard link is created, the hard link files have one copy on the disk, but two separate links to the files. When a hard link to a file is created, the file is not deleted unless both links are deleted.

The benefit of hard links is that the system manipulates the hard links much quicker than it would if it had to copy the files. This provides significant improvement in the speed of the migration.

The overall process of hard-link migration is shown in the following table.

**TIP:** Hard-link migration stores cannot be compressed. When using the **/hardlink** option, you must also use the **/nocompress** option.

| Hard-Link Migration Process | Description |
|---|---|
| **scanstate** captures data with the **/hardlink** option. | An additional link is created for all the files in the store. Because the actual files aren't copied, this does not take much space. For example, data in the store might actually take 10 GB of space on the drive, but the hard links might take only 5 MB of space. |
| New operating system is installed. | The partition holding the hard links must not be modified. For example, the partition holding the hard-link store is not resized or formatted. The existing data and hard-link migration store remains intact. |
| **loadstate** restores data with the **/hardlink** option. | The hard links from **scanstate** are modified to the new locations required by Windows 7. For example, links to data in the C:\ Documents and Settings folders are changed to the C:\Users folders. Because data is not copied, the migration is much quicker. |

**TIP:** Encrypted migration stores must be compressed and password protected, but hard-link migration stores cannot be compressed. In other words, hard-link migration stores cannot be encrypted.

Another benefit of using a hard-link migration store is that the data can be browsed by a user. Figure 24-4 shows a hard-link migration store created with the following command:

```
C:\usmtx86>scanstate c:\hard /hardlink /nocompress
```

Notice that the path starts in the c:\hard folder. It captured data from the C: drive as shown in the path of C:\usmt\file\c$. The folders in the c$ folder are the exact folders that existed in the original installation.

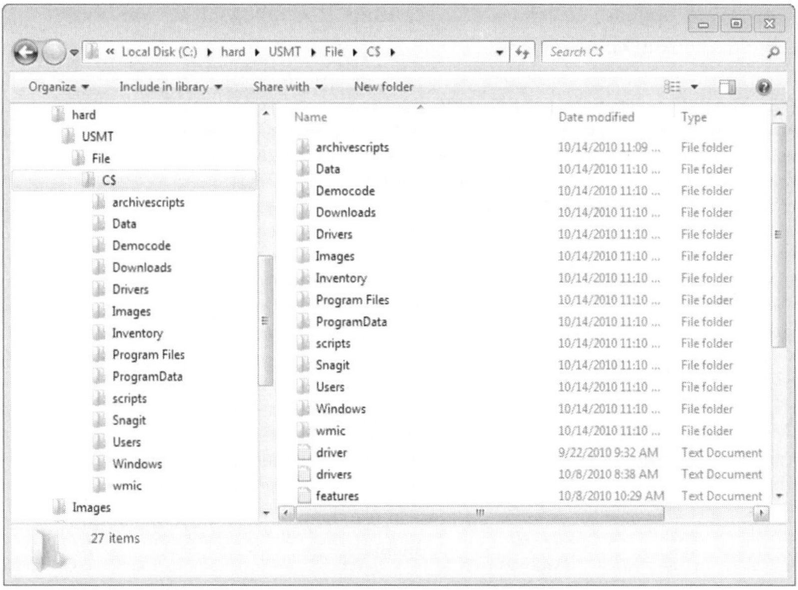

**Figure 24-4**   A Hard-Link Migration Store in Windows Explorer

## Capturing Migration Data with scanstate

The USMT tool used to save migration data is scanstate. The basic syntax is

```
scanstate storepath [options]
```

> **NOTE: scanstate** is installed with the WAIK. The 32-bit version is located in the C:\
> Program Files\Windows AIK\Tools\USMT\x86 folder, and the 64-bit version is located in
> the C:\Program Files\Windows AIK\Tools\USMT\amd64 folder.

The store path can be a folder on the local system or a share identified by a UNC path.
For example, either of the following two commands will work. The first command stores
the migration in a folder named migstore on the local C: drive:

```
scanstate c:\migstore
```

This command stores the migration store on a share named migstore on a computer
named win7pcg:

```
scanstate \\win7pcg\migstore
```

There are several options you can use with **scanstate**. The following sections show many of the commonly used options.

> **NOTE:** The path to **scanstate** is not known by the system by default. In the following examples, the contents of the C:\Program Files\Windows AIK\Tools\USMT\x86 folder have been copied to the c:\usmtx86 folder. This folder includes all of the USMT files and allows the demonstration path to be shorter (C:\usmtx86 instead of C:\Program Files\Windows AIK\Tools\USMT\x86).

## Specifying XML Files

You can use XML files to specify additional settings when migrating user documents and application data. The following table shows the syntax for the different XML files.

| XML File Switches | Description |
|---|---|
| Migrate user documents and application data<br><br>`/i:migdocs.xml /i:migapp.xml`<br>`C:\usmtx86>scanstate c:\migstore`<br>`/i:c:\usmtx86\migdocs.xml /i:c:`<br>`\usmtx86\migapp.xml`<br>`C:\usmtx86>scanstate c:\migstore`<br>`/i:migdocs.xml /i:migapp.xml` | The migdocs.xml and migapp.xml files exist in the usmt folder by default. You can use them as they exist, or modify them.<br><br>The migdocs.xml file identifies documents to migrate.<br><br>The migapp.xml file identifies application data to migrate. You can modify this if you have custom applications to migrate. |
| Identify specific user folders, files, and file types<br><br>`/i:miguser.xml`<br>`C:\usmtx86>scanstate c:\migstore`<br>`/i:c:\usmtx86\miguser.xml /i:c:`<br>`\usmtx86\migapp.xml` | The miguser.xml file identifies user folders, files, and file types to migrate. It does not specify which users to migrate.<br><br>**NOTE:** The miguser.xml file cannot be used with the migdocs.xml file. |
| Set path of XML files<br><br>`/auto:path`<br>`/auto:c:\usmtx86`<br>`C:\usmtx86>scanstate c:\migstore`<br>`/auto:c:\usmtx86` | You can use the **/auto** switch to specify the location of XML files once.<br><br>The example command automatically uses the migdocs.xml and migapp.xml files in the c:\usmtx86 folder. It also sets the verbosity logging level to 13 (the same as **/v:13**), which enables all logging. |

## Modifying XML Files

You can alter the default data files that are migrated by either modifying the existing migdocs.xml file or creating your own. For example, if you wanted to include all files except for .mp3 files, you could create the following file:

```
<migration urlid="http://www.microsoft.com/migration/1.0/migxmlext/
mp3files">
    <!-- This component migrates all files except those with .mp3 exten
      sion-->
    <component type="Documents" context="System">
        <displayName _locID="miguser.sharedvideo">MP3 Files</display
          Name>
        <role role="Data">
            <rules>
                <include filter='MigXmlHelper.IgnoreIrrelevantLinks()'>
                    <objectSet>
                        <pattern type="File">C:\* [*]</pattern>
                    </objectSet>
                </include>
                <exclude>
                    <objectSet>
                        <pattern type="File">C:\* [*.mp3]</pattern>
                    </objectSet>
                </exclude>
            </rules>
        </role>
    </component>
</migration>
```

> **TIP:** You can cut and paste this file from the "Exclude Files and Settings" section of the *User State Migration Tool (USMT) 4.0 User's Guide*. Name it something like excludemp3.xml and include that filename with the **/i** switch.

You can also just add an exclude node to the existing migdocs.xml file. The following table shows some examples.

> **NOTE:** If you specify an exclude rule, you must also have an include rule. Include filters are included by default in the migdocs.xml file.

| migdocs.xml File Nodes | Description |
|---|---|
| Exclude document types with an exclude node <br><br>`<exclude>`<br>`    <objectSet>`<br>`        <pattern type="file">c:\*`<br>`[*.mp3]</pattern>`<br>`    </objectSet>`<br>`</exclude>` | The migdocs.xml and migapp.xml files exist in the usmt folder. You can use them as they exist, or modify them.<br><br>This example excludes all .mp3 files, but **\*.mp3** can be replaced with any file type. |

| Exclude specific folders<br><br>```<exclude>```<br>  ```<objectSet>```<br>    ```<pattern type="File">c:\archive\```<br>```temp\* [*]</pattern>```<br>  ```</objectSet>```<br>```</exclude>``` | This example excludes the c:\archive\ temp folder. You can specify any folder to exclude. |
|---|---|
| Exclude specific files (from any location)<br><br>```<include>```<br>  ```<objectSet>```<br>    ```<pattern type="File"> C:\*```<br>```[exclude.doc] [*]</pattern>```<br>  ```</objectSet>```<br>```</include>``` | This example excludes any instance of the file named exclude.doc on the C: drive. |

## Identifying Users to Migrate with scanstate

By default, all users are migrated with **scanstate**. However, you can modify which users are migrated with various switches.

| scanstate Option to Identify Users | Description |
|---|---|
| Include all users except for a specific user<br><br>`/ue:user`<br>`C:\usmtx86>scanstate c:\hard`<br>`/hardlink /nocompress /ue:dgibson`<br>`C:\usmtx86>scanstate c:\hard`<br>`/hardlink /nocompress /ue:pearson\`<br>`dgibson`<br>`C:\usmtx86>scanstate c:\hard`<br>`/hardlink /nocompress /ue:pearson\*` | The **/ue** switch can be used to exclude specific users.<br><br>The first example excludes the local user account named dgibson.<br><br>The second example excludes the domain user account named dgibson in the Pearson domain.<br><br>You can also use the * wildcard. The third example excludes all user accounts from the Pearson domain. |
| Migrate only specific users<br><br>`/ue:*\* /ui:user`<br>`/ue:*\* /ui:pearson\dgibson`<br>`C:\usmtx86>scanstate c:\hard`<br>`/hardlink /nocompress /ue:*\*`<br>`/ui:pearson\dgibson` | You can combine the **/ue** switch with the **/ui** switch to include specific users.<br><br>First, use the **/ue:*\*** switch to exclude all users.<br><br>Second, use the **/ui** switch to include specific users. |

| Exclude users that have not logged in recently | The **/uel** switch can be used to exclude users that haven't logged in within the specified period. |
| --- | --- |
| `/uel:`*numberofdays*<br>`/uel:60`<br>`C:\usmtx86>`**`scanstate c:\hard`**<br>**`/hardlink /nocompress /uel:60`** | **TIP:** This is an effective way of ensuring that old, unused profiles are not migrated. |
| Exclude users that have not logged in since a specific date | If you specify a date with the **/uel** switch, users that have not logged in since that date will be excluded. |
| `/uel:`*date*<br>`/uel:2010/10/14`<br>`C:\usmtx86>`**`scanstate c:\hard`**<br>**`/hardlink /nocompress /uel:2010/10/14`** | The date must be in the format of yyyy/mm/dd. |

## Encrypting the Migration Store with scanstate

If the user data is valuable or holds confidential data, you can encrypt it. Users will not be able to access the data without either the encryption key or the encryption file.

**TIP:** Encrypted migration stores must be compressed and password protected. Hard-link migration stores cannot be encrypted.

| scanstate Encryption Option | Description |
| --- | --- |
| Encrypt the store with a password<br><br>`/encrypt:[`*algorithm*`] /key:`*password*<br>`C:\usmtx86>`**`scanstate c:\store`**<br>**`/encrypt /key:Pa$$w0rd`**<br>`C:\usmtx86>`**`scanstate c:\store`**<br>**`/encrypt:AES_256 /key:Pa$$w0rd`** | The first example command encrypts the store using 3DES (the default). You must have the password to decrypt it with **loadstate**.<br><br>You can also specify the encryption algorithm. The second example uses 256-bit AES as the encryption algorithm. |
| Encrypt the store with a key within a file<br><br>`/encrypt:[`*algorithm*`] /keyfile:`*filename*<br>`C:\usmtx86>`**`scanstate c:\store`**<br>**`/encrypt /keyfile:c:\usmtx86`**<br>**`\password.txt`**<br>`C:\usmtx86>`**`scanstate c:\store`**<br>**`/encrypt:AES_256 /keyfile:c:\usmtx86`**<br>**`\password.txt`** | The key file is a simple text file.<br><br>**TIP:** Placing the key in the file makes it accessible to anyone that can open the file. You need to protect access to the file. |
| Identify supported encryption algorithms<br><br>`C:\usmtx86>`**`usmtutils /ec`** | This command provides a list of supported algorithms. Possible algorithms are 3DES, 3DES_112, AES_128, AES_192, and AES_256. |

## Simple Error Handling with scanstate

When things don't go as planned, you can use the logs to understand why. You also can increase the verbosity level to get more details in the logs. The following table shows some basic switches used for the logs.

| scanstate Error-Handling Switch | Description |
| --- | --- |
| Set logging verbosity level<br><br>/v:*verbosity level*<br>C:\usmtx86>**scanstate** c:\hard /hardlink /nocompress /v:13 | Valid verbosity levels are 0, 1, 4, 5, 8, 9, 12, and 13.<br><br>The default is 0 and it provides only default errors and warnings. Level 13 provides a verbose logging level that includes status and debugger output. |
| Continue if errors occur<br><br>/c<br>C:\usmtx86>**scanstate** c:\hard /hardlink /nocompress /c | By default, **scanstate** aborts if any errors occur.<br><br>The /c switch allows **scanstate** to continue if any nonfatal errors occur. |
| Overwrite existing folders<br><br>C:\usmtx86>**scanstate** c:\hard /hardlink /nocompress /o | By default, **scanstate** creates the target folder. However, if the folder already exists, it will abort.<br><br>The /o switch causes **scanstate** to overwrite the existing folder. |
| Log results<br><br>/l:*logname*<br>C:\usmtx86>**scanstate** c:\hard /hardlink /nocompress /l:c:\data\ scan.log | You can specify a different location or different name of the **scanstate** log.<br><br>**TIP:** By default, the log is named loadstate.log and is stored in the same folder as scanstate.exe. |

## Handling EFS Files

Files on NTFS drives can be encrypted using the NTFS Encrypting File System (EFS). By default, **scanstate** aborts if any EFS files are encountered. If the system has EFS files, or you suspect it might, you need to use the /efs switch.

| scanstate efs Option | Description |
| --- | --- |
| Create a hard link to encrypted files<br><br>/efs:hardlink<br>C:\usmtx86>**scanstate** c:\hard /hardlink /nocompress /efs:hardlink | The EFS file is not copied.<br><br>You can only use this option with the **/hardlink** and **/nocompress** options. |
| Ignore EFS files<br><br>/efs:skip<br>C:\usmtx86>**scanstate** c:\hard /hardlink /nocompress /efs:skip | EFS files are skipped. |

| Decrypt EFS files<br><br>`/efs:decryptcopy`<br>`C:\usmtx86>scanstate c:\store`<br>`/efs:decryptcopy` | If access allows the action, EFS files will be decrypted. **scanstate** will fail if the file can't be decrypted. |
| Migrate the encrypted file<br><br>`/efs:copyraw`<br>`C:\usmtx86>scanstate c:\store`<br>`/efs:copyraw` | **scanstate** copies the encrypted files. If users have their original EFS certificates, they will have access to the encrypted files.<br><br>**TIP:** You should use this option only if the destination computer is running Windows Vista or Windows 7. |

## Migrating Data from the Windows.old Folder

When Windows 7 is installed on a computer with an existing operating system, it detects the original operating system. It then creates a folder named Windows.old and moves key files and folders into the Windows.old folder. Even if you didn't run **scanstate** before the new installation, you can now run **scanstate** against the Windows.old folder.

| Windows.old Option | Description |
| --- | --- |
| Retrieve migration data from Windows.old<br><br>`/offlinewinold:`*`windows.oldpath`*<br>`C:\usmtx86>scanstate c:\store`<br>`/offlinewinold:c:\windows\old`<br>`\windows\` | Relevant data is retrieved from the Windows.old folder and migrated to the c:\store folder.<br><br>Data can then be migrated using **loadstate**.<br><br>**TIP:** If multiple Windows.old folders exist, the second and subsequent Windows.old folders are appended with three-digit numbers. For example, the first folder will be named Windows.old. The second folder will be named Windows.old.001, the third will be named Windows.old.002, and so on. |
| Use hard-link migration with windows.old<br><br>`C:\usmtx86>scanstate c:\hard`<br>`/offlinewinold:c:\windows\old`<br>`\windows\ /hardlink /nocompress` | Hard links will be created in the c:\hard folder for the relevant data. |

**TIP:** If you want to delete the Windows.old folder after the migration, you can use the **takeown /f c:\windows.old\\* /r /a /d y** and **rd /s /q c:\Windows.old\** commands. This is covered in Chapter 4, "Manipulating Files and Folders."

This chapter provides information and commands concerning the following topics:

- Running **loadstate**
- Specifying XML files
- Specifying hard-link options
- Deleting the hard-link store
- Identifying users to migrate
- Decrypting an encrypted migration store
- Handling errors

## Running loadstate

Chapter 24, "Capturing User Data with scanstate," covers the overall migration process and the use of **scanstate** to capture the migration data. As a reminder, Figure 25-1 shows the overall process. This chapter covers the **loadstate** commands.

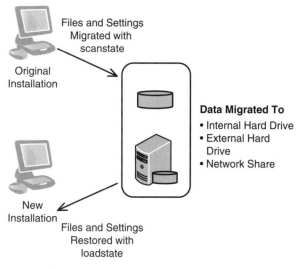

**Figure 25-1** Migration of Data with USMT

The basic syntax of the **loadstate** command is

```
loadstate storepath [options] /lac
```

> **TIP:** The **/lac** switch must be used if local accounts are in the migration store and they don't exist on the target system. If it is omitted, **loadstate** fails with an error code of 14.

The following command will load the migration data from the C:\migstore folder.

```
loadstate c:\migstore /lac
```

This command restores the migration store from a share on another computer using a standard UNC path:

```
loadstate \\win7pcg\migstore /lac
```

> **NOTE:** In the examples in this chapter, the contents of the C:\Program Files\Windows AIK\Tools\USMT\x86 folder have been copied to the C:\usmtx86 folder. This includes all of the USMT tools and allows the demonstration path to be shorter (C:\usmtx86 instead of C:\Program Files\Windows AIK\Tools\USMT\x86).

# Specifying XML Files

You can use XML files to specify additional settings when migrating user documents and application data. The following table shows the syntax for the different XML files.

| Specifying XML File Switches | Description |
|---|---|
| Migrate user documents and application data<br><br>`/i:migdocs.xml /i:migapp.xml`<br>`C:\usmtx86>loadstate c:\migstore`<br>`/i:c:\usmtx86\migdocs.xml /i:c:`<br>`\usmtx86\migapp.xml /lac`<br>`C:\usmtx86>loadstate c:\migstore`<br>`/i:migdocs.xml /i:migapp.xml /lac` | The migdocs.xml and migapp.xml files exist in the usmt folder by default. You can use them as they exist, or modify them.<br><br>**NOTE:** These are the same migdocs.xml and migapp.xml files used with **scanstate**. However, you can modify them to use with **loadstate** even if you didn't modify them before running **scanstate**. |
| Specify specific user folders, files, and file types<br><br>`/i:miguser.xml`<br>`C:\usmtx86>loadstate c:\migstore`<br>`/i:c:\usmtx86\miguser.xml /i:c:`<br>`\usmtx86\migapp.xml /lac` | The miguser.xml file identifies user folders, files, and file types to migrate. It does not specify which users to migrate.<br><br>**NOTE:** The miguser.xml file cannot be used with the migdocs.xml file. |

| Set path of XML files<br><br>`/auto:path`<br>`/auto:c:\usmtx86`<br>`C:\usmtx86>loadstate c:\migstore`<br>`/auto:c:\usmtx86   /lac` | You can use the **/auto** switch to specify the location of XML files once.<br><br>The example command automatically uses the migdoc.xml and migapp.xml files in the c:\usmtx86 folder. It also sets the verbosity logging level to 13 (the same as **/v:13**), which enables all logging. |

## Specifying Hard-Link Options

If the migration store was captured using hard-link options, you restore the migration data with the **/hardlink** and **/nocompress** switches.

| loadstate Hard-Link Option | Description |
|---|---|
| Migrate from a hard-link store<br><br>`/hardlink /nocompress`<br>`C:\usmtx86>loadstate c:\hard`<br>`/hardlink /nocompress /lac` | This performs the migration from a **/hardlink** store. You can only use **loadstate** to migrate from a **/hardlink** store if you captured a hard-link store with **scanstate**. |

**NOTE:** The **/nocompress** switch is required with the **/hardlink** switch. This is required with both **loadstate** and **scanstate**.

## Deleting the Hard-Link Store

After you've completed the migration, you'll want to delete the folder holding the hard-link store. Normally, this is a simple process using the **rd** command.

**TIP:** The basic command to remove a folder is **rd**. For example, if the folder was named c:\hard, you could use this command to remove it: **rd /s /q c:\hard**. The **/s** switch specifies subfolders. The **/q** switch suppresses prompts.

However, there are occasions when the path to the hard-link store becomes locked and it can't be deleted. You can use the **usmtutils** tool included with USMT to delete a locked hard-link store.

| usmtutils Command | Description |
|---|---|
| `/rd:storedir`<br>`/rd:c:\hard`<br>`C:\usmtx86>usmtutils /rd c:\hard` | The **usmtutils** command overrides existing sharing locks. |

## Identifying Users to Migrate

By default, all users are migrated with **loadstate**. However, you can modify which users are migrated with **loadstate**. This is similar to how you can modify which users are migrated with **scanstate**.

| loadstate Option to Identify Users | Description |
|---|---|
| Include all users except for a specific user<br><br>/ue:*user*<br>/ue:*domain\user*<br>C:\usmtx86>loadstate c:\hard<br>/hardlink /nocompress /ue:dgibson<br>/lac<br>C:\usmtx86>loadstate c:\hard<br>/hardlink /nocompress /ue:pearson<br>\dgibson /lac<br>C:\usmtx86>loadstate c:\hard<br>/hardlink /nocompress /ue:pearson\*<br>/lac | The **/ue** switch can be used to exclude specific users.<br><br>The first example excludes the local user account named dgibson.<br><br>The second example excludes the domain user account named dgibson in the Pearson domain.<br><br>You can also use the * wildcard. The third example excludes all user accounts from the Pearson domain. |
| Migrate only specific users<br><br>/ue:*\* /ui:*user*<br>/ue:*\* /ui:pearson\dgibson<br>C:\usmtx86>loadstate c:\hard<br>/hardlink /nocompress /ue:*\*<br>/ui:pearson\dgibson /lac | You can combine the **/ue** switch with the **/ui** switch to include specific users.<br><br>First, use the **/ue:*\*** switch to exclude all users.<br><br>Second, use the **/ui** switch to include specific users. |
| Move users into a new domain<br><br>/md:*olddomain:newdomain*<br>C:\usmtx86>loadstate c:\<br>hard /hardlink /nocompress<br>/md:publisher:pearson /lac | If the domain is changing as part of the migration, you can have the user account profile moved with the new domain name. |
| Exclude users that have not logged in recently<br><br>/uel:*numberofdays*<br>/uel:60<br>C:\usmtx86>loadstate c:\hard<br>/hardlink /nocompress /uel:60 /lac | The **/uel** switch can be used to exclude users that haven't logged in within the specified period.<br><br>**TIP:** This is an effective way of ensuring that old, unused profiles are not migrated. |
| Exclude users that have not logged in since a specific date<br><br>/uel:*date*<br>/uel:2010/10/14<br>C:\usmtx86>loadstate c:\hard<br>/hardlink /nocompress /uel:2010/10/14<br>/lac | If you specify a date with the **/uel** switch, users that have not logged in since that date will be excluded.<br><br>The date must be in the format of yyyy/mm/dd. |

| Create local accounts<br><br>`/lac:[`*`password`*`]`<br>`C:\usmtx86>loadstate c:\hard`<br>`/hardlink /nocompress /lac` | The **/lac** switch specifies that local accounts are created.<br><br>An empty password is used and the account is disabled by default. If a password is specified, all migrated users are given the same password.<br><br>**TIP:** If the migration store includes local accounts that don't already exist on the new system and the **/lac** switch is not used, the migration fails. |
|---|---|
| Enable local accounts<br><br>`/lae /lac:`*`password`*<br>`C:\usmtx86>loadstate c:\hard`<br>`/hardlink /nocompress /lae:`<br>`/lac:Pa$$w0rd` | You can combine **/lac** with the **/lae** switch to enable migrated local accounts.<br><br>If enabling the account, you should provide a password. Some systems will have password policies that prevent the creation of the account with a blank password. |

# Decrypting an Encrypted Migration Store

If the migration store was encrypted with **scanstate**, you must decrypt it with **loadstate**.

| loadstate Decryption Option | Description |
|---|---|
| Decrypt the store with a password<br><br>`/decrypt:[`*`algorithm`*`] /key:`*`password`*<br>`C:\usmtx86>loadstate c:\store /decrypt`<br>`/key:Pa$$w0rd /lac`<br>`C:\usmtx86>loadstate c:\store`<br>`/decrypt:AES_256 /key:Pa$$w0rd /lac` | The first example decrypts the store using the default algorithm of 3DES. You must have the password to decrypt it with **loadstate**.<br><br>If the store was encrypted with a different algorithm (such as AES_256), you need to specify the algorithm in the command.<br><br>Possible algorithms are 3DES, 3DES_112, AES_128, AES_192, and AES_256. |
| Decrypt the store with a key within a file<br><br>`/decrypt:[`*`algorithm`*`] /keyfile:`*`filename`*<br>`C:\usmtx86>loadstate c:\store /decrypt`<br>`/keyfile:c:\usmtx86\password.txt /lac`<br>`C:\usmtx86>loadstate c:\store /`<br>`decrypt:AES_256 /keyfile:c:\usmtx86\`<br>`password.txt /lac` | The key file is a simple text file. |

## Handling Errors

The following table shows some basic switches you can use to manipulate the logs.

| loadstate Error-Handling Switch | Description |
|---|---|
| Set logging verbosity level<br><br>`/v:verbosity level`<br>`C:\usmtx86>loadstate c:\hard`<br>`/hardlink /nocompress /v:13 /lac` | Valid verbosity levels are 0, 1, 4, 5, 8, 9, 12, and 13.<br><br>The default is 0 and it provides only default errors and warnings. Level 13 provides a verbose logging level that includes status and debugger output. |
| Retry on busy networks<br><br>`/r:timestoretry`<br>`C:\usmtx86>loadstate \\server1\`<br>`migstore /r:5 /lac` | If the network is busy, you can specify how many times to retry before aborting the migration. |
| Wait before retrying<br><br>`/w:secondsbeforeretry`<br>`C:\usmtx86>loadstate \\server1\`<br>`migstore /r:5 /w:60 /lac` | If you specify a retry option, you can also specify a waiting period before retrying. The default is 1 second.<br><br>The example causes it to wait 60 seconds before retrying and will retry as many as five times before aborting the migration. |
| Log results<br><br>`/l:logname`<br>`C:\usmtx86>loadstate c:\hard`<br>`/hardlink /nocompress /l:c:\data\`<br>`load.log /lac` | You can specify a different location or different name of the **loadstate** log.<br><br>**TIP:** By default, the log will be named loadstate.log and it will be stored in the same folder as loadstate.exe. |

This chapter provides information and commands concerning the following topics:

- Launching PowerShell
- Understanding PowerShell verbs and nouns
- Tabbing through PowerShell commands
- Understanding the different types of PowerShell commands
- Creating aliases
- Discovering Windows PowerShell commands
- Exploring **get-member**
- Redirecting output with Windows PowerShell
- Understanding PowerShell errors
- Understanding PowerShell variables
- Using comparison operators
- Understanding pipelining

## Launching PowerShell

PowerShell is an advanced command-line tool. It's integrated with many of the internal Windows components such as Windows Management Interface (WMI), the .NET Framework, and built-in COM objects. It includes more than 400 commands you can enter from the PowerShell prompt. You can launch PowerShell by choosing **Start**, **All Programs**, **Accessories**, **Windows PowerShell**, **Windows PowerShell**.

**TIP:** Many PowerShell commands require administrative permissions. You can launch Windows PowerShell with elevated permissions by right-clicking **Windows PowerShell** and selecting **Run As Administrator**.

Figure 26-1 shows the Windows PowerShell window after the **get-help** command was executed.

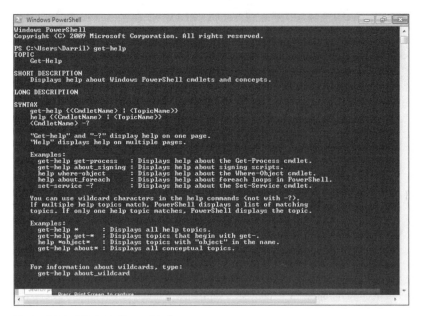

**Figure 26-1** Windows PowerShell

**NOTE:** Windows 7 includes Windows PowerShell v2.0 and this chapter covers version 2.0 commands. Windows Vista and Windows Server 2008 use PowerShell v1.0 but can be upgraded to Windows PowerShell v2.0 by following the steps at this link: http://support.microsoft.com/kb/968930.

# Understanding PowerShell Verbs and Nouns

Windows PowerShell commands use basic verbs and nouns. You can usually determine what the command does just by its name. For example, the **get-help** command combines the get verb with the help noun, and just as you'd expect, it gets help.

**NOTE:** PowerShell commands follow Pascal casing rules, which are also known as camel casing. Pascal casing joins words without spaces but uses uppercase to distinguish them. For example, camel case is written as CamelCase. However, PowerShell commands are mostly case insensitive, so they are shown in all lowercase here to match the style of this book.

Common verbs in PowerShell are outlined in the following table.

| Verb with Example | Description |
|---|---|
| Get | Retrieves information. |
| get-command<br>PS C:\>get-command | For example, the **get-command** cmdlet retrieves a listing of all PowerShell commands.<br><br>**NOTE:** PowerShell commands are called cmdlets. |

| Set | Configures a setting. |
|---|---|
| `set-executionpolicy` *policy*<br>`PS C:\>set-executionpolicy`<br>`remotesigned` | The example sets the PowerShell execution policy to remote signed, allowing local scripts to run. |
| Format | Formats output. |
| `format-table` *columns*<br>`PS C:\>get-service |`<br>`format-table name, status,`<br>`dependentservices -auto` | The example gets a listing of all services but picks specific columns to include in the table.<br><br>**TIP:** The **-auto** switch helps the output fit on the screen. |
| Out | Sends data out to a file. |
| `out-file` *filename*<br>`PS C:\>get-process |`<br>`out-file processes.txt` | The example retrieves a listing of all running processes including key data, and sends it to a text file. |
| Test | Tests various conditions, such as the existence of a file or the existence of a registry key. |
| `test-path` *path*<br>`PS C:\>test-path c:\data\`<br>`processes.txt` | The example tests to see if the path and filename exist. If they exist, the command returns a true. If they don't exist, it returns a false. |
| Write | Writes data to various sources, such as the screen or event logs. |
| `write-warning` *message*<br>`PS C:\>write-warning "Help`<br>`I'm stuck inside this`<br>`computer."` | The example writes the warning to the screen in yellow text. |
| Start | You can use this to start jobs, processes, services, and more. |
| `start-service` *servicename*<br>`PS C:\>start-service`<br>`wsearch` | The example starts the Windows Search service using the service name.<br><br>**TIP:** You can get a list of all services (including their service names) with the **get-service** command. The service name is displayed in the Name column. |
| Stop | You can use this to stop jobs, processes, services, and more. |
| `stop-service` *servicename*<br>`PS C:\>stop-service wsearch` | The example stops the Windows Search service using the service name. |
| Measure | Provides counts, averages, and more measures for various objects. |
| `measure-object`<br>`PS C:\>get-command |`<br>`measure-object` | The example command counts the number of Windows PowerShell commands and outputs the number 417 or more. |

**NOTE:** This is not a complete list of verbs available in Windows PowerShell. You can get a complete list of all commands by entering **get-command** at the PowerShell command prompt.

The following table shows a couple more advanced **get** commands combined with the gridview verb.

**TIP:** The **gridview** commands are available in Windows PowerShell 2.0 but not in Windows PowerShell version 1.

| gridview Commands | Description |
|---|---|
| Showing the gridview<br><br>`get-service | out-gridview`<br>`PS C:\>get-service |`<br>`where-object {$_.status -eq`<br>`"running"} | sort-object`<br>`-property displayname |`<br>`out-gridview` | Sends the output to a gridview window similar to that shown in Figure 26-2.<br><br>The example command uses the **where-object** cmdlet to list only running services, the **sort-object** cmdlet to sort on the display name, and the **out-gridview** cmdlet to send the output to a gridview window.<br><br>**TIP:** The gridview window allows dynamic sorting by simply clicking any column to reorder the data. |
| Limiting columns in gridview<br><br>`get-process | select columns`<br>`| out-gridview`<br>`PS C:\>get-process | select-`<br>`object name, description,`<br>`handles, vm, ws, pm, npm,`<br>`cpu, totalprocessortime |`<br>`out-gridview` | This example shows how to select specific columns in the gridview by using the **select-object** cmdlet. The output of this command is shown in Figure 26-3.<br><br>**TIP:** You can view a list of all selectable columns (and their names in the header) by running **get-process | select-object * | out-gridview**. |

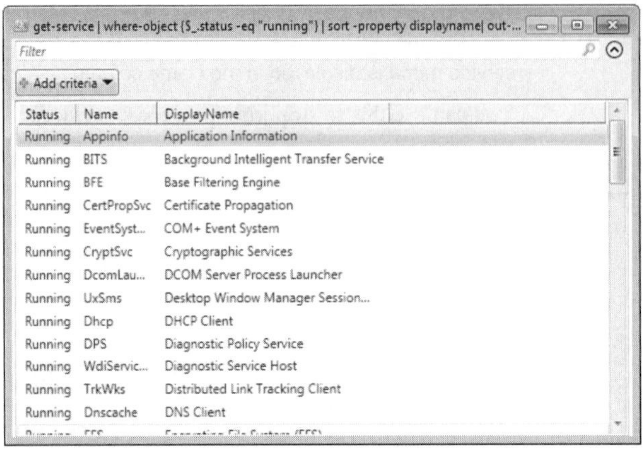

**Figure 26-2** Windows PowerShell Gridview Output

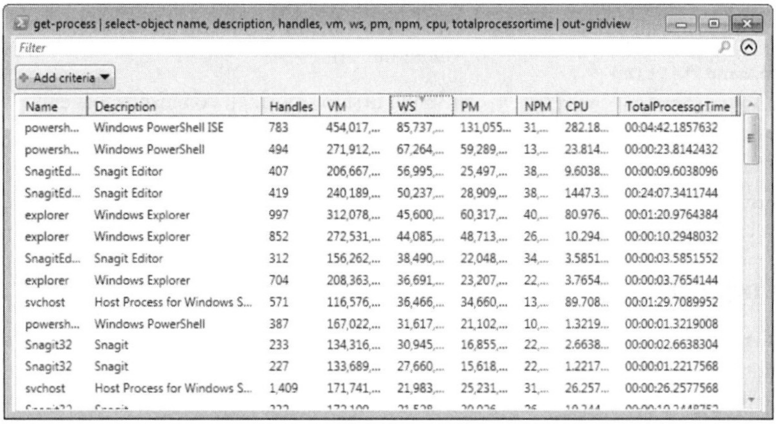


| Name | Description | Handles | VM | WS | PM | NPM | CPU | TotalProcessorTime |
|---|---|---|---|---|---|---|---|---|
| powersh... | Windows PowerShell ISE | 783 | 454,017,... | 85,737,... | 131,055... | 31,... | 282.18... | 00:04:42.1857632 |
| powersh... | Windows PowerShell | 494 | 271,912,... | 67,264,... | 59,289,... | 13,... | 23.814... | 00:00:23.8142432 |
| SnagitEd... | Snagit Editor | 407 | 206,667,... | 56,995,... | 25,497,... | 38,... | 9.6038... | 00:00:09.6038096 |
| SnagitEd... | Snagit Editor | 419 | 240,189,... | 50,237,... | 28,909,... | 38,... | 1447.3... | 00:24:07.3411744 |
| explorer | Windows Explorer | 997 | 312,078,... | 45,600,... | 60,317,... | 40,... | 80.976... | 00:01:20.9764384 |
| explorer | Windows Explorer | 852 | 272,531,... | 44,085,... | 48,713,... | 26,... | 10.294... | 00:00:10.2948032 |
| SnagitEd... | Snagit Editor | 312 | 156,262,... | 38,490,... | 22,048,... | 34,... | 3.5851... | 00:00:03.5851552 |
| explorer | Windows Explorer | 704 | 208,363,... | 36,691,... | 23,207,... | 22,... | 3.7654... | 00:00:03.7654144 |
| svchost | Host Process for Windows S... | 571 | 116,576,... | 36,466,... | 34,660,... | 13,... | 89.708... | 00:01:29.7089952 |
| powersh... | Windows PowerShell | 387 | 167,022,... | 31,617,... | 21,102,... | 10,... | 1.3219... | 00:00:01.3219008 |
| Snagit32 | Snagit | 233 | 134,316,... | 30,945,... | 16,855,... | 22,... | 2.6638... | 00:00:02.6638304 |
| Snagit32 | Snagit | 227 | 133,689,... | 27,660,... | 15,618,... | 22,... | 1.2217... | 00:00:01.2217568 |
| svchost | Host Process for Windows S... | 1,409 | 171,741,... | 21,983,... | 25,231,... | 31,... | 26.257... | 00:00:26.2577568 |

**Figure 26-3** Selected Columns in Windows PowerShell Gridview

You can also use **get-command** to retrieve information on commands with specific verbs or with specific nouns.

| **get-command Options** | **Description** |
|---|---|
| Get verbs<br><br>**get-command -verb** *verb*<br>PS C:\>**get-command -verb get**<br>PS C:\>**get-command -verb out**<br>PS C:\>**get-command -verb write** | Provides a listing of all commands associated with a specific verb.<br><br>The examples show all the commands using the **get** verb, the **out** verb, and the **write** verb. You can also use other verbs such as **set**, **select**, **start**, and **stop**.<br><br>**TIP:** You can get a list of all verbs, including the number of commands using the verb, with the following command:<br><br>**get-command \| group-object verb \| sort-object count -descending** |
| Get nouns<br><br>**get-command -noun** *noun*<br>PS C:\>**get-command -noun event** | Provides a listing of all commands associated with a specific noun.<br><br>The example shows all the commands using the noun **event**. You can also use other nouns, such as **service**, **variable**, and **error**.<br><br>**TIP:** You can get a list of all nouns, including the number of commands using the noun, with the following command:<br><br>**get-command \| group-object noun \| sort-object count -descending** |

| Look for strings with wildcards<br><br>`get-command *string`<br>`PS C:\>get-command *service`<br>`PS C:\>get-command *object*` | Provides a listing of all commands associated with the string.<br><br>In the first example, all commands that end in **service** are shown. The second example shows all commands with the word **object** anywhere in the command. |

## Tabbing Through PowerShell Commands

One of the benefits of knowing the verbs is that it enables you to easily discover the commands using the tab completion, or tab expansion feature. With more than 400 commands, you simply can't remember them all. However, you can remember common verbs such as **get**, **set**, **start**, and **stop**. You enter the name of the verb, and then simply press the Tab key to discover all the available commands.

Try these steps:

| Step | Remarks |
| --- | --- |
| 1. Launch PowerShell. | Click **Start**, type **PowerShell** in the Search Programs and Files text box, and double-click **Windows PowerShell**. |
| 2. Type **get-**. | **get** is a common verb. It retrieves information. |
| 3. Press the **Tab** key. | The command **get-** will change to **Get-Acl**. If you were to press Enter at this point, it would execute the **get-acl** command.<br><br>**NOTE:** PowerShell is not case sensitive, but it does automatically change to Pascal casing (camel case) for easier readability. |
| 4. Continue to press the **Tab** key to discover all of the commands beginning with **get-**. | There are more than 50 **get** commands that you can discover using this method.<br><br>**NOTE:** The command **get-command get\* \| measure-object** shows a count of 51 commands. |
| 5. Press the **Esc** key to clear the PowerShell command. | Pressing Esc clears the command line the same way in PowerShell as it works from the command prompt. |
| 6. Type **set-**. | **set** is another common verb. It can be used to configure settings. |

| 7. Press the **Tab** key. | The command **set-** will change to **Set-Acl**. If you were to press Enter at this point, it would try to execute the **set-acl** command. However, because the **set-acl** command requires additional parameters, it wouldn't complete.<br><br>**TIP:** You can get additional help on any command by entering the **get-help** command. For example, **get-help set-acl** retrieves information on this command. |
| --- | --- |
| 8. Continue to press the **Tab** key to discover all of the commands beginning with **set-**. | There are 35 **set** commands that you can discover using this method.<br><br>**NOTE:** The command **get-command set\* \| measure-object** shows a count of 35 commands. |
| 9. Try the same method with any of the other verbs. | This is one of the core self-discovery methods built into Windows PowerShell. |

**TIP:**  Windows PowerShell has the equivalent of the command prompt's doskey program. It keeps a history of previous commands, and you can use the Up Arrow, Down Arrow, F7, Home, End, Page Up, and Page Down keys to navigate through the history. The **get-command \*history\*** command shows all the commands that have been entered in this session.

## Understanding the Different Types of PowerShell Commands

All PowerShell commands aren't the same. There are actually three distinct types of commands, as shown in the following table.

| Type | Description |
| --- | --- |
| Cmdlet | Cmdlets are mini-programs. They are created as objects with properties and methods. Properties describe the object and methods perform actions. |
| Alias | Aliases are simpler names for common commands. For example, the command **get-alias** lists all aliases. The **get-alias** command actually has two aliases that you can execute instead of **get-alias**, **gal** and **alias**. All three commands perform the same function. |
| Function | Functions perform a specific action. For example, the **E:** function changes the drive to E:. The **clear-host** function clears the screen. |

**NOTE:**  You can create your own cmdlets, aliases, and functions. Creating cmdlets can be complex, whereas creating aliases and functions is very easy. The next section shows how to create aliases. The "Creating and Modifying the Global PowerShell Profile" section in Chapter 28, "Creating a Running PowerShell Scripts," shows how to add functions to the profile.

## Creating Aliases

Although Windows PowerShell includes many built-in aliases, you can also create your own. The following table shows you how to list the aliases and create your own.

| Command | Description |
|---------|-------------|
| alias<br>PS C:\>alias | Provides a listing of all aliases. It includes built-in aliases and user-defined aliases. This returns the same data as **get-alias** and **get-command -commandtype alias**. |
| set-alias *alias command*<br>PS C:\>set-alias gh get-help | Creates or changes an alias.<br><br>The example creates an alias named **gh** that can be entered instead of **get-help**. |

## Discovering Windows PowerShell Commands

Very few people will ever master all of the PowerShell commands. However, you can master a basic self-discovery method used to learn and master any specific command. This method includes three important commands.

| PowerShell Discovery Command | Description |
|------------------------------|-------------|
| get-command [*switches*]<br>PS C:\>get-command<br>PS C:\>get-command -commandtype cmdlet<br>PS C:\>get-command -commandtype alias<br>PS C:\>get-command -commandtype function | The **get-command** cmdlet shows all of the possible commands.<br><br>You can list the cmdlets, aliases, or functions separately, as shown by the three examples. |

| | |
|---|---|
| ```get-help get-help command [-full  | -detailed  | -examples] PS C:\>get-help set-execution- policy -full PS C:\>get-help get-process -detailed PS C:\>get-help start-service -examples``` | The **get-help** command provides access to a rich set of built-in help.<br><br>You can follow **get-help** with the name of any command. By default, it provides basic help. However, you can also add the **-full**, **-detailed**, or **-examples** switch.<br><br>The **-detailed** switch expands the basic information with more details and includes examples.<br><br>The **-full** switch provides verbose help, including technical information. It includes all available help information, including examples. It often includes online links for more information.<br><br>The -**examples** switch shows a brief synopsis with the examples. |
| ```get-member command or object  | get-member PS C:\>get-service  | get-member $variable  | get-member PS C:\>$profile  | get-member``` | The **get-member** command provides information about commands. Almost all of the commands are objects, meaning they have properties and methods.<br><br>Properties are descriptions that you can retrieve and sometimes configure.<br><br>Methods are actions you can take with the item. |

There are also many help topics available on conceptual PowerShell topics. These are called "about" topics and they all start with **about_**.

| about_ Topic Commands | Description |
|---|---|
| List all about topics<br><br>```PS C:\>get-help about_*``` | The **\*** wildcard can be used to list all about topics (all topics that start with **about_**). |
| View any specific about topic<br><br>```get-help about_topic``` <br>```PS C:\>get-help about_execution_policies``` | You can then use the **get-help** command to view the **about_** topic. |

## Exploring get-member

The **get-member** cmdlet shows what properties and events are available for a command. The following listing shows a partial output of the **get-date | get-member** command:

```
PS C:\>get-date | get-member


   TypeName: System.DateTime

Name               MemberType  Definition
----               ----------  ----------
Add                Method      System.DateTime
                                           Add(System.TimeSpan
value)
AddDays            Method      System.DateTime AddDays(double value)
AddHours           Method      System.DateTime AddHours(double value)


        . . .


ToShortDateString  Method      string ToShortDateString()
ToShortTimeString  Method      string ToShortTimeString()


        . . .


Date               Property    System.DateTime Date {get;}
Day                Property    System.Int32 Day {get;}
DayOfWeek          Property    System.DayOfWeek DayOfWeek {get;}
DayOfYear          Property    System.Int32 DayOfYear {get;}
Hour               Property    System.Int32 Hour {get;}
Kind               Property    System.DateTimeKind Kind {get;}
Millisecond        Property    System.Int32 Millisecond {get;}
Minute             Property    System.Int32 Minute {get;}
Month              Property    System.Int32 Month {get;}
Second             Property    System.Int32 Second {get;}
Ticks              Property    System.Int64 Ticks {get;}
TimeOfDay          Property    System.TimeSpan TimeOfDay {get;}
Year               Property    System.Int32 Year {get;}
```

If you want to identify what you can do with the **get-date** cmdlet, you can use the **get-member** command to list the members (properties and methods) of the **get-date** cmdlet The following table shows how you can use this information retrieved with the **get-member** cmdlet by accessing properties or executing methods.

> **NOTE:** Most properties and methods can be accessed using the dot operator, which is simply a period.

| Steps | Description |
|---|---|
| 1. Get available members<br><br>`PS C:\>get-date | get-member`<br>`PS C:\>get-date | get-member`<br>`-force` | This shows all of the members of the **get-date** cmdlet. The MemberType column identifies the members as methods and properties.<br><br>The Definition column identifies how the member can be used, such as {get;} to indicate a property can be retrieved, {set;} to indicate a property can be configured, or both.<br><br>**-force** shows all members, including intrinsic members. |
| 2. Format member output to view definitions<br><br>`PS C:\>get-date | get-member |`<br>`format-list` | Displayed data often won't fit on the screen and instead ends with an ellipsis (…), which usually simply means "there's more." You can use the **format-list** command to view all the data in a list format instead of a table format. |
| 3. Retrieve a property<br><br>`(command).property`<br>`PS C:\>(get-date).hour`<br>`19` | Most properties can be retrieved simply by enclosing the cmdlet in parentheses and using a dot and the property name.<br><br>The example shows the hour as 19 (or 7 PM) on a 24-hour clock.<br><br>**TIP:** This works when there is only one instance of a class. There is only one current date and time, so this works. It wouldn't work for **get-service** because there are multiple instances of services running. The next table shows how to handle objects with multiple instances. |
| 4. Execute a method<br><br>`(command).method()`<br>`PS C:\>(get-date).`<br>`toshorttimestring()`<br>`9:13 AM` | Methods are executed with parentheses, (), at the end. Some methods accept (and require) parameters that can be included in the parentheses, but an empty parameter list often works.<br><br>**NOTE:** The **get-member** output shows that the **toshorttimestring()** method has an empty parameter list in the description.<br><br>The example shows the output of the **toshorttimestring()** method. |

| 5. Execute a method with a parameter<br><br>`(command).method(parameter)`<br>`PS C:\>(get-date).addhours(5).`<br>`toshorttimestring()`<br>`2:13 PM` | The **addhours()** method requires a parameter and adds the provided number to the current hours.<br><br>**NOTE:** The **get-member** output (from step 1) shows that the **addhours()** method requires a parameter of type double. Double is a number.<br><br>Notice that you can sometimes use more than one method by separating them with a dot. The example adds five hours to the current time of 9:13 AM and then converts it to a short time string (as 2:13 PM). |
|---|---|

There is a difference between objects with just a single instance and objects with multiple instances. For example, there is only one date that is ever returned with the **get-date** cmdlet. However, there are always multiple services returned when executing the **get-service** cmdlet.

Different procedures are required when you have multiple instances. The following table shows some examples.

| Steps | Description |
|---|---|
| 1. Get available members<br><br>`PS C:\>get-service | get-member` | This shows all the members of the **get-service** cmdlet. The MemberType column identifies the members as methods and properties.<br><br>The Definition column identifies how the member can be used, such as {get;} to indicate a property can be retrieved. |
| 2. Retrieve a property<br><br>`(command -name name).property`<br>`(get-service -name servicename`<br>`).status`<br>`PS C:\>(get-service -name`<br>`mpssvc).status`<br>`Running` | Properties of specific services can be retrieved using a unique identifier such as the name. The **(get-service).status** command returns a null value.<br><br>You substitute the name of any service shown after running the **get-service** command.<br><br>The example checks the status of the Windows Firewall service (mpssvc). It will return Running, Stopped, or Paused. |

| 3. Execute a method<br><br>(`command` -**name** `name`).`method`()<br>PS C:\>(**get-service -name**<br>**wuauserv**).**stop**()<br>PS C:\>(**get-service -name**<br>**wuauserv**).**start**() | Methods are executed with parentheses, (),<br>at the end. Some methods accept parameters<br>that can be included in the parentheses, but<br>an empty parameter list often works.<br><br>**NOTE:** The **get-service \| get-member** output<br>shows that the **stop()** and **start()** methods have<br>empty parameter lists.<br><br>These examples show how to stop and start<br>a service. |
|---|---|

# Redirecting Output with Windows PowerShell

Often you'll want data sent to a file. The Windows PowerShell redirection operators are
as follows.

| Operator and Example | Description |
|---|---|
| ><br>`command` > `filename`<br>PS C:\> **get-help about_execution_policies** ><br>**exec.txt** | Send output to a file. The file<br>is created if it doesn't exist<br>and overwritten if it exists. |
| >><br>`command` >> `filename`<br>PS C:\>**get-help about_execution_policies** >><br>**about.txt** | Append output to a file.<br>Existing data is not overwrit-<br>ten. |

# Understanding PowerShell Errors

PowerShell provides excellent feedback when you make an error. However, unless you
know what to look for, it can look just like a huge red blob.

**NOTE:** Errors are displayed in red text on a black background and clearly indicate
something is wrong with the previous command.

Figure 26-4 shows an example of what an error looks like; this error is explained in the
following table.

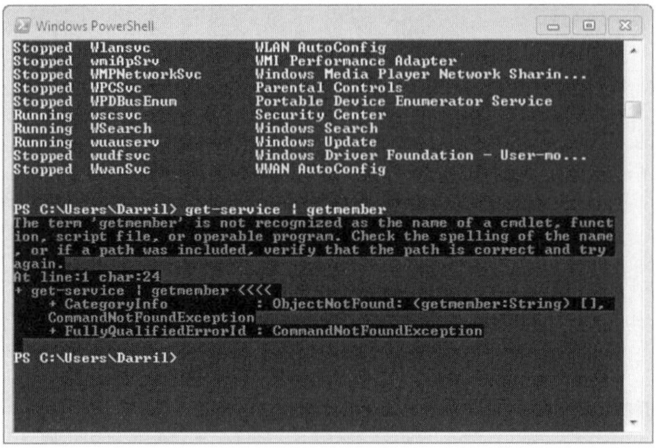

**Figure 26-4**   Windows PowerShell Error

| Errors | Description |
|---|---|
| Command with an error:<br><br>`PS C:\>get-service \| getmember` | This command is missing the dash between **get** and **member**. It results in an error. |
| First part of error message:<br><br>`The term 'getmember' is not recognized as the name of a cmdlet, function, script file, or operable program. Check the spelling of the name, or if a path was included, verify that the path is correct and try again.` | The first line indicates what PowerShell doesn't understand, in this case **getmember**. |
| Second part of error message, showing location:<br><br>`At line:1 char:23` | This gives the specific line number and character number where the error was encountered. In this case, it gives the character number where the unknown command (**getmember**) ended.<br><br>**NOTE:** Most commands will be on line 1, but if you're running a script, this will tell you which line of the script is at fault. |
| Third part of error message, pointing at error:<br><br>`+ get-service \| getmember <<<<` | The <<<< characters are arrows or pointers to the offending command. In this case, the arrows are pointing directly at **getmember**. |
| Additional information:<br><br>`   + CategoryInfo          :`<br>`ObjectNotFound:`<br>`(getmember:String) [],`<br>`CommandNotFoundException` | The error closes with some technical information. If you're writing a script, this can be useful, but usually, the first lines will give you the information you need to resolve the problem. |

## Understanding PowerShell Variables

*Variables* are units within memory that hold different values. Both built-in and user-defined variables are available within PowerShell.

**NOTE:** All PowerShell variables start with the dollar sign (**$**).

The following table shows some of the commonly used variables built into Windows PowerShell.

| Built-in Variable | Description |
| --- | --- |
| `$pshome`<br>`PS C:\>cd $pshome`<br>`PS C:\Windows\System32\`<br>`WindowsPowerShell\v1.0>` | Shows the location of the PowerShell command and associated configuration files. A profile can be placed here.<br><br>The example changes the directory to the location of $pshome. |
| `$profile`<br>`PS C:\>$profile`<br>`C:\Users\Darril\Documents\`<br>`WindowsPowerShell\Microsoft.`<br>`PowerShell_profile.ps1`<br>`PS C:\>test-path $profile` | Shows the perceived location of the profile. ps1 file. This path does not exist by default. The **test-path $profile** command returns false if the file does not exist, and true if the file does exist.<br><br>**NOTE:** If the profile.ps1 file exists in the C:\ Windows\System32\WindowsPowerShell\v1.0 folder, it will execute. |
| `$error` | Displays an array of all the errors from the current session. The most recent error can be retrieved with **$error[0]** (the first item in the array). |
| `$_ .`<br>`PS C:\>Get-Service | where`<br>`{$_.status -eq "stopped" }` | Identifies the current cmdlet being piped.<br><br>In the example, the **get-service** command retrieves all services and is then piped to the **where** clause. The **$_** variable is used with dot notation to identify the status of each service and see if it is stopped. |
| `$pwd` | Current working directory. |

**NOTE:** You can retrieve a full list of variables with the **get-variable** cmdlet or the **variable** alias. The output lists the variables and their current values.

You can create your own variables. Variables are assigned with the equal sign (=) and prefixed with the dollar sign (**$**). You can then use the variable in the current session, or within a script.

The following table shows the methods used to assign and manipulate variables.

| Assigning Variables | Description |
|---|---|
| `PS C:\>$d = get-date`<br>`PS C:\>$d` | Assigns the current date and time value to **$d**.<br><br>You can view the value of the variable by entering it by itself. |
| `PS C:\>$counter = 0` | Assigns the value 0 to a counter. |
| `PS C:\>$counter = $counter + 1`<br>`PS C:\>$counter++`<br>`PS C:\>$counter` | Increments a variable by 1. |
| `PS C:\>$counter = $counter - 1`<br>`PS C:\>$counter--`<br>`PS C:\>$counter` | Decrements a variable by 1. |
| `PS C:\>$msg = "Success!"`<br>`PS C:\>$msg` | Assigns a string of characters to a variable. |

When working with numeric variables, you can use different mathematical assignment values, as shown in the following table.

| Working with Numeric Variables | Description |
|---|---|
| `=`<br>`PS C:\>$x = 10` | Assignment.<br><br>If $x started at 10, the value of $x is 10 after this command. |
| `+`<br>`PS C:\>$x = $x +5` | Addition.<br><br>If $x started at 10, the value of $x is 15 after this command. |
| `-`<br>`PS C:\>$x = $x - 5` | Subtraction.<br><br>If $x started at 10, the value of $x is 5 after this command. |
| `*`<br>`PS C:\>$x = $x * 5` | Multiplication.<br><br>If $x started at 10, the value of $x is 50 after this command. |
| `/`<br>`PS C:\>$x = $x / 5` | Division.<br><br>If $x started at 10, the value of $x is 2 after this command. |
| `%`<br>`PS C:\>$x = $x % 3` | Module (remainder).<br><br>If $x started at 10, the value of $x is 1 after this command. |

| | |
|---|---|
| `+=`<br>`PS C:\>$x += $x` | Additive assignment.<br><br>If $x started at 10, the value of $x is 20 after this command. |
| `-+`<br>`PS C:\>$x -= $x` | Subtractive assignment.<br><br>If $x started at 10, the value of $x is 0 after this command. |
| `*=`<br>`PS C:\>$x *= 10` | Multiplicative assignment.<br><br>If $x started at 10, the value of $x is 100 after this command. |
| `/=`<br>`PS C:\>$x /= 2` | Quotient assignment.<br><br>If $x started at 10, the value of $x is 1 after this command. |
| `%=`<br>`PS C:\>$x /= 3` | Remainder assignment.<br><br>If $x started at 10, the value of $x is 1 after this command. |
| `++`<br>`PS C:\>$x ++` | Increment.<br><br>If $x started at 10, the value of $x is 11 after this command. |
| `--`<br>`PS C:\>$x --` | Decrement.<br><br>If $x started at 10, the value of $x is 9 after this command. |

## Using Comparison Operators

When you're trying to compare two values, you have to use specific syntax. For example, you can't use the equal sign (=) as a comparison operator. The equal sign is used as an assignment operator to assign a value to a variable (such as **$x = 10** to assign the value of 10 to the **$x** variable).

This command will work to compare two strings:

```
PS C:\scripts>If ("abc" -eq "abc") {write-host "equal"}
equal
```

However, this command fails with an error:

```
PS C:\scripts>If ("abc" = "abc") {write-host "equal"}
```

The following table lists the commonly used comparison operators.

| Comparison Operator | Description |
| --- | --- |
| -eq | Equal |
| -ne | Not equal |
| -gt | Greater than |
| -lt | Less than |
| -le | Less than or equal |
| -ge | Greater than or equal |

# Understanding Pipelining

Pipelines enable you to combine multiple commands together. The output of one command is used as the input for another command.

> **NOTE:** These are called pipelines for two reasons: as a metaphor of data being sent through a pipe to another location, and because the character (|) looks similar to a pipe.

This chapter has already demonstrated many uses of the pipeline. This table shows some of the examples used, and adds a few others.

| Pipeline Example | Description |
| --- | --- |
| Retrieve list of services<br><br>`PS C:\>get-service | format-table name, status, dependent-services -auto` | The output of the **get-service** cmdlet is used as the input for the **format-table** cmdlet. The **format-table** cmdlet gives you the ability to format the output. |
| Retrieve list of processes and send to file<br><br>`PS C:\>get-process | out-file processes.txt` | The output of **get-process** is piped to **out-file** to send the data to a file. |
| Count commands<br><br>`PS C:\>get-command | measure-object`<br>`PS C:\>get-command -type cmdlet | measure-object` | The **measure-object** cmdlet counts the number of commands retrieved by **get-command**. |
| Learn properties and methods for commands<br><br>`PS C:\>get-service | get-member` | The **get-member** cmdlet is used to retrieve all the members of the **get-service** cmdlet. |

| | |
|---|---|
| Identify running services<br><br>`PS C:\>get-service \| where`<br>`{$_.status -eq "running" }` | The **$_** combination is a special pipeline variable that allows you to use dot notation with pipelines. The **$_.** refers to the cmdlet being piped (**get-service**).<br><br>This example retrieves a list of running services.<br><br>**NOTE**: The **get-service** cmdlet by itself returns a list of all services, whether they are running or not. |
| Count list of running services<br><br>`PS C:\>get-service \| where`<br>`{$_.status -eq "running" } \|`<br>`measure-object` | This pipes all the services to the **where** filter to identify only the running services. It then pipes this result to the **measure-object** command to count the result. It returns an integer indicating the number of services that are running. |
| Sort a list of running processes<br><br>`PS C:\>get-process \| sort-`<br>`object -property handles` | This retrieves a listing of running processes and sorts the output on the property **handles** property. |
| Retrieve verbose details on any running process<br><br>`PS C:\>get-process \| where-`<br>`object { $_.processname -eq`<br>`"powershell" } \| format-list *` | This lists all data (**format-list** *) on any running process (**get-process**) identified by the process name (**$_.processname -eq** *"name"*). |
| Retrieve top 10 list of memory-consuming processes<br><br>`PS C:\>get-process \| sort-`<br>`object workingset -descending \|`<br>`select-object -first 10` | This uses two pipelines. It starts by getting a listing of all processes. It then uses the **sort-object** cmdlet with descending sort order to list only the processes using the most memory (**workingset**). It then limits the output to only the top 10 with the **select-object** cmdlet. |
| Retrieve list of processes using more than 30 MB of memory<br><br>`PS C:\>get-process \|`<br>`where-object {$_.workingset -gt`<br>`30000000}` | This uses **where-object** to list only the processes that are using more than 30 MB of memory (**working set -gt 30000000**). |
| Retrieve last 10 log entries from System log<br><br>`PS C:\>get-eventlog system`<br>`-newest 10 \| Format-List *` | The **format-list** * cmdlet formats the last 10 System event log entries in a list format. The * ensures that all items are listed. |
| Get a listing of files and folders in a wide format<br><br>`PS C:\>get-childitem \|`<br>`format-wide` | This retrieves a directory listing of the current folder, and uses the **format-wide** cmdlet to format the output. |

| Get a listing of folders only<br><br>`PS C:\>get-childitem \|`<br>`where-object`<br>`{ $_.psiscontainer }` | This gets a listing of folders in the current directory using the **psiscontainer** (PowerShell is container) value. |
|---|---|
| Get a listing of files only<br><br>`PS C:\>get-childitem \|`<br>`where-object`<br>`{ !$_.psiscontainer }` | This gets a listing of files in the current directory. It uses the not operator (!) to look for all items that aren't folders using the **psiscontainer** (PowerShell is container) value. |
| List drives, including type, capacity, and free space<br><br>`PS C:\>get-wmiobject`<br>`win32_volume \| select name,`<br>`drivetype, capacity, freespace`<br>`\| export-csv drivelist.csv` | This uses the **get-wmiobject** cmdlet to retrieve a list of volumes with specific columns. The **export-csv** cmdlet formats the output as a comma-separated value file. |

**TIP:** You can get more detailed help on pipelines with the command **get-help about_ pipelines**.

**TIP:** A great source for more information is "Windows PowerShell Tips" in the Microsoft TechNet Library, at http://technet.microsoft.com/library/ee692948.aspx.

This chapter provides information and commands concerning the following topics:

- Launching the ISE
- Exploring the ISE
- Executing commands in the ISE
- Creating and saving a script in the ISE

## Launching the ISE

The Windows PowerShell Integrated Scripting Environment (ISE) is a handy little tool you can use to create, test, and debug PowerShell scripts. You can launch the ISE by choosing **Start**, **All Programs**, **Accessories**, **Windows PowerShell**, **Windows PowerShell ISE**.

Figure 27-1 shows the ISE in action with the different areas labeled.

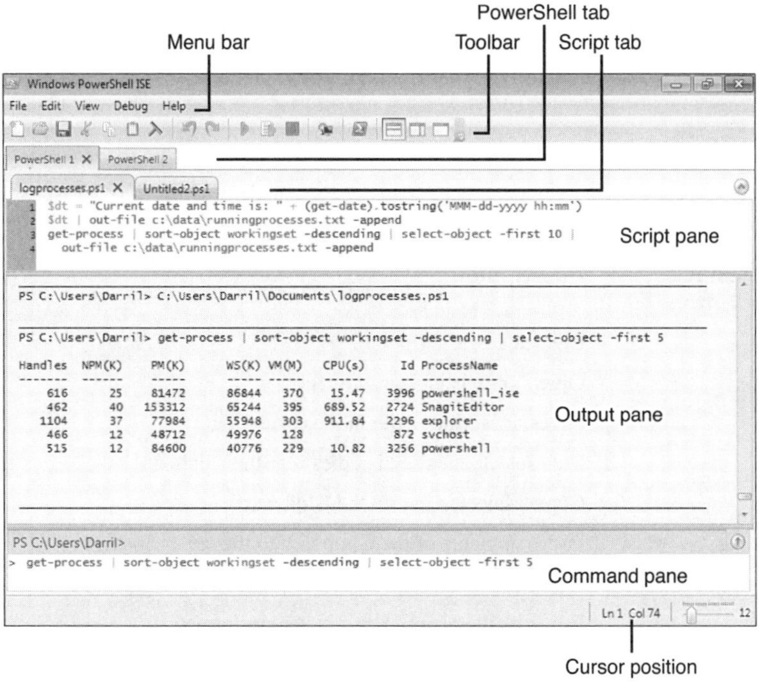

**Figure 27-1** Windows PowerShell ISE

| PowerShell ISE GUI Element | Description |
|---|---|
| Menu bar | Windows drop-down menus. |
| Toolbar | Buttons for key tools. |
| PowerShell tab | Different PowerShell tabs can have separate scripts and variables. It's common to create a different PowerShell tab when connecting to a remote computer.<br><br>**NOTE:** You can have as many as eight PowerShell tabs open at a time. |
| Script tab | Shows the name of the script you're currently working on. Multiple scripts can be open at a time.<br><br>**TIP: If you** hover over the tab, the full path to the script appears in a tooltip. |
| Script pane | Shows the script you're currently working on. The line numbers automatically appear in the script pane, but are not in the script. |
| Output pane | The script output goes here when scripts or PowerShell commands are executed. |
| Command pane | A regular PowerShell command prompt. Any PowerShell commands can be executed here. |
| Cursor position | Shows the current position of the cursor.<br><br>**NOTE:** PowerShell error outputs show the cursor position. You can use this hint to get right to the source of the problem when troubleshooting a script. |

# Exploring the ISE

The following table lists and describes the default buttons on the toolbar, in order from left to right.

| PowerShell ISE Toolbar Button | Description |
|---|---|
| New | Creates a new script tab. |
| Open | Opens an existing script or file. |
| Save | Saves the script or file in the current tab. |
| Cut | Cuts selected text and copies it to the Clipboard. |
| Copy | Copies selected text to the Clipboard. |
| Paste | Pastes contents of the Clipboard to the cursor location. |
| Clear Output Pane | Clears all content in the output pane. |
| Undo | Reverses the action that was just performed. |
| Redo | Performs the action that was just undone. |

| Run Script (green arrow) | Runs a script. Pressing the F5 key also runs the script. |
|---|---|
| Run Selection | Runs a selected portion of a script.<br><br>**TIP:** You can select any portion of a script and run it by itself by clicking this button or by pressing the F8 key. |
| Stop Execution | Stops a script that is running. The Ctrl+Break and Ctrl+C combinations also stop the script. |
| New Remote PowerShell Tab | Creates a new PowerShell tab that establishes a session on a remote computer. A dialog box appears and prompts you to enter details required to establish the remote connection. |
| Start PowerShell.exe | Opens a PowerShell console. |
| Show Script Pane Top | Moves the script pane to the top in the display. This is the default display. |
| Show Script Pane Right | Moves the script pane to the right in the display. The output pane moves to the top, with the command pane at the bottom. |
| Show Script Pane Maximized | Maximizes the script pane. |

You can use several keyboard shortcuts with the ISE. The following tables list and describe many of these.

| PowerShell Shortcut Key or Key Combination | Description |
|---|---|
| F1 | Launches Help. |
| F3 | Launches the Find dialog box to search the script. |
| F5 | Runs the script. |
| F8 | Runs a selected portion of a script. |
| Ctrl+T | Creates a new PowerShell tab. |
| Ctrl+Shift+P | Starts PowerShell. |
| Ctrl+N | Creates a new script tab. |

Breakpoints enable you to pause a script when it reaches the breakpoint. You can set breakpoints on any line in the script. The following keyboard shortcuts are used with breakpoints.

| Breakpoint Shortcut Key or Key Combination | Description |
|---|---|
| F9 | Toggles the breakpoint. Position the cursor where you want the breakpoint and press **F9** to create it. The script will pause at the breakpoint. |
| Ctrl+Shift+F9 | Removes all breakpoints. |

| Ctrl+Shift+L | Lists all breakpoints. |
| --- | --- |
| F10 | Steps over a loop. This enables you to run the current loop completely. |
| F11 | Steps into a loop. This enables you to step through a loop one command at a time. |
| Shift+F11 | Steps out of a loop. This enables you to complete a current loop that you are stepping through. |
| F5 | Runs/continues. This runs the entire script or resumes a script if it was paused by a breakpoint. |
| Shift+F5 | Stops the debugger. |
| Ctrl+Shift+D | Displays the call stack. |

## Executing Commands in the ISE

You can execute any commands in the ISE that you can execute from the normal PowerShell prompt. Simply enter the command in the command pane and press **Enter**. Also, the command pane keeps a running history of your commands just as the normal PowerShell prompt does. Figure 27-2 shows the result of the **get-wmiobject win32_bios** command.

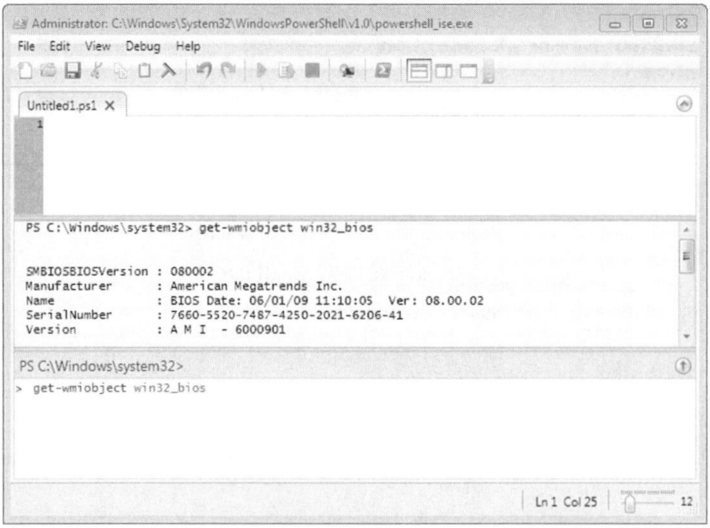

**Figure 27-2**   Executing Commands in the Windows PowerShell ISE

**NOTE:** Whereas the figure indicates the **get-wmiobject win32_bios** command on the command line, it actually disappears after the command is entered. The Up Arrow was pressed before the screenshot was captured to show the command.

# Creating and Saving a Script in the ISE

You can build scripts and test the progress from within the ISE. The steps in the following table show how to build a script that will do the following:

- Read a text file of computer names

- Store the computer names in an array

- Start writing output to a text file, beginning with the date

- Loop through the list of computer names, retrieving a list of hotfixes and writing them to the text file

| Step | Remarks |
|------|---------|
| 1. Use Notepad to create a text file named computerlist.txt in the c:\data folder. | This text file will include a list of computer names in your network. To start, you can use a text file with just two computer names, such as computer1 and computer2.<br><br>**NOTE:** The computers should be reachable by your computer or the script will fail and give an error when it tries to reach them. |
| 2. Launch the Windows PowerShell ISE with administrative permissions. | Click **Start**, enter **PowerShell** in the Search Programs and Files text box, right-click **Windows PowerShell ISE**, and click **Run As Administrator**. |
| 3. Enter the following line in the script pane:<br><br>`$list = get-content "c:\`<br>`data\computerlist.txt"` | This reads the text file and stores the list in the variable named **$list**. Because there is more than one name in the list, the variable is created as an array. |
| 4. Press **F5** to run the script. | This should run successfully.<br><br>**NOTE:** You can view the contents of the array by entering **$list** in the command pane and pressing **Enter**. |
| 5. Enter the following three lines in the script pane:<br><br>`$outputline = "Hotfix list`<br>`as of: " + (get-date).`<br>`tostring('MMM-dd-yyyy`<br>`hh:mm')`<br>`$outputline | out-file c:\`<br>`data\hotfixlist.txt -append`<br>`$outputline = "-----------`<br>`----------" | out-file c:\`<br>`data\hotfixlist.txt -append` | The first line creates a variable and populates it with some text and the current date. It then appends it to a text file.<br><br>**TIP:** The **MMM** in the date format field must be entered as all caps to ensure the month is displayed. |

| | The third line uses pipelining to send a line of dashes to the text file. It could also be entered as two lines similar to how the first two lines are used. In other words, instead of entering it as one line (**$outputline = "--------------------" \| out-file c:\data\hotfixlist.txt -append**) you could enter it as two lines: |
|---|---|
| | `$outputline = "--------------------"`<br>and<br>`$outputline \| out-file c:\data\hotfixlist.txt -append` |
| 6. Select the three lines you just entered and press the **F8** key to execute just these three lines. | This should run successfully.<br><br>**NOTE:** You can view the output of this by entering **notepad c:\data\hotfixlist.txt** in the command pane and pressing **Enter**. |
| 7. Enter the following line in the command pane and press **Enter**:<br><br>`get-wmiobject win32_quick-`<br>`fixengineering -computername`<br>`localhost` | This command retrieves a list of hotfixes installed on the local computer.<br><br>**TIP:** The term **localhost** runs this command on the local computer. However, you can substitute the name of any computer in place of **localhost**.<br><br>The purpose of this line is to ensure that the **get-wmiobject** command is formatted correctly prior to placing it in the **foreach** loop in the next step. |
| 8. Enter the following lines in the script pane:<br><br>`foreach ($i in $list)`<br>`{`<br>`   $outputline =`<br>`"Computername: " + $i ;`<br>`   $outputline \| out-file`<br>`c:\data\hotfixlist.txt -ap-`<br>`pend;`<br>`   $outputline = get-`<br>`wmiobject win32_quickfixen-`<br>`gineering -computername $i`<br>`   $outputline = get-`<br>`wmiobject win32_quickfix-`<br>`engineering -computername`<br>`$i \|`<br>`      sort-object`<br>`-descending installedon`<br>`   $outputline \| out-file`<br>`c:\data\hotfixlist.txt`<br>`-append;`<br>`   }` | The **foreach** command loops through the script lines within the curly brackets ({ }). The **$list** variable is an array of all the computers read from the text file. The **$i** holds the value of the first computer name in the list the first time it loops, then the second name on the next loop, and continues until the computer list is exhausted.<br><br>The loop starts by writing the name of the computer in the file with the first two **$outputline** lines.<br><br>It then populates the **$outputline** with the hotfix information for the computer after sorting the output in descending order on the installedon column. This lists the most recent hotfixes first.<br><br>**NOTE:** If your computerlist.txt file doesn't include names of valid computers, or these computers can't be reached, the **get-wmiobject** command will fail.<br><br>The last line writes the hotfix information to the file. |

| | |
|---|---|
| 9. Press **F5** to run the script. | At this point, your display will look similar to Figure 27-3.<br><br>**TIP:** It's common to have typos. A simple spaced added in the wrong place causes problems. Use the error output to determine the location of the error. As a reminder, the current cursor position is displayed in the lower-right corner of the ISE. |
| 10. Save your script. Click the **Save** button. Browse to a location on your computer and save the script as **hotfix. ps1**. | **NOTE:** You might not be able to run the script if the execution policy hasn't been modified. The "Setting the Security Context" section of Chapter 28, "Creating a Running PowerShell Scripts," covers how to set the execution policy if necessary.<br><br>If the execution policy has been modified, you can execute the script from the command prompt with the following command:<br><br>`c:\data\hotfix.ps1`<br><br>If the script is in the same path as your current path, you can run it with this command:<br><br>`./hotfix.ps1` |

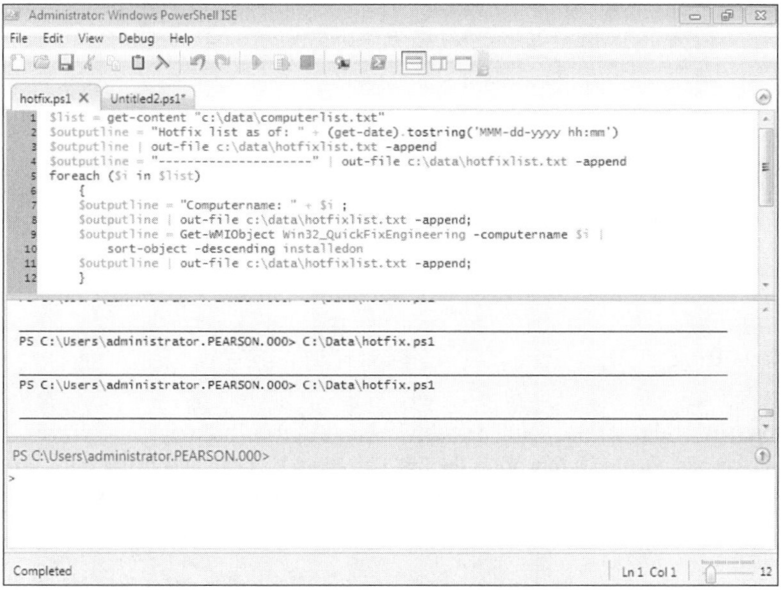

**Figure 27-3**  Building a Script in the Windows PowerShell ISE

The file that was created in Notepad from your hotfix.ps1 script will look something like this:

```
Hotfix list as of: Oct-21-2010 07:32
--------------------
Computername: Win7pcg


Source          Description     HotFixID      InstalledBy
InstalledOn
------          -----------     --------      -----------      -----
------
WIN7PCG         Security Update KB2281679     NT AUTHORITY\SYSTEM
10/12/2010 12:00:00 AM
WIN7PCG         Update          KB2345886   NT AUTHORITY\SYSTEM
10/12/2010 12:00:00 AM
WIN7PCG         Security Update KB2296011     NT AUTHORITY\SYSTEM
10/12/2010 12:00:00 AM
WIN7PCG         Security Update KB2387149     NT AUTHORITY\SYSTEM
10/12/2010 12:00:00 AM


Computername: dc1
Source          Description     HotFixID      InstalledBy
InstalledOn
------          -----------     --------      -----------      -----
------
DC1             Security Update KB2378111     NT AUTHORITY\SYSTEM
10/14/2010 12:00:00 AM
DC1             Security Update KB2387149     NT AUTHORITY\SYSTEM
10/14/2010 12:00:00 AM
DC1             Security Update KB2360131     NT AUTHORITY\SYSTEM
10/14/2010 12:00:00 AM
DC1             Security Update KB2296011     NT AUTHORITY\SYSTEM
10/14/2010 12:00:00 AM
DC1             Update          KB2345886   NT AUTHORITY\SYSTEM
10/14/2010 12:00:00 AM
```

After you start writing scripts, you'll probably realize that there is always an improvement you can add. Getting it to work is the first objective. You can then tweak it to make it better. For example, after you see the output of the hotfix.ps1 script, you might want to adjust it. The following table shows how you can tweak it.

| Script Modifications | Description |
|---|---|
| Test this line from the command pane:<br><br>`Get-WMIObject Win32_`<br>`QuickFixEngineering  \|`<br>`format-table -property hotfixid,`<br>`description, installedon,`<br>`installedby` | This changes the output using the **format-table** cmdlet to pick specific columns.<br><br>When you're happy with the output, you can then put the line into the script.<br><br>**TIP:** You can use **\| format-table \*** to view all the possible columns that you can add to the **format-table -property** list. |
| Modify the line in the script so that it looks like this:<br><br>`    $outputline = Get-WMIObject`<br>`Win32_QuickFixEngineering`<br>`-computername $i  \|`<br>`        sort-object -descending`<br>`installedon  \|`<br>`        format-table -property`<br>`hotfixid, description,`<br>`installedby, installedon` | You can now run the script with the modified line by pressing the F5 key. |

At this point, the modified script looks like the following text:

```
$list = get-content "c:\data\computerlist.txt"
$outputline = "Hotfix list as of: " + (get-date).tostring('MMM-dd-yyyy
hh:mm')
$outputline | out-file c:\data\hotfixlist.txt -append
$outputline = "--------------------" | out-file c:\data\hotfixlist.txt
-append
foreach ($i in $list)
    {
    $outputline = "Computername: " + $i ;
    $outputline | out-file c:\data\hotfixlist.txt -append;
    $outputline = Get-WMIObject Win32_QuickFixEngineering -computername
$i |
        sort-object -descending installedon |
        format-table -property hotfixid, description, installedby,
installedon
    $outputline | out-file c:\data\hotfixlist.txt -append;
    }
```

This chapter provides information and commands concerning the following topics:

- Setting the security context
- Creating a PowerShell profile
- Creating and modifying the Global PowerShell profile
- Running PowerShell Scripts
- Flushing the DNS cache
- Creating a list of domain computers
- Logging processes with a **get-process** script
- Testing for the existence of a file
- Creating output as HTML
- Running a script against multiple computers
- Creating a PowerShell message box
- Scheduling PowerShell scripts

## Setting the Security Context

PowerShell has different levels of security set by an execution policy. If you don't modify the execution policy, you won't be able to run any scripts. These security contexts or security levels define what PowerShell scripts can run. The following table shows the available security contexts that you can configure.

**TIP:** By default, PowerShell scripts cannot run until the execution policy is changed. It's common to change the policy to remote-signed.

| Execution Policy | Description |
| --- | --- |
| Restricted | No scripts can run. PowerShell does not load configuration files or run scripts.<br>**NOTE:** This is the default. |
| Unrestricted | All configuration files are loaded and any scripts can run. If you run an unsigned script that was downloaded from the Internet, you will be prompted for permission before it runs. |

| Remote-signed | Local scripts can run without being signed. All scripts and configuration files downloaded from the Internet must be signed by a trusted publisher. |
|---|---|
| All-signed | All scripts and configuration files must be signed by a trusted publisher. This includes scripts running on the local computer. |
| Bypass | Nothing is blocked and there are no warnings or prompts. This works like the unrestricted policy without the prompts. |
| Undefined | The currently assigned execution policy is removed from the current scope. It does not remove an execution policy that is set in a Group Policy scope. |

You can view and set the execution policy with the following commands:

| PowerShell Command | Description |
|---|---|
| PS C:\>get-executionpolicy | Returns the currently assigned execution policy. |
| PS C:\>get-executionpolicy -list | Lists the state of the execution policy for all scopes including the machine policy, the user policy, the process, the current user, and the local machine. |
| set-executionpolicy (restricted \| remotesigned \| allsigned \| unrestricted \| bypass) <br> PS C:\>set-executionpolicy remotesigned | Sets the execution policy. The example sets the policy to allow local scripts to run. You will be prompted to confirm the change. Press **Y** and the change will be committed. <br><br> **NOTE:** You need to start PowerShell with administrative permissions to change the execution policy. |

# Creating a PowerShell Profile

The PowerShell profile is a PowerShell script file (named profile.ps1 or Microsoft. PowerShell_profile.ps1) that creates the PowerShell environment every time Windows PowerShell is started. It can include aliases, PowerShell functions, or any other type of PowerShell modifications you want.

> **TIP:** The default location of the user's PowerShell profile is C:\Users\*username*\ Documents\WindowsPowerShell\Microsoft.PowerShell_profile.ps1. However, it doesn't exist by default.

You can view the location and name of the profile by using the $profile variable executed at the PowerShell prompt as follows:

```
PS C:\>$profile
C:\Users\Darril\Documents\WindowsPowerShell\Microsoft.PowerShellISE_
profile.ps1
```

The following steps show how to test for and create a profile used for the current user.

**NOTE:** You can also modify the profile using Notepad or the Windows PowerShell Integrated Scripting Environment (covered in Chapter 26, "Understanding PowerShell Commands"). These steps use Notepad.

| PowerShell Command | Description |
|---|---|
| Step 1.<br><br>`PS C:\>$profile`<br>`C:\Users\Darril\Documents\`<br>`WindowsPowerShell\Microsoft.`<br>`PowerShellISE_profile.ps1` | Displays the path and name of the profile. |
| Step 2.<br><br>`PS C:\>test-path $profile` | Identifies whether the path exists. Returns true if it exists and false if not. |
| Step 3.<br><br>`PS C:\>new-item -path`<br>`$profile -type file -force` | Creates the path and the profile. If **test-path $profile** returned false before, it will return true now. |
| Step 4.<br><br>`PS C:\>notepad $profile` | Opens the profile file with Notepad. If it was just created, it will be blank.<br><br>At this point, you can modify the profile as desired. |

Both local and global PowerShell profiles can exist. The following table compares these two profiles.

| Profile Type | Description |
|---|---|
| Global profile<br><br>C:\Windows\Ssystem32\WindowsPowerShell\v1.0\profile.ps1<br><br>Open with:<br><br>`PS C:\>notepad c:\windows\`<br>`system32\windowspowershell\`<br>`v1.0\profile.ps1` | If a global profile exists, it will be used for all users.<br><br>**NOTE:** Even though the path includes v1.0, this profile does apply to Windows PowerShell v2, which is installed on Windows 7. |
| Local profile<br><br>C:\Users\username\Documents\WindowsPowerShell\Microsoft.powershell_profile.ps1<br><br>Open with:<br><br>`PS C:\>notepad $profile` | This profile applies to the currently logged-in user and takes precedence over the global profile. The **$profile** variable holds the path for the local profile.<br><br>**TIP:** If PowerShell profiles exist in both locations, the local profile will take precedence over the global profile, if there are any conflicts. For example, if the global profile set the location to c:\data, but the local profile set the location to c:\scripts, the location would be set to c:\scripts. |

# Creating and Modifying the Global PowerShell Profile

The steps in the following table show how to create and modify the global profile.

**TIP:** You can use most of these steps to modify the local profile too, if desired.

| Step | Remarks |
|------|---------|
| 1. Launch PowerShell with administrative permissions. | Some of the steps will not work correctly if PowerShell is not started using **Run As Administrator**. |
| 2. Create the global profile:<br><br>`PS C:\>notepad c:\windows\`<br>`system32\windowspowershell\`<br>`v1.0\profile.ps1` | If the file doesn't exist, Notepad will prompt you to create the file. Click **Yes**. |
| 3. Change the PowerShell starting folder:<br><br>`set-location c:\scripts` | **cd** is an alias for **set-location**, so you enter **cd c:\scripts** instead.<br><br>Press **Ctrl+S** to save the file. Close and restart PowerShell and you'll see the default path is changed.<br><br>**NOTE:** The path must exist for this to work. In other words, if c:\scripts isn't a valid folder, PowerShell will give an error when it launches. |
| 4. Add an alias to the profile:<br><br>`set-alias gh get-help` | This creates an alias called **gh** that will execute **get-help**. After this alias is created, you can use the following line to get help on the **set-alias** command:<br><br>`PS C:\>gh set-alias` |
| 5. Add a function to the profile:<br><br>`function get-topprocesses`<br>`{`<br>`get-process | sort-object`<br>`-property ws -descending |`<br>`select-object -first 10 |`<br>`out-gridview`<br>`}` | After this is added to the profile, you can enter the following line at the PowerShell prompt:<br><br>`PS C:\>get-topprocesses`<br><br>You'll see a display similar to Figure 28-1. If you want all processes displayed, remove the **select-object -first 10** clause.<br><br>**TIP:** You can name the function anything you like. For example, you could name it something shorter, like **gtp**, for get top processes. Additionally, you can have multiple lines of code in the function. |
| 6. Run other scripts from the profile.<br><br>Add a dot, a space, and then the path to the script:<br><br>`. c:\scripts\env.ps1` | You can run other scripts from within the PowerShell profile by typing a dot, a space, and the path to the script.<br><br>**TIP:** If there is not a space after the dot, the command will fail and you'll see an error message when PowerShell is launched. |

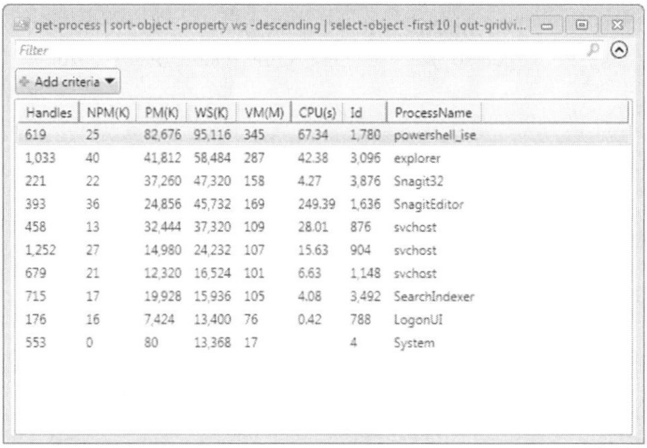

**Figure 28-1**  Top Running Processes Shown in Gridview

**NOTE:** The profile is loaded only when Windows PowerShell is first launched. In other words, if you modify the profile, the modifications won't take effect until you close and restart PowerShell.

## Running PowerShell Scripts

Unlike normal command-prompt commands, PowerShell doesn't look in the current path to run commands. In other words, you have to include one of two prefixes when running a PowerShell script from the PowerShell prompt (the full path, or the .\ combination). You can also run a script from the command prompt or from the Start Search text box. The following table shows the different methods of running a PowerShell script named test.ps1 located in the C:\scripts folder.

| Script Execution Methods | Description |
|---|---|
| Include the full path as a prefix<br><br>`PS C:\>c:\scripts\test.ps1` | You can run the script by including the full path as a prefix to the command. In this case, the full path is **c:\scripts\**. |
| Use the .\ prefix<br><br>`PS C:\scripts>.\test.ps1` | If the file is in the current path, you can use the full path or the .\ prefix.<br><br>**NOTE:** There are no spaces between the dot, the backslash, or the script name. |
| Run from the command prompt<br><br>`c:\>powershell c:\scripts\`<br>`test.ps1` | You can run PowerShell scripts from the command prompt.<br><br>**TIP:** You can also access PowerShell interactively from the command prompt by just entering **PowerShell**. You will then have the PowerShell prompt, from which you can enter any PowerShell commands. |

| Run from the Start Search Programs and Files text box<br><br>`powershell -noexit c:\`<br>`scripts\test.ps1` | The -**noexit** switch leaves the command prompt open so that you can see the results of the script. |

## Flushing the DNS Cache

You can create a PowerShell script from any PowerShell command or group of commands. Just as a batch file is one or more command-line commands, a PowerShell script is one or more PowerShell lines. The following steps show you how to create and run a script that will flush the DNS cache.

> **NOTE:** This is a simplistic script. However, the same steps can be used to create and run any script.

| Step to Create and Run Script to Flush Cache | Remarks |
|---|---|
| 1. Launch PowerShell with administrative permissions. | The script requires elevated permissions to run. |
| 2. Enter the following command to create the script file:<br><br>`PS C:\>notepad c:\scripts\`<br>`flushdns.ps1` | If the file doesn't exist, PowerShell prompts you to create the file. Click **Yes**. |
| 3. Add the following line to the script:<br><br>`ipconfig /flushdns` | PowerShell recognizes the **ipconfig** command and can run it from within a script.<br><br>**NOTE:** The **ipconfig /flushdns** command can also be entered at the command prompt. It will flush the DNS cache. |
| 4. Save the file by pressing **Ctrl+S**. | The file is saved as c:\scripts\flushdns.ps1. |
| 5. Run the script from PowerShell:<br><br>`PS C:\>c:\scripts\flushdns.ps1` | The script runs, flushes the cache, and returns the PowerShell prompt. |

# Creating a List of Domain Computers

You can use the following script to create a list of computers in a domain.

> **TIP:** You must run this on a computer that is joined to a domain, with an account that has permissions to query the domain.

```
$strfilter = "computer"
$dom = [adsi]""

$searcher = new-object system.directoryservices.directorysearcher
$searcher.searchroot = $dom
$Searcher.searchscope = "Subtree"
$searcher.filter = "(objectCategory=$strfilter)"
$results = $searcher.findall()
foreach ($entry in $results)
    {
        $computer = $entry.getdirectoryentry().name
        $computer | out-file c:\data\computerlist.txt -append
    }
```

The following table provides brief explanations of this code, including how you can slightly modify it for other uses.

| Script to List Domain Computers | Description |
| --- | --- |
| `$strfilter = "computer"` | If you wanted to get a list of all users in the domain, you could change this to **$strFilter = "user"**. |
| `$dom = [adsi]""` | This line uses the ADSI accelerator to get the current domain. |
| `$searcher = new-object system.directoryservices.directorysearcher`<br>`$searcher.searchroot = $dom`<br>`$Searcher.searchscope = "Subtree"` | These lines set up the Active Directory searcher object to search the entire domain. |
| `$searcher.filter = "(objectCategory=$strfilter)"`<br>`$results = $searcher.findall()` | The filter specifies computer objects from the first line in the script (**$strfilter = "computer"**). The **$results** variable is an array that contains all computer objects in the domain. |

<table>
<tr>
<td>

```
foreach ($entry in $results)
{
        $computer =
$entry.getdirectoryentry().name
        $computer | out-file c:\
data\computerlist.txt -append
}
```

</td>
<td>

The **foreach** loop then loops through the array (**$results**) that holds all the computer objects. Each computer object is named $i on each pass through the loop.

The name of the computer is retrieved using the **$entry.getdirectoryentry().name** line.

It is then written to the computerlist.txt file with the **-append** switch. If you don't use the **-append** switch, only the last computer will be in the file.

**NOTE:** The file should start empty or as a nonexistent file. You can check for the existence of the file at the beginning of the script, and delete it if it exists. The "Testing for the Existence of a File" section, later in the chapter, shows how.

You can get the distinguished name using this line:

```
$ocomputer = $i.getdirectoryentry().
distinguishedname
```

You can get the LDAP path using this line:

```
$ocomputer = $i.getdirectoryentry().
path
```

</td>
</tr>
</table>

## Logging Processes with a get-process Script

You can use the following script to capture all of the running processes at any given time. For example, if you suspect that a rogue process is running at random times and causing problems, you can schedule this script to run once an hour for a week to log running processes. At the end of the week, you can analyze the file.

```
$dt = "Current date and time is: "
$dt = $dt + (get-date).tostring('MMM-dd-yyyy hh:mm')
$dt | out-file c:\data\runningprocesses.txt -append
get-process | out-file c:\data\runningprocesses.txt -append
```

**TIP:** You can also use this script to identify a process with a memory leak. The script will record the amount of memory the process uses, and if a memory leak exists, the memory usage will steadily increase.

| Script to Log Processes | Description |
|---|---|
| `$dt = "Current date and time is: "` | The script starts by creating a variable (**$dt**) that will be used to record the current date and time in the file. |
| `$dt = $dt + (get-date).tostring('MMM-dd-yyyy hh:mm')` | The **get-date** cmdlet is used with dot notation to get the actual day and time and convert it to a string. The plus (**+**) character concatenates (or appends) the data.<br><br>**NOTE:** The **MMM** for Month must be in upper case, and the **mm** for minutes must be in lower case. If you use three Ms (MMM), it will list the month with letters such as Jan for January. If you use two Ms (MM), it will list the month as a number such as 01 for January.<br><br>You could also combine the line in the previous row with the command in this column so that it is a single line as:<br><br>`$dt = "Current date and time is: " + (get-date).tostring('MMM-dd-yyyy hh:mm')` |
| `$dt | out-file c:\data\ runningprocesses.txt -append` | This line writes the current date and time to the file using the **out-file** cmdlet and the variable created in the previous step. The value of the string will be something like:<br><br>Current date and time is: Oct-17-2010_09:02<br><br>The **-append** switch ensures the data is added to the file and it doesn't overwrite the file. |
| `get-process | out-file c:\data\ runningprocesses.txt -append` | This line gets a list of all current running processes and outputs them to the same file using the **-append** switch.<br><br>Of course, you can get fancier with the **get-process** command. For example, if you only wanted to record the top 10 processes based on memory usage, you could use this command:<br><br>`get-process | sort-object -property ws -descending | select-object -first 10 | out-file c:\data\ runningprocesses.txt -append` |

**TIP:** You can use the same script to record the activity of a specific process. For example, if you wanted to see the activity of the lsass process, you can modify the last line so that it looks like this:

```
get-process | where-object { $_.processname -eq "lsass" } | out-file
c:\data\runningprocesses.txt -append
```

## Testing for the Existence of a File

You can use the following script snippets to test for the existence of a file and either delete or rename the file depending on which code snippet you choose. This has multiple uses. For example, if you want to create a listing of computers in the domain, but you don't want the new listing appended to the current file, you can either delete or rename the existing file. Similarly, if you have a script that writes data to a file for logging, you can use one of these scripts to handle preexisting files.

| Delete or Rename Existing Files | Description |
|---|---|
| Delete a file if it exists<br><br>`If (test-path c:\data\computerlist.txt)`<br>`{`<br>`remove-item c:\data\computerlist.txt`<br>`}` | The **test-path** cmdlet checks for the existence of the file. If it exists, it returns true.<br><br>If the file exists, the lines within the curly brackets execute.<br><br>You can use the **remove-item** cmdlet to delete file. |
| Rename a file if it exists<br><br>`If (test-path c:\data\computerlist.txt)`<br>`{`<br>`$dt = (get-date).tostring('MMM_dd_yyyy_`<br>`hh_mm')`<br>`$newname = "computerlist_" + $dt + ".txt"`<br>`rename-item -path c:\data\computerlist.`<br>`txt -newname $newname`<br>`}` | Alternatively, you could archive the item by renaming it with the **rename-item** cmdlet.<br><br>**NOTE:** Use this code *instead* of the **remove-item** code in the preview row.<br><br>This code renames the file by appending the date and time to the filename. |

## Creating Output as HTML

You can use the following script to capture the data and send the output to an HTML file. Although this script captures the output of a get-service command, you can use it for other commands as well.

```
$computer = get-content env:computername
get-service |
sort-object -property status -descending |
```

```
convertto-html -title "Running Services" -body "<h1>Running Services on
$computer</h1> " -property DisplayName, Name, Status  |
   foreach   {
      if($_ -like "*<td>Running</td>*")
          {$_ -replace "<tr>", "<tr bgcolor=ffffcc >"}
      elseif($_ -like "*<td>Stopped</td>*")
          {$_ -replace "<tr>", "<tr bgcolor=ffccff >"}
      else{$_}
   }   >   c:\scripts\get-service.html
c:\scripts\get-service.html
c:\democode\get-service.html
```

| Script to Send Output to HTML | Description |
|---|---|
| `$computer = get-content`<br>`env:computername` | This line retrieves the name of the computer and stores it in the **$computer** variable. |
| `get-service   |` | The rest of the script is a single line with several pipes. The first cmdlet is the familiar **get-service** ending with the pipe symbol (\|). |
| `sort-object -property status`<br>`-descending  |` | Next, the output is sorted based on the status (running or stopped), in descending order, so that running services are listed first. It finishes with a pipe. |
| `convertto-html -title "Running`<br>`Services" -body "<h1>Running Services`<br>`on $computer</h1> " -property`<br>`DisplayName, Name, Status  |` | The **convertto-html** cmdlet converts the output to HTML with some HTML codes. The title is in the title bar of the web browser. The **<h1>** code provides a heading at the top of the page, with the **$computer** variable displaying the name. Last, the **-property** switch identifies the three columns to include and lists them as column headings.<br><br>**NOTE:** The column headings are not case sensitive, but will be displayed in the same case you enter them. If you use this script for something other than the **get-service** applet, you'll need to modify the columns in the **-property** list. |

| | |
|---|---|
| ```foreach   {`<br>`     if($_ -like "*<td>Running</`<br>`td>*")`<br>`          {$_ -replace "<tr>", "<tr`<br>`bgcolor=ffffcc >"}`<br>`      elseif($_ -like "*<td>Stopped</`<br>`td>*")`<br>`          {$_ -replace "<tr>", "<tr`<br>`bgcolor=ffccff >"}`<br>`      else{$_ }`<br>`  }  > c:\scripts\get-service.html` | The **foreach** command loops through the page to change the background colors of the rows. If the service is running, the row is changed to a light yellow color. If the service is not running, the row is changed to a reddish color.<br><br>The redirector (>) then sends the output to the c:\scripts\get-service.html file. |
| ```c:\democode\get-service.html``` | The file is opened. It will look similar to Figure 28-2. Because it is an HTML file, it automatically launches the default web browser. |

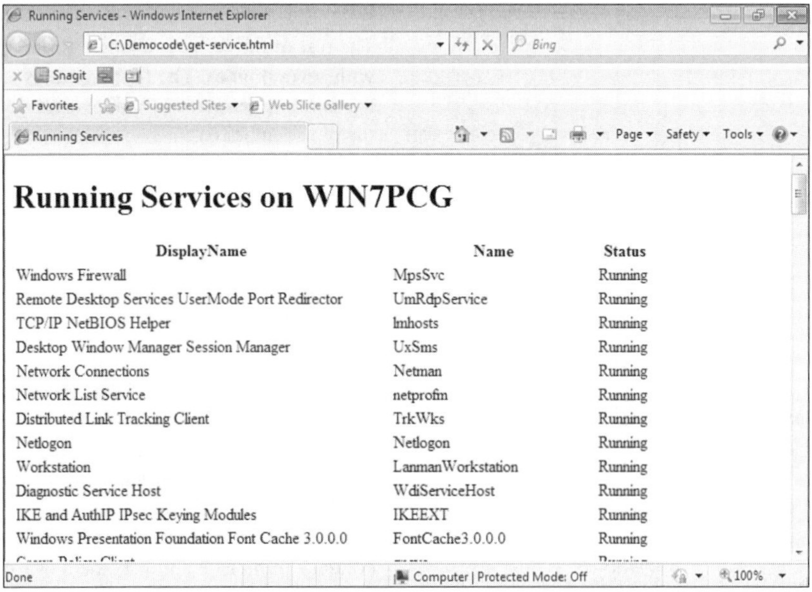

**Figure 28-2**   Display Running Services in an HTML File

# Running a Script Against Multiple Computers

Occasionally, you need to run a single script against multiple computers. One way of doing so is to read a list of the computers from a text file.

This script shows how to read the computer list from a text file and then run the script against each computer in the list. Although this script records the BIOS information for each computer in the list, you can use it to do any other task by modifying the content of the **foreach** loop.

**TIP:** You can combine this script with the earlier script used to create a list of domain computers. Use the computerlist.txt file created from that script as the source input for this script, or you can manually create a text file named computerlist.txt with the computer names.

The script is presented here, with some comments on the lines in the following table:

```
$computers = get-content "c:\data\computerlist.txt"
"BIOS Information as of " + (get-date).tostring('MMM-dd-yyyy') |
out-file c:\data\computerbios.txt
foreach ($computer in $computers){
"Computer name: " + $computer | out-file c:\data\computerbios.txt
-append
get-wmiobject win32_bios -computername $computer | out-file c:\data\
computerbios.txt -append
}
```

| Script to Run Command Against Multiple Computers | Description |
|---|---|
| `$computers = get-content "c:\data\`<br>`computerlist.txt"` | This command reads the list of computer names from a file named computerlist.txt and places the names in an array named $computers. You can view the array contents by entering **$computers**.<br><br>**NOTE:** If the file doesn't exist, the script will fail. |
| `"BIOS Information as of " + (get-`<br>`date).tostring('MMM-dd-yyyy') |`<br>`out-file c:\data\computerbios.txt` | Next, a file header line is added to indicate what the file contains. The **get-date** cmdlet is used to add the month and year to the header to identify when it was created.<br><br>**NOTE:** The **-append** switch is not used, so any existing data in the file will be deleted. |
| `foreach ($computer in $computers){`<br>`"Computer name: " + $computer`<br>`-computername $computer | out-file`<br>`c:\data\computerbios.txt -append`<br>`get-wmiobject win32_bios | out-file`<br>`c:\data\computerbios.txt -append`<br>`}` | The **foreach** command will loop through the $computers array. For each computer name in the array, it will output data.<br><br>First, it outputs the name of the computer.<br><br>Next, it uses the **get-wmiobject** cmdlet to retrieve information on the BIOS. |
| You can view the file with this command:<br><br>`PS C:\>notepad`<br>`c:\data\computerbios.txt` | |

**TIP:** There are thousands of commands you can execute using **get-wmiobject**. You can't know them all. However, Marc van Orsouw (also known as The PowerShell Guy) wrote a great script known as the PowerShell WMI Explorer. You can read about it and download it from here: http://thepowershellguy.com/blogs/posh/archive/2007/03/22/powershell-wmi-explorer-part-1.aspx. Figure 28-3 shows a screenshot of the WMI Explorer in action.

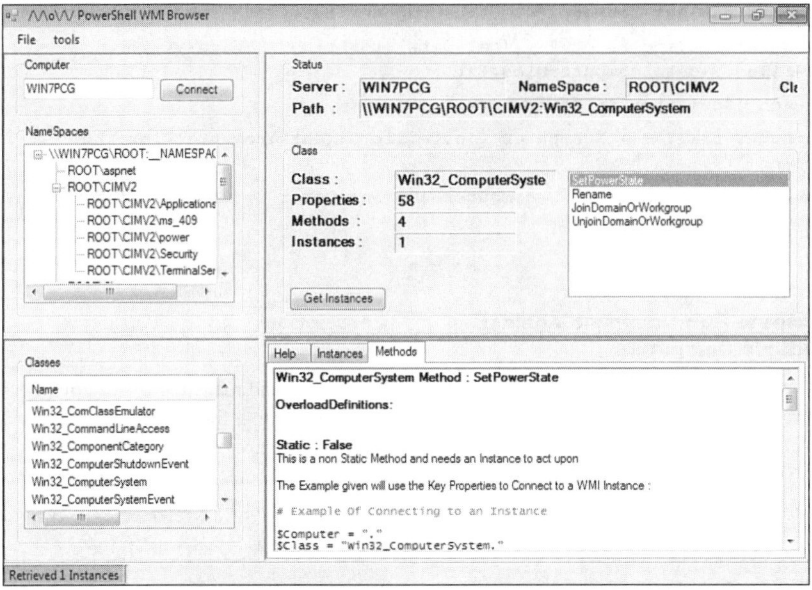

**Figure 28-3**  PowerShell WMI Explorer

# Creating a PowerShell Message Box

There may be times when you want to provide feedback to the user in a message box, or even get some response from a user with a message box. This is relatively easy to do. The following script shows basic syntax to create a message box, and then check to see what button the user clicked:

```
$obj = new-object -comobject wscript.shell
$intButton = $obj.popup("Do you want to continue?",0,"A question for
you", 4)
If ($intbutton -eq 6)
    { write-host "User pressed yes" }
elseif ($intbutton -eq 7)
    { write-host "User pressed no" }
```

| Script to Create a Message Box | Description |
|---|---|
| `$obj = new-object -comobject wscript.shell` | The **new-object** cmdlet creates other objects. In this case, it's creating a wscript shell. |
| `$intbutton = $obj.popup("Do you want to continue?",0,"A question for you", 4)` | The **$intbutton** variable will hold the value of the message box after the user clicks either Yes or No.<br><br>Figure 28-4 shows the message box that is displayed. |
| `If ($intbutton -eq 6)`<br>`    { write-host "User pressed yes" }`<br>`elseif ($intbutton -eq 7)`<br>`    { write-host "User pressed no" }` | After the user clicks a button, you can check the value of **$intbutton** to determine what button the user clicked.<br><br>The Yes button has an integer value of 6.<br><br>The No button has an integer value of 7. |

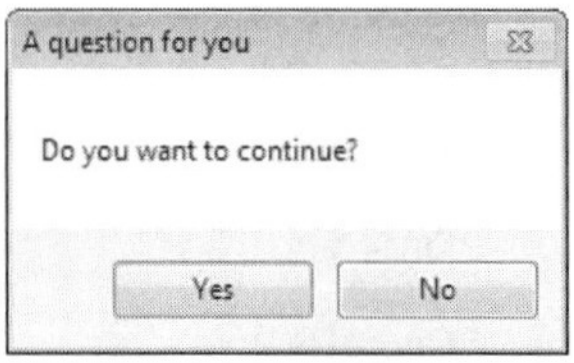

**Figure 28-4**   Basic Message Box from PowerShell

The **popup** object has four parameters, as shown in the following syntax and described in the table.

`$obj.popup(msg, [secondstowait], [title], [ntype])`

| popup Object Parameter | Description |
|---|---|
| `msg` | This is the message that is displayed in the message box. It is the only option that is required. |
| `secondstowait` | You can enter a number here to cause the dialog box to automatically dismiss itself. If it is 0, the dialog box will remain until dismissed by the user.<br><br>Any number between 0 to about 1999999999 will work. |
| `title` | The string entered here will be in the title bar of the message box. |
| `ntype` | This is an important parameter that identifies what buttons and icons are displayed. The number 4 shows Yes and No buttons, as shown in Figure 28-4. The default, 0, is an OK button. |

As long as the user clicks a button (and doesn't just close the message box), the **$intbutton** variable will hold the value of the button. It's important to know what this value is so that you can check to see what button the user clicked. The previous example uses an *ntype* of 4 to display Yes and No buttons. If the user clicked Yes, the value of **$intbutton** would be 6. If the user clicked No, the value of **$intbutton** would be 7.

However, what if you want to use other buttons? What are the *ntype* codes for those buttons, and what is the value of the clicked buttons? These values are shown in the following table.

| *ntype* Value | Button(s) Displayed | Value of Button(s) if Clicked |
|---|---|---|
| 0 | OK button | OK = 1 |
| 1 | OK and Cancel buttons | OK = 1 <br> Cancel = 2 |
| 2 | Abort, Retry, and Ignore buttons | Abort = 3 <br> Retry = 4 <br> Ignore = 5 |
| 3 | Yes, No, and Cancel buttons | Yes = 6 <br> No = 7 <br> Cancel = 2 |
| 4 | Yes and No buttons | Yes = 6 <br> No = 7 |
| 5 | Retry and Cancel buttons | Retry = 4 <br> Cancel = 2 |
| 6 | Cancel, Try Again, and Continue buttons | Cancel = 2 <br> Try Again = 10 <br> Continue = 11 |

**TIP:** If a button isn't clicked, a value of -1 is returned. This can occur if a timer is used and it times out before the user responds, or if the user closes the message box another way, such as with Task Manager.

You can display icons by adding numbers to the *ntype* value. For example, if you want to display Yes and No buttons with a question mark, you combine the value of 32 (for a question mark) to the value of 4 (for the Yes and No buttons) to get a value of 36:

```
$obj = new-object -comobject wscript.shell
$buttonpresssed = $obj.popup("Message",0,"Title",36)
```

The following table shows the get different buttons and icons by manipulating the *ntype* value.

| *ntype* Value | Button(s) and Icon Displayed |
| --- | --- |
| 16 | Shows a Stop symbol and an OK button. |
| | The Stop icon has a value of 16 and the OK button has a value of 0, so the total value is 16. |
| 20 | Shows a Stop symbol and Yes and No buttons. |
| | The Stop icon has a value of 16 and the Yes and No button combination has a value of 4. |
| 32 | Shows a question mark symbol and an OK button. |
| | The question mark icon has a value of 32 and the OK button has a value of 0, so the total value is 32. |
| 33 | Shows a question mark symbol and OK and Cancel buttons. |
| | The question mark icon has a value of 32 and the OK and Cancel button combination has a value of 1. |
| 36 | Shows a question mark symbol and Yes and No buttons. |
| | The question mark icon has a value of 32 and the Yes and No button combination has a value of 4. |
| 48 | Shows an exclamation mark symbol and an OK button. |
| | The exclamation mark icon has a value of 48 and the OK button has a value of 0, so the total value is 48. |
| 50 | Shows an exclamation mark symbol and Abort, Retry, and Continue buttons. |
| | The exclamation mark icon has a value of 48 and the Abort, Retry, and Continue button combination has a value of 2. |
| 64 | Shows an information mark with an OK button. |
| | The information icon has a value of 64 and the OK button has a value of 0, so the total value is 64. |
| 70 | Shows an exclamation mark symbol and Cancel, Try Again, and Continue buttons. |
| | The exclamation mark icon has a value of 48 and the Cancel, Try Again, and Continue button combination has a value of 6. |

You could add a row for the *ntype* of 36 example that was replaced earlier by the Figure 28-5 example.

Basically, the code in the left column is the same for each row, with only a change to the *msg* and *ntype* parameters.

**Figure 28-5**   Message Box with a Stop Icon and OK Button

## Scheduling PowerShell Scripts

You can schedule PowerShell scripts through Task Scheduler, but it is a little trickier than scheduling simple batch files. If you try to schedule the .ps1 file, Notepad will open the file instead of the script running.

As an example, imagine that you created the following script and named it c:\scripts\ feedback.ps1:

```
$obj = new-object -comobject wscript.shell
$intButton = $obj.Popup("Your message",0,"Title", 0)
```

> **TIP:** You can test your script from the command prompt by entering **powershell c:\ scripts\feedback.ps1**.

Now you want to schedule it with Task Scheduler. You can use the following steps.

| Step | Remarks |
|------|---------|
| 1. Launch Task Scheduler with administrator permissions. | Click **Start**, enter **Schedule** in the Start Search text box, right-click **Task Scheduler**, and select **Run As Administrator**. |
| 2. Select **Task Scheduler Library**. Click **Create Basic Task**. | The Create Basic Task button is in the right pane. Clicking it starts the Create Basic Task Wizard. |
| 3. Name the task **Testing** and click **Next**. | |
| 4. Select **Daily** and click **Next**. | This is just for testing, but you could create a schedule for a live script. |
| 5. Accept the default daily schedule and click **Next**. | |

| 6. Ensure **Start a Program** is selected and click **Next**. | |
|---|---|
| 7. Enter **powershell** in the Program/Script text box. Enter **c:\scripts\feedback.ps1** in the Add Arguments text box. Click **Next**. | This has the net effect of entering the following command from the command prompt:<br><br>```powershell c:\scripts\feedback.ps1```<br><br>Before you click Next, your display should look similar to Figure 28-6. |
| 8. Click **Finish** to create the task. | |
| 9. Locate the **Testing** task in **Task Scheduler**. Right-click it and select **Run**. | The script will run and the message box will appear. However, it doesn't appear as the top window, so you may have to look for it. While this isn't elegant for a message box, it does show how to make a PowerShell script run. |
| 10. Close all the open windows and delete the task you created. | |

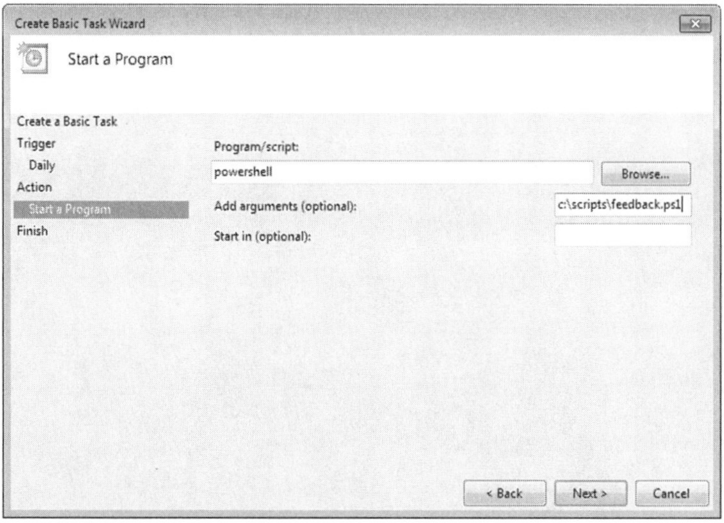

**Figure 28-6**   Scheduling a PowerShell Script with Task Scheduler

The previous procedure creates a noninteractive command-line prompt in the background while the script runs.

You can also run the PowerShell script by creating a batch file to run the script. The batch file has the following line:

```
powershell -noexit c:\scripts\feedback.ps1
```

> **TIP:** **powershell** is a command-line command. You can see a full range of help on **powershell** by entering the command **powershell /?**.

The -noexit switch keeps the PowerShell window open after the script runs.

> **TIP:** While not a native feature, you can download a free copy of the specops tool, which enables you to schedule scripts similarly to how you can with Task Scheduler, but with a few more features. You can check it out at http://technet.microsoft.com/en-us/library/ff730969.aspx.

This chapter provides information and commands concerning the following topics:

- Understanding Group Policy settings
- Blocking inheritance
- Enforcing GPOs
- Using loopback processing
- Running scripts with Group Policy
- Running PowerShell scripts via Group Policy

## Understanding Group Policy Settings

Administrators use Group Policy to administer and manage users and computers within a domain. There are literally thousands of Group Policy settings. The goal isn't to know them all, but instead to understand a few key Group Policy settings and how they're created.

Figure 29-1 shows the Local Computer Policy. You can access this on Windows 7 by clicking **Start**, typing **Policy** in the Start Search text box, and selecting **Edit Group Policy**. To reach the screen shown in Figure 29-1, browse to **Computer Configuration**, **Windows Settings**, **Security Settings**, **Local Policies**, **Audit Policy** and double-click **Audit Object Access**.

You can configure any setting by double-clicking it. Most settings have built-in help. For example, as shown in Figure 29-1, the Audit Object Access setting has an Explain tab that provides additional information on this setting.

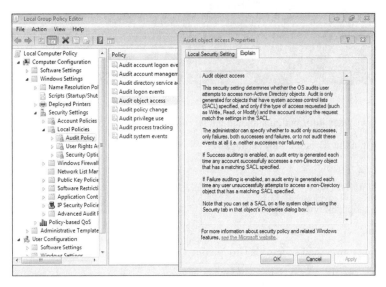

**Figure 29-1** Local Group Policy Editor for Local Computer Policy

Figure 29-2 shows the Default Domain Policy for a domain with the Audit Policy node. Many of the configurable settings in the local Group Policy are the same in domain policies. You can access this in a domain by launching the Group Policy Management console via the **Administrative Tools** menu, expanding the domain, right-clicking over the **Default Domain Policy** and selecting **Edit**.

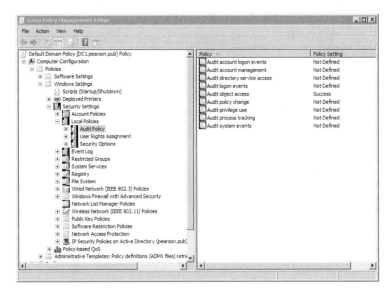

**Figure 29-2** Group Policy Management Editor Displaying the Default Domain Policy

**NOTE:** Group Policies in a domain are configured in Group Policy objects (GPOs). There are two default GPOs in any domain: the Default Domain Policy and the Default Domain Controllers Policy.

The following table shows the different levels, or *scopes*, where Group Policy can be applied.

| Group Policy Scope | Description |
| --- | --- |
| Local Computer Policy | This is applied first and only applies to the local computer.<br><br>Local computer policies are overwritten by any Group Policy settings in the domain. |
| Site | GPOs linked to a site apply to all computers and users in the site.<br><br>There aren't any default site policies in a domain. |
| Domain | GPOs linked to a domain apply to all computers and users in the domain. Domains include a Default Domain Policy by default. |
| Organizational unit (OU) | GPOs linked to an OU apply to all computers and users in the OU.<br><br>The Default Domain Controllers Policy applies to the Domain Controllers OU. When a server is promoted to a domain controller, it is automatically placed in the Domain Controllers OU. |

When multiple GPOs are applied, all of the settings in each of the GPOs are applied. If there is a conflict between the GPOs, the last one applied wins in most situations.

**TIP:** Two exceptions exist to the "last GPO applied wins" rule: when a higher-level setting is enforced, and when loopback processing is enabled.

The following is the order in which GPOs are applied:

- Local Computer Policy
- Site GPOs
- Domain GPOs
- OU GPOs (parent OUs first and child OUs last)

Consider the following scenario:

| Group Policy | Description |
| --- | --- |
| Local Computer Policy of Computer1 | Access to the Control Panel is removed. |
| Default Domain Policy applied to the domain | Access to the Control Panel is granted. |

| | |
|---|---|
| Sales GPO applied to an OU named Sales | Access to the Control Panel is removed. |
| Marketing OU (no other GPOs applied) | Access to the Control Panel is granted (inherited from the Default Domain Policy). |

You should be able to determine the resulting GPO settings for different users in the domain when conflicting GPOs are applied. The simplest rule to remember is that, by default, the last GPO applied wins.

> **NOTE:** These results assume the Group Policies listed in the previous table are applied.

| User Account Location | Result |
|---|---|
| User logged onto Computer1 locally | Access to the Control Panel is removed.<br><br>If the user is logged onto the computer locally, domain Group Policy settings are not applied. |
| Users in the domain Users container | Access to the Control Panel is granted.<br><br>Because the Default Domain Policy is applied after the local policy, it takes precedence. The user is in the Users container, so no other GPOs are applied. |
| Users in the Sales OU | Access to the Control Panel is removed.<br><br>Users in this OU have two GPOs applied. The Default Domain Policy grants access, but the Sales GPO (applied last) removes it. |
| Users in the Marketing OU | Access to the Control Panel is granted.<br><br>Because the Default Domain Policy is applied after the local policy, it takes precedence. |

Default permissions for GPOs are automatically assigned so that they will apply to all members of the Authenticated Users group.

> **TIP:** As soon as a user logs into the domain, the user account is automatically added to the Authenticated Users group. In other words, all GPOs automatically apply to any user that logs in because the GPOs apply to the Authenticated Users group by default.

Figure 29-3 and the following table show the key permissions that are applied to new GPOs. When both Read and Apply Group Policy permissions are set to Allow, the policy applies.

| Default Permission for Authenticated Users Group | Description |
|---|---|
| Read | Settings in the GPO can be read. |
| Apply Group Policy | Settings in the GPO are applied. |

**TIP:** You can filter Group Policy by changing the Apply Group Policy Allow permission to Deny for any group. For example, if you don't want the policy to apply to members of the Administrators group, select the group and then select Deny for Apply Group Policy.

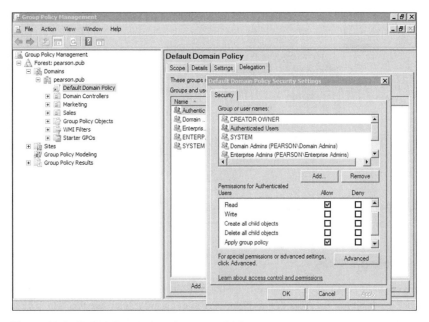

**Figure 29-3**   Default Permissions for a New GPO

## Blocking Inheritance

By default, GPO settings from GPOs at higher levels are automatically inherited at lower levels. For example, each organizational unit automatically inherits all GPO settings set at the domain level. In this context, each OU is a child of the domain. Similarly, children OUs automatically inherit GPO settings from parent OUs. However, you can block this behavior.

Figure 29-4 shows how to enable Block Inheritance for a child OU. In this figure, the West Region OU is a child OU of the Sales OU. The exclamation icon next to the OU and the check mark next to Block Inheritance show that Block Inheritance is enabled.

**NOTE:** You can set Block Inheritance on an OU, but not on a GPO.

**TIP:** When Block Inheritance is selected, it blocks all GPOs, with one exception. If a GPO from any parent is set to Enforced, the Enforced GPO is not blocked.

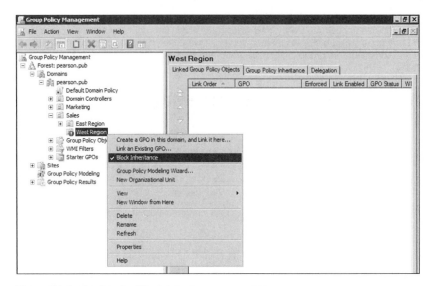

**Figure 29-4**   Configuring Block Inheritance on an OU

# Enforcing GPOs

There might be times when you want to ensure that settings from a GPO take precedence no matter when they are applied. For example, you might want to ensure that Group Policy settings set at the domain level are not overwritten by settings at an OU level. Similarly, you might want to ensure that GPOs are not blocked even if an OU has Block Inheritance configured. You can do so by configuring Enforced on the GPO.

Figure 29-5 shows the setting as Enforced for the Default Domain Policy. Notice that the GPO has a lock icon indicating it is enforced. Of course, you can right-click it as shown in the figure and see the check mark next to Enforced.

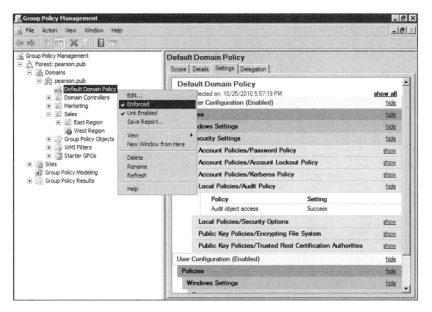

**Figure 29-5**   Configuring Enforced for a GPO

## Using Loopback Processing

Group Policy settings applied to users normally take precedence over Group Policy settings that apply to computers. As a reminder, the last Group Policy that is applied is the one that takes precedence. Because a computer boots up before a user can log in, the Group Policy settings for the computer is applied first, and the Group Policy settings for the user are applied last.

However, there might be times when you want this reversed. In other words, you might want the Group Policy settings for the computer to take precedence over the Group Policy settings for the user. You can do so by enabling Loopback Processing. Figure 29-6 shows the location of this setting.

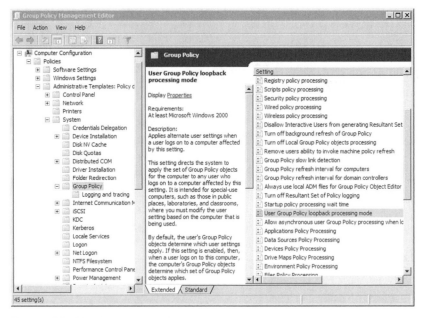

**Figure 29-6**   Enabling Loopback Processing

# Running Scripts with Group Policy

You can write scripts and have them automatically run via Group Policy. The great strength of this is that you write and configure the script once, and it'll run on all the computers in your domain or all the computers in a specific OU, depending on where you link the GPO holding the script.

Figure 29-7 shows the locations of these GPO settings.

| Group Policy Script Event | Description |
| --- | --- |
| Computer startup | The script runs when the computer starts.<br><br>The Group Policy setting for a domain GPO is in the Computer Configuration, Policies, Windows Settings, Scripts node. |
| Computer shutdown | The script runs when the computer shuts down.<br><br>The Group Policy setting for a domain GPO is in the Computer Configuration, Policies, Windows Settings, Scripts node. |
| User logon | The script runs when the user logs on.<br><br>The Group Policy setting for a domain GPO is in the User Configuration, Policies, Windows Settings, Scripts node. |

| User logoff | The script runs when the user logs off. |
| --- | --- |
| | The Group Policy setting for a domain GPO is in the User Configuration, Policies, Windows Settings, Scripts node. |

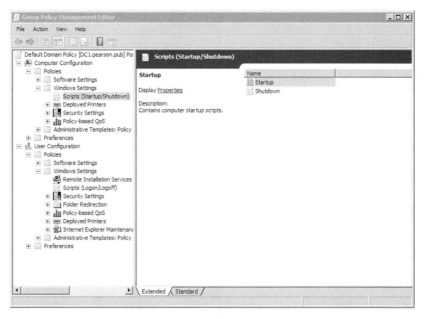

**Figure 29-7**  Group Policy Settings for Scripts

Scripts can run either synchronously or asynchronously.

| Script Behavior Type | Description |
| --- | --- |
| Synchronous | Scripts run one after the other. |
| | Users cannot interact with the system until all scripts have completed. |
| Asynchronous | Multiple scripts run at the same time. |
| | Users can interact with the system before the scripts have completed. |

All scripts run asynchronously by default on Windows 7. This includes both computer startup and user logon scripts.

> **TIP:** The default behavior for computer startup and user logon scripts before Windows Vista was synchronous. Users could not interact with the system until all scripts completed. However, computers boot quicker with this set to asynchronous, and the behavior is changed in Windows Vista and Windows 7. You can modify the new default behavior if needed.

The following table shows the overall steps to schedule a script to run for all users.

| Step | Remarks |
|---|---|
| 1. Launch the Group Policy Management Console (GPMC). | On a Windows Server 2008 or Windows Server 2008 R2 system, choose **Start**, **Administrative Tools**, **Group Policy Management**.<br><br>**TIP:** If you've installed and configured the Remote Server Administration Tools (RSAT) on Windows 7, you can also launch the GPMC on the Windows 7 computer. |
| 2. Right-click **Default Domain Policy** and select **Edit**. | You might need to expand the forest and domain to access the Default Domain Policy. |
| 3. Browse to the **User Configuration**, **Policies**, **Windows Settings**, **Scripts** node. | Ensure you're in the User Configuration node. |
| 4. Double-click **Logon** to open it. | |
| 5. On the Logon Properties page, click **Show Files**. | This opens Windows Explorer in the Logon folder.<br><br>**TIP:** This is a deep Windows Explorer folder labeled with GUID. It is very difficult to browse to this folder, but the Show Files button takes you there easily. |
| 6. Right-click in the folder and choose **New**, **Text Document**. Double-click the new text document to open it in Notepad. | **NOTE:** Instead of creating the script file from scratch, you can also copy a script file using Windows Explorer and paste it into the folder. |
| 7. Enter the following line in Notepad:<br><br>`msgbox "Your Message",,"Title"` | This line creates a simple message box.<br><br>Alternately, you can have a script do something else depending on your needs. |
| 8. Save the file as **test.vbs**. | Ensure the file is saved with a .vbs extension and not as a text file. |
| 9. Delete the New Text Document. Close Windows Explorer. | Because you saved the script file as test.vbs, the original New Text Document still exists in the folder. |
| 10. Click **Add** in the Logon Properties dialog box. Click **Browse**. | This opens Windows Explorer in the same Logon folder where you created the test.vbs script. |
| 11. Select the **test.vbs** script and click **Open**. Click **OK** twice. | That's it, the script is scheduled. |

## Running PowerShell Scripts via Group Policy

You can run PowerShell scripts with Group Policy, but not directly.

**NOTE:** PowerShell scripts end with the .ps1 extension, but .ps1 files are not treated as executable files. Instead, the .ps1 extension is mapped to Notepad, so if you try to run it, it opens in Notepad.

The following table shows the overall steps to run a PowerShell script via Group Policy.

| Step | Remarks |
|---|---|
| 1. Create the PowerShell script and place it on a network share. | The script can be any .ps1 script. You need to place it on a network share so that it is available to any user or computer in the domain.<br><br>For this example, imagine that you have placed a script named psscript.ps1 on a share named scripts on a server named server1. It is accessible via the UNC path \\server1\scripts\psscript.ps1. |
| 2. Open Notepad and add the following two lines:<br><br>`Set objShell =`<br>`CreateObject("Wscript.Shell")`<br>`objShell.Run("powershell.exe`<br>`\\server1\scripts\psscript.ps1")`<br>Save the file as **callps.vbs**. | This is a mini Visual Basic script that Group Policy can run.<br><br>It will create an instance of PowerShell, run the PowerShell script, and then close. |
| 3. Schedule the batch file using Group Policy. | You can use the same procedure shown previously to schedule it as a startup, shutdown, logon, or logoff script. |

This chapter provides information and commands concerning the following topics:

- Viewing Group Policy settings with **gpresult**
- Refreshing Group Policy settings with **gpupdate**

## Viewing Group Policy Settings with gpresult

You can view current Group Policy settings with the **gpresult** command. The syntax is

```
gpresult [switches]
```

Common switches are shown in the following table.

| gpresult Switch | Description |
|---|---|
| gpresult<br>C:/>gpresult | Shows the help file if no switches are included. At least one switch needs to be provided to actually see Group Policy results. |
| /r<br>C:/>gpresult /r | Displays Resultant Set of Policy (RSoP) summary data.<br><br>The summary data doesn't include the settings. |
| /x file.xml<br>C:/>gpresult /x gprx.xml | Saves the report in XML format.<br><br>You can then open the file in Internet Explorer by just entering the filename at the command prompt. |
| /h file.html<br>C:/>gpresult /h gprh.html | Saves the report in HTML format.<br><br>You can then open the file in Internet Explorer by just entering the filename at the command prompt. |
| /f<br>C:/>gpresult /x gprx.xml /f<br>C:/>gpresult /h gprh.html /f | Forces **gpresult** to overwrite an existing file. This is used with the **/x** or **/h** command. |

| `/v`<br>`C:/>gpresult /v` | Returns results on the local computer in verbose mode.<br><br>This provides additional details on Group Policy settings. |
|---|---|
| `/z`<br>`C:/>gpresult /z` | Specifies that super-verbose mode is used.<br><br>This provides significantly more details on Group Policy settings than verbose mode. |
| `/s computername`<br>`C:/>gpresult /z /s dc1` | Specifies a remote system to connect to for Group Policy details.<br><br>**NOTE:** This option can only be used when also using one of the following switches: **/x, /h, /r, /v,** or **/z.** |
| `/u {user \| domain\user}`<br>`C:/>gpresult /s DC1 /z /u`<br>`pearson\administrator` | Runs **gpresult** with a different user account. You will be prompted to provide the password.<br><br>**NOTE:** The **/u** option can only be used when using the /s switch, which also requires one of the following switches: **/x, /h, /r, /v,** or **/z.** |
| `/u {user \| domain\user} /p pass-`<br>`word`<br>`C:/>gpresult /z /u pearson\ad-`<br>`ministrator /p P@ssw0rd` | Runs **gpresult** with a different user account without prompting for a password.<br><br>**NOTE:** This can't be used with the **/x** or **/h** switch. |
| `/scope {user \| computer}`<br>`C:/>gpresult /z /scope user`<br>`C:/>gpresult /z /scope computer` | Retrieves only the user or only the computer settings with the /scope switch. |

**TIP:** You can output the settings to a text file with the **redirect** command. For example, **gpresult /z > gpr.txt** sends the output to a text file named gpr.txt.

The Group Policy Management Console (GPMC) allows you to view these settings in a GUI. Figure 30-1 shows the GPMC with a Group Policy Results report.

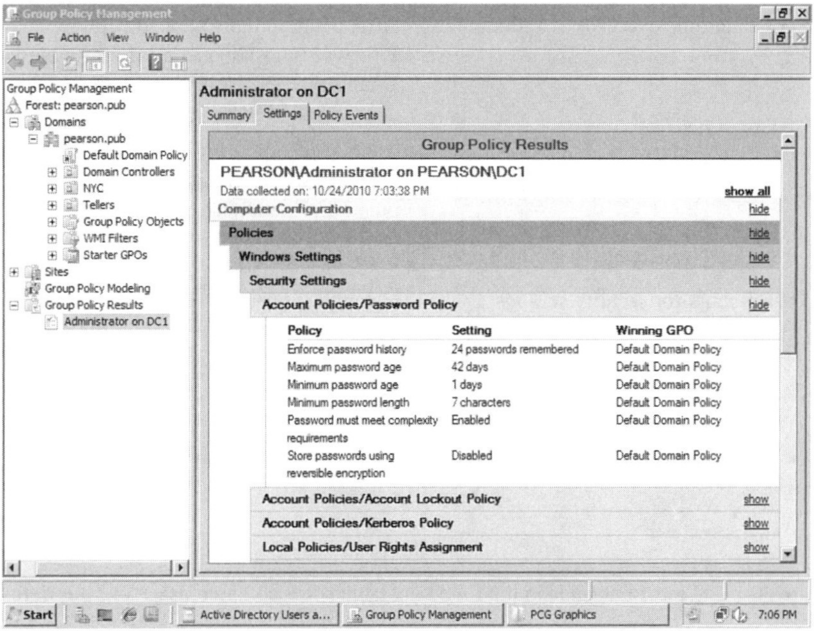

**Figure 30-1**   Group Policy Results in the GPMC

# Refreshing Group Policy Settings with gpupdate

Group Policy settings are applied at different times for computers within a domain, as shown in the following table.

| Automatic Group Policy Update Interval | Description |
|---|---|
| When the computers starts | Group Policy settings for computers are applied when the computer starts. The logon screen appears after the settings are applied. |
| When the user logs on | Group Policy settings for users are applied when the user logs on. The desktop appears after the settings are applied. |

| At a random time every 90 to 120 minutes | After being initially applied, Group Policy settings are queried from Active Directory every 90 minutes with a random offset of 30 minutes. If there are any changes, the changes are applied.<br><br>**NOTE:** These are default times for all computers except domain controllers. Settings are reapplied to domain controllers every 5 minutes by default. |
| --- | --- |
| Every 16 hours for security settings | Computers query Active Directory every 16 hours to retrieve security settings. These are reapplied whether they have been changed or not. |

You can reapply Group Policy settings to a computer by using the **gpupdate** command. The syntax is

```
gpupdate [switches]
```

Figure 30-2 and the commands in the following table show common usage of **gpupdate**.

```
gpupdate /force
```

| gpupdate Switch | Description |
| --- | --- |
| `gpupdate`<br>`C:/>gpupdate` | This queries Active Directory for any changes in Group Policy settings and reapplies any changed settings. |
| `gpupdate /force`<br>`C:/>gpupdate /force` | This queries Active Directory and reapplies all policy settings, even settings that haven't changed. |
| `gpupdate /force /target {computer | user}`<br>`C:/>gpupdate /force /target computer`<br>`C:/>gpupdate /force /target user` | You can specify either computer or user Group Policy settings with the **/target** switch.<br><br>With **/target computer**, only computer Group Policy settings are reapplied. With **/target user**, only user Group Policy settings are reapplied. |
| `gpupdate /force /logoff`<br>`C:/>gpupdate /force /logoff` | Some Group Policy settings such as software installation are not applied unless the user logs off and back on, or the computer is rebooted. You can specify the **/logoff** switch to force a logoff if necessary to apply the settings. |

| | |
|---|---|
| `gpupdate /force /boot`<br>`C:/>gpupdate /force /boot` | Some Group Policy settings are not applied unless the computer shuts down and restarts. The /boot switch forces a reboot if necessary to apply the settings. |

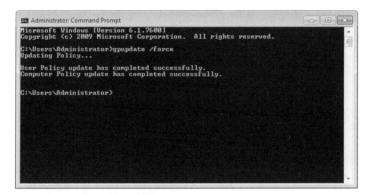

**Figure 30-2**   Executing the **gpupdate /force** Command

Use this appendix to make notes about your day-to-day tasks and information specific to your job to make this journal truly your own.

_____

_____

_____

_____

_____

_____

_____

_____

_____

_____

_____

_____

_____

_____

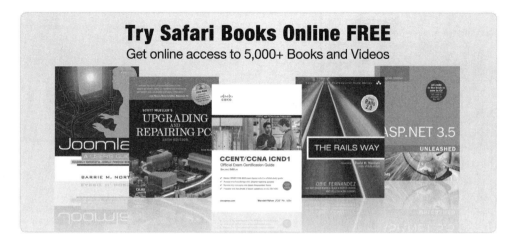

# FREE Online Edition

Your purchase of **Windows 7 Portable Command Guide: MCTS 70-680, and MCITP 70-685 and 70-686** includes access to a free online edition for 45 days through the Safari Books Online subscription service. Nearly every Pearson IT Certification book is available online through Safari Books Online, along with more than 5,000 other technical books and videos from publishers such as Addison-Wesley Professional, Cisco Press, Exam Cram, IBM Press, O'Reilly, Prentice Hall, and Sams.

**SAFARI BOOKS ONLINE** allows you to search for a specific answer, cut and paste code, download chapters, and stay current with emerging technologies.

## Activate your FREE Online Edition at
## www.informit.com/safarifree

> **STEP 1:** Enter the coupon code: NHTTQGA.

> **STEP 2:** New Safari users, complete the brief registration form. Safari subscribers, just log in.

If you have difficulty registering on Safari or accessing the online edition, please e-mail customer-service@safaribooksonline.com

**Safari**
Books Online